Materials of Construction

G. D. Taylor
Ewell County Technical College

Longman

London and New York

This book was edited by C. R. Bassett of Guildford County College of Technology.

Also under his Editorship are:

Environmental Physics Series

Heating   C. R. Bassett and M. D. W. Pritchard
Lighting   D. C. Pritchard
Acoustics   B. J. Smith

Longman Construction Series

Construction Science, Volume 2   B. J. Smith
Construction Mathematics, Volume 1   M. K. Jones
Construction Surveying   G. A. Scott
Materials and Structures   R. Whitlow
Construction Technology, Volume 1   R. Chudley
Construction Technology, Volume 2   R. Chudley

048 08967

LONGMAN GROUP LIMITED
London

Published in the United States of America by
Longman Inc., New York.
Associated companies, branches and representatives
throughout the world.

First published 1974
Second Impression 1975

ISBN 0582 42130 6

Set in IBM Press Roman 10 on 12pt

Printed in Great Britain by
Lowe & Brydone (Printers) Ltd.,
Thetford, Norfolk.

D
624.18
TAY

Acknowledgements

We are grateful to the following for permission to reproduce copyright material:

Extracts from *BS 882, 1201: 1965,* Aggregates from natural sources for concrete; *CP 110, 1972,* The Structural use of concrete, reproduced by permission of the British Standards Institution, 2 Park Street, London W1A 2BS, from whom copies of the complete standards and Codes of Practice may be obtained; British Steel Corporation for Figures 13 to 19 from *Simple Guide to the Structure and Properties of Steel;* Cement and Concrete Association for extracts based on the following: 'The determination of the proportions of aggregates approximating to any required grading', 'Basic mix method', 'Winter concreting', Introduction to statistical methods for quality control of concrete' and 'Lean concrete bases for roads'; Director of the Building Research Establishment for Fig. 6 of *BRS* current paper 12/71; John Laing Research and Development Limited for references made to the incorporation of polypropylene fibres in concrete for the modification of plastic and hardened properties; Portland Cement Association for a table from *Design and Control of Concrete Mixtures* and a table from *Properties of Materials* and West's Piling and Construction for the mention of polypropylene fibres used in piling shells.

Contents

Preface

The need for the modern builder to have a thorough knowledge of scientific aspects of building is reflected by the current Materials and Environmental Science syllabus for the Membership, Part I, of the Institute of Building. The environmental science subjects are already well served by the 'Environmental Physics' series and this book has been produced as an adjunct to the series to cover materials properties at this level. It is now widely appreciated that the thorough understanding of materials, which is so important to their correct use, must hinge at least to some degree on a study of underlying structure and properties. Although in the early stages such a study must involve some extra time and effort, the knowledge so gained will result in a greater ability of the builder to tackle and overcome new problems or to assess new materials as they become available. Also, many of the basic principles can be applied to groups of materials, thereby reducing the amount of detailed learning required in order to acquire a working knowledge of individual materials.

This book is concerned with principles such that to some degree, space has not permitted inclusion of what might be regarded as desirable detail. It must be emphasised, however, that to obtain an intimate knowledge of materials properties it is essential to be involved with their use as well as to read trade and reference literature.

In addition to building students the book should be of value to more advanced students of Architecture, Civil and Constructional Engineering and to all those who are concerned with building or engineering materials and who wish to obtain a deeper insight into their principles and uses.

The author is indebted to many colleagues for assistance and suggestions in producing the book and to his wife for typing the manuscript.

Chapter 1
INTRODUCTION

Recent years have seen the beginning of considerable changes in the construction industry, and materials for construction are no exception. Traditionally, the use of building materials has been based to some degree on long-term experience rather than on intimate understanding and, as a result, generous allowances have been made against known modes of failure. This approach is not surprising if one appreciates the enormous complexity of materials such as clay products or cements, even though they are made by basically simple techniques. Indeed, the success of the vast majority of materials and methods in the past is borne out by such terms as 'safe as houses' and the fact that old buildings are rarely demolished due to a condition of advanced deterioration. Developments which have occurred in materials and techniques have been based not so much on any inferiority in the traditional approach but rather on great technological advances in many fields which, together with rising prices, have forced the engineer and builder to consider very carefully other possible ways of achieving given standards of performance. At the same time, because larger buildings are often economically more viable than small buildings—and more dangerous if defects are present—attention has been paid to studies of the structural properties of materials. In particular, statistical laws have been applied to quantify the inherent variability of most materials and to arrive at sensible definitions of the word 'safe' in a given situation. Recently published codes of practice typify the changes which are being made while standards for materials reflect attempts to describe more accurately their relevant properties. An important requirement of codes of practice is that they should consider and allow for all modes of failure. There have been examples in recent times of problems arising because, owing to greater production control, property requirements of components, such as average strength, have justifiably been reduced. In some cases this has led to adverse changes in other properties (perhaps durability) such that, although the component is satisfactory in respect of strength, it may not be able to fulfil its total requirements.

Changes of manufacturing techniques are by no means the only ones to affect the building industry. New products appear on the market continuously and the user must be able to make some judgement as to their suitability for his purpose.

This book attempts to provide an understanding, as well as a knowledge, of the performance of materials in a given situation. The most important single factor in determining properties is chemical structure, which in turn depends on the atomic structure of the constituent elements. Materials may be classified according to the basic bond types which they exhibit. Silicaceous and related materials form the largest group and are conveniently described under two chapter headings. Remaining chapters describe metals, organic materials and fibre reinforcement. In each case, a simple understanding of structure will allow a more accurate prediction of performance than a much wider superficial knowledge which is not so based. This chapter is devoted entirely to the subject of atomic structure and forms the basis of remaining chapters.

ATOMIC STRUCTURE

In much the same way as the structural properties and performance of a completed building depend on the individual units which it comprises and on the way these are assembled, so the behaviour of a single component, for example a brick or steel beam, depends on the 'building units' which form it. These units or atoms are entirely responsible for every property of the material whether it be physical, chemical or mechanical. Atoms are made up of still smaller units, the three main ones being protons, neutrons and electrons. These particles are important in their role as building units in atoms and in some cases are used to test materials. Table 1.1 shows their properties.

Table 1.1
Properties of the fundamental particles which comprise atoms

Particle	Charge (Coulomb)	Mass (kg)	Relative Mass
Proton	$+ 1{\cdot}602 \times 10^{-19}$	$1{\cdot}672 \times 10^{-27}$	$1{\cdot}000$
Neutron	0	$1{\cdot}675 \times 10^{-27}$	$1{\cdot}002$
Electron	$- 1{\cdot}602 \times 10^{-19}$	$9{\cdot}109 \times 10^{-31}$	$\dfrac{1}{1836}$

Structure of the atom

Atoms consist of a central core or nucleus which contains the protons and neutrons, and a relatively large area of space around the outside which is occupied by electrons moving in orbits. An unbonded atom will be stable only if the number of protons is balanced by the number of electrons. The neutrons also have a role since they minimise the repulsion of the protons which are concentrated in a small space in the nucleus. Nuclear reactions occur naturally in the form of radioactivity and can be stimulated by many artificial means. The physical and chemical properties of materials are, however, due to processes in which the electrons in their orbits are modified in some way. These electrons are governed by certain laws which limit the number of ways in which orbits can be formed. Certain properties of the electrons are also 'quantised', that is, they may take only certain discreet values, whereas similar macroscopic or bulk properties may apparently take a continuum of values. These properties of electrons are referred to by quantum numbers:

Principal quantum number—n. Although held in an orbit by the electrostatic attraction of the nucleus, it was found that the electron can only exist in certain orbits or shells. These shells are classified by the principal quantum number n. The lowest orbit nearest the nucleus corresponds to the least energy and is hence most stable. Here $n = 1$ and the orbit is called the K shell. The others, $n = 2, 3, 4, 5, 6, 7$, are labelled L, M, N, O, P, Q respectively. There is no theoretical limit to the number of orbits but the atoms in general become unstable when very large.

Angular momentum quantum number—l. It is commonly understood that electron orbits are circular and well defined. Circular orbits do exist, known as 's' states, but other shapes are possible. These shapes correspond to different angular momentum (l) values of the electron, these values also being quantised. Values may be 0, 1, 2, etc., angular momentum units, with the requirement that l cannot be larger than $n-1$. Table 1.2 shows these values together with the letter code. It is fallacious to regard

Table 1.2

Quantum number descriptions of electrons in orbit around the nucleus

Shell	K	L		M			N			
n-value	1	2		3			4			
Subshell	s	s	p	s	p	d	s	p	d	f
l value	0	0	1	0	1	2	0	1	2	3
No. of electrons per subshell	2	2	6	2	6	10	2	6	10	14
Total electrons per shell	2	8		18			32			

electrons as small hard particles; they should be regarded as moving charges represented by a probability diagram rather than by a certain fixed orbit (Fig. 1.1). Notice that the p orbital is symmetrical about the x–x axis. There are three possible axes at right angles, so that three electrons could occupy p_x, p_y and p_z orbitals without overlapping. It can be shown similarly that d orbitals ($l = 2$) comprise five possible independent orbits, f orbitals seven and so on.

Spin-m_s. The electron may be regarded as spinning. It thus has a spin quantum number m_s equal to $\pm \frac{1}{2}$ (rather than 1) corresponding to clockwise and anticlockwise spin directions.

Formation of atoms—The Pauli exclusion principle

The above partially interdependent descriptions of an electron's character are responsible for the formation of atoms. Electrons fill the shells to balance the nuclear proton

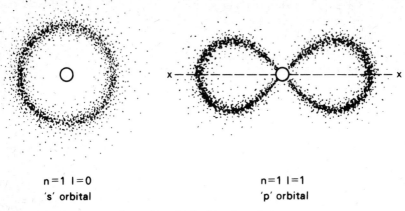

n=1 l=0
's' orbital

n=1 l=1
'p' orbital

Fig. 1.1 Charge clouds corresponding to 's' and 'p' orbits of an electron

charge, occupying lowest energy sites first and subject to the Pauli exclusion principle, that no two electrons may occupy identical orbits (i.e. having all three quantum numbers equal). This principle is logical since, if electrons occupied two identical orbits in the same atom, there would be enormous electron–electron repulsion— hence a high energy state. Although the principal quantum number n is primarily responsible for the energy of a certain orbit, l also affects this since the larger numbers of electrons involved in higher l values repel one another and hence raise the energy of that state. Figure 1.2 shows the energies of various l and n values in atoms, as well as the available 'sites' for electrons.

The periodic table can be built up easily from the above. The atomic number, given first in each case, is the number of protons (or electrons in the uncharged atom). Each electron is designated by a number equal to the 'n' value and a letter describing the orbital shape. Whenever any sub-group is completed, a very stable (inert) element is produced.

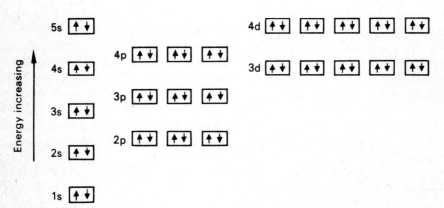

Fig. 1.2 Orbital energies of electrons. The numbers represent the 'n' values. Note that for any one shell, the energy increases in order s, p, d. . . . The arrows represent the opposite spins of each pair of electrons

1	Hydrogen	(H)	1s
2	Helium	(He)	$(1s)^2$ (i.e. 2 1s electrons) Inert
3	Lithium	(Li)	$(1s)^2 2s$
4	Beryllium	(Be)	$(1s)^2 (2s)^2$
5	Boron	(B)	$(1s)^2 (2s)^2 2p$
6	Carbon	(C)	$(1s)^2 (2s)^2 (2p)^2$
7	Nitrogen	(N)	$(1s)^2 (2s)^2 (2p)^3$
8	Oxygen	(O)	$(1s)^2 (2s)^2 (2p)^4$
9	Fluorine	(F)	$(1s)^2 (2s)^2 (2p)^5$
10	Neon	(Ne)	$(1s)^2 (2s)^2 (2p)^6$ —L shell complete—inert.

When subshell 3d begins to fill, Fig. 1.2 shows that, since this shell is approximately equal in energy to 4s, these two shells tend to fill together (Table 1.3). Similarly, 5s is approximately equal to 4d and these fill together. Subshell 5p fills before 4f since it is lower in energy. The process could continue indefinitely except that the nucleus becomes unstable when very large. Several elements contain variable numbers of neutrons in the nucleus but have the same number of protons and electrons. They are known as isotopes. Normally one isotope is more stable than the others and tends to predominate. For example, carbon normally has six neutrons, though a small percentage exists with seven neutrons and cosmic radiation in the atmosphere produces some with eight neutrons—the radioactive element C^{14}. The number 14 here refers to the atomic mass—eight neutrons and six protons.

Properties of the elements

It is perhaps tempting at this stage to look for systematic changes in, for example, density or some mechanical property in the periodic table, but apart from some very general observations (e.g. the densities of atomic numbers 21 to 30 in which the 3d shell is filling comparative to 39 to 48 in which the 4d shell is filling) this cannot be successful because the physical and mechanical properties of materials are largely dependent on the ways in which atoms interact, forming real materials. The periodic table in the form shown in Table 1.3 after Mendleef, however, leads to an understanding of the interaction of atoms. In this table the elements are listed in groups I–VII and then 0 corresponding to the numbers of filled electron sites in a shell. This leads to a classification of properties of elements. For example, it is known that the lowest energy configurations and hence the most stable are those in which a shell is complete—the inert gases. These are extremely unreactive. Argon for example is used in incandescent lamps since the metal filament would tend to combine chemically with atmospheric gases at its high operating temperature. The valency of an element is normally the difference between the number of electrons in the outermost shell and the number of electrons in the nearest stable state: for example, sodium and potassium; fluorine and chlorine have a valency of one while magnesium and calcium; sulphur and oxygen have a valency of two. Occasionally valency is complicated when several orbits interact or become 'hybridised'; for example carbon, atomic number 6; $(1s)^2 (2s)^2 (2p)^2$. Normally one would expect a valency of two—$(2p)^2$ electrons but in fact the two 2s and two 2p electrons mix making a valency of four. Iron (Fe) is another more complicated element since, as shown by reference to the periodic

Table 1.3   Periodic Table after Mendleef

IA	IIA	IIIB	IVB	VB	VIB	VIIB	VIIIB	VIIIB	VIIIB	IB	IIB	IIIA	IVA	VA	VIA	VIIA	0
1 H 1s																	2 He $(1s)^2$
3 Li 2s	4 Be $(2s)^2$											5 B 2p	6 C $(2p)^2$	7 N $(2p)^3$	8 O $(2p)^4$	9 F $(2p)^5$	10 Ne $(2p)^6$
11 Na 3s	12 Mg $(3s)^2$											13 Al 3p	14 Si $(3p)^2$	15 P $(3p)^3$	16 S $(3p)^4$	17 Cl $(3p)^5$	18 Ar $(3p)^6$
19 K 4s	20 Ca $(4s)^2$	21 Sc $(4s)^2 3d$	22 Ti $(4s)^2(3d)^2$	23 V $(4s)^2(3d)^3$	24 Cr $4s(3d)^5$	25 Mn $(4s)^2(3d)^5$	26 Fe $(4s)^2(3d)^6$	27 Co $(4s)^2(3d)^7$	28 Ni $(4s)^2(3d)^8$	29 Cu $(4s)^1(3d)^{10}$	30 Zn $(4s)^2(3d)^{10}$	31 Ga 4p	32 Ge $(4p)^2$	33 As $(4p)^3$	34 Se $(4p)^4$	35 Br $(4p)^5$	36 Kr $(4p)^6$
37 Rb 5s	38 Sr $(5s)^2$	39 Y $(5s)^2 4d$	40 Zr $(5s)^2(4d)^2$	41 Nb $5s(4d)^4$	42 Mo $5s(4d)^5$	43 Tc $5s(4d)^6$	44 Ru $5s(4d)^7$	45 Rh $5s(4d)^8$	46 Pd $(4d)^{10}$	47 Ag $5s(4d)^{10}$	48 Cd $(5s)^2(4d)^{10}$	49 In 5p	50 Sn $(5p)^2$	51 Sb $(5p)^3$	52 Te $(5p)^4$	53 I $(5p)^5$	54 Xe $(5p)^6$
55 Cs 6s	56 Ba $(6s)^2$	57	72 Hf $(6s)^2(5d)^2$	73 Ta $(6s)^2(5d)^3$	74 W $(6s)^2(5d)^4$	75 Re $(6s)^2(5d)^5$	76 Os $(6s)^2(5d)^6$	77 Ir $(6s)^2(5d)^7$	78 Pt $6s(5d)^9$	79 Au $6s(5d)^{10}$	80 Hg $(6s)^2(5d)^{10}$	81 Tl 6p	82 Pb $(6p)^2$	83 Bi $(6p)^3$	84 Po $(6p)^4$	85 At $(6p)^5$	86 Rn $(6p)^6$
87 Fr 7s	88 $(7s)^2$	89															

Row labels (by shell filling): 1s, 2s, 3s, 4s, 5s, 6s, 7s; 3d, 4d, 5d, 6d; 2p, 3p, 4p, 5p, 6p.

71 — Lanthanides (4f filling) (57 ○—71)

103 — Actinides (5f filling) (89 ○—103)

The atomic number is indicated above each element. Subshells above or to the left of each element are complete. Lead (Atomic number number 82) is the largest stable element

table, it contains a partially complete inner subshell (3d) with a complete 4s shell. It may be di- or trivalent. In general, however, elements in the lower groups are reactive, tending to lose electrons, while those in the upper groups are reactive, tending to gain electrons. Group 0 is of course stable. The B groups are similar to the A groups in that the shells which are filling contain the same number of electrons as corresponding shells in the A groups. The IB group is not as reactive, however, as IA because a stable state is not achieved with loss of a group IB electron, as with a group IA electron. Group IA elements are highly reactive. A 'Group VIII' is necessary once d shells begin to fill since the d shell may contain 10 electrons.

Excitation and ionisation

It is possible that if energy is supplied to an atom, for example by irradiation, electrons may be raised to higher orbits. This situation exists in a discharge tube when the excitation is by electron collisions. When an electron returns to the ground state from a certain excited state, there will be an emission of the appropriate wavelength of light, the wavelength being shorter for a bigger jump. In a sodium discharge tube, for example, there is a substantial amount of the yellow colour of wavelength 589 nm which occurs when an electron jumps from the 3p level to the 3s level (that is, the ground state), hence the yellow colour of sodium lights. In some cases, excitation may take place to the extent that an electron completely leaves the atom. The atom is then said to be ionised. Ionisation also plays an important part in the operation of discharge tubes.

RADIOACTIVITY

The stability of the nucleus depends on the balance between two opposite tendencies which exist inside it. The nucleus in the first instance is held together by very short range attractive forces between protons and neutrons alike. This produces a surface tension effect whereby larger nuclei tend to be more stable. However, a second effect—that of proton-proton repulsion—also exists and above iron in the periodic table (atomic number 26), becomes important so that heavier elements than iron become less stable and tend to disintegrate into smaller, more stable units. Therefore light elements tend to group together or fuse (nuclear fusion) and heavy elements tend to break up (nuclear fission). In practice, the actual probability of most nuclei changing in this manner is so small that the rate of modification towards iron is negligible. Many isotopes are, however, unstable and may emit particles; elements above lead in the periodic table decay in this way. The following types of emission may take place:

Alpha particles

These consist of two protons and two neutrons and are themselves tightly bound structures. Hence they are often emitted in preference to loose protons or neutrons. Alpha particles are heavy relative to other forms of radioactive emission and do not have wide use in the construction industry since their penetration of materials is very low.

Beta particles

These are high energy electrons and are emitted by a nucleus that has too many neutrons. The reaction may be expressed:

$$n \rightarrow e^- + p^+$$

neutron   beta   proton

particle

Beta particles are often emitted after one or a series of alpha particle emissions. They travel with high speeds, often as high as 99 per cent of the speed of light and will penetrate a few millimetres of low-density materials such as aluminium.

Gamma rays

Some nuclei may end up in an excited state as a result of a radioactive transformation. This will lead to a rapid emision of energy normally of a very low wavelength called gamma rays, as electrons return to the ground state. These rays have high energy, are similar to X rays and will penetrate dense materials such as concrete. Gamma rays may be produced by artificial means and a commonly used isotope is cobalt 60:

$$_{27}Co^{60} \rightarrow {}_{28}Ni^{60} + \beta \text{ particle} + \text{energy}$$

$$_{28}Ni^{60} \rightarrow {}_{28}Ni^{60} + \gamma \text{ ray}$$

In each case, the superscript refers to the atomic mass and subscript to the atomic number.

Gamma rays are extensively used in the construction industry, applications being based on the fact that the absorption of gamma rays by materials increases with their density. There are two applications: radiography, where steel and concrete are irradiated to find flaws; and *in situ* density measurement of concrete and soil.

Gamma radiography (BS 4408)

Concrete up to half a metre thick can be tested in this way. A small-diameter gamma source is placed in front of the structure to be photographed and an X ray film enclosed in a flat cassette behind it (Fig. 1.3). Lead-intensifying screens are normally used in front of and behind the film. These emit electrons when irradiated and they effectively make the film more sensitive. The gamma rays are not focused and for maximum sharpness the source should be as far as possible from the specimen, subject to obtaining satisfactory exposure times. The technique is particularly useful for examining grouting in pre-stressed concrete and for locating the position of steel.

Density measurement

This is a direct application of the effect of density of materials on their gamma ray absorption. The density may be obtained by a transmission technique or by measuring

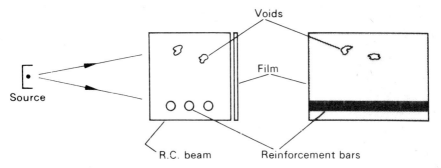

Fig. 1.3 Gamma radiography of pre-stressed concrete. Dense materials produce darker shadows

backscattered radiation. In the transmission technique, a source of gamma rays is placed on one side of the structure and a detector on the other (Fig. 1.4). The count rate decreases as density increases (Fig. 1.5). In the backscatter method, the source is placed on the surface with the counter adjacent to it but shielded from direct radiation by a lead screen (Fig. 1.6). The counter then measures backscattered radiation, the detector response depending on the instrument geometry. The variation of count rate with density is shown in Fig. 1.7. Some instruments are designed such that the density of concrete occurs on the positive gradient portion and others such that it occurs on the negative gradient portion. The backscatter method is particularly suitable for density measurement of structures with only one accessible surface such as concrete slabs. Material up to between 50 and 100 mm from the surface contributes towards backscattered radiation and corrections may be necessary if other materials lie within this region. There is also a tendency for different types of materials to produce different density response characteristics. Greatest accuracy in these cases is obtained by calibration of each material used.

Artificial radioactivity, fast neutrons

Although neutrons are not emitted normally by radioactive materials, some light elements can be stimulated into emitting them as a result of bombardments with alpha particles:

$$_4\text{Be}^9 \quad + \quad _2\text{He}^4 \rightarrow \quad _6\text{C}^{12} \quad + \quad _0\text{n}^1$$

beryllium   alpha   carbon fast neutron
particle

The neutron has the property of being unaffected by the electron shell of an atom because it is uncharged. As a result fast neutrons penetrate to the nucleus and are slowed down by collision with it. The element which causes greatest loss of energy of neutrons is the hydrogen atom since this has a mass similar to that of the neutron. Hence neutrons will be slowed down or 'moderated' dependent on the number of hydrogen atoms in a given volume of material. The formula for water makes it immediately evident that in inorganic materials (which, when dry, contain no hydrogen

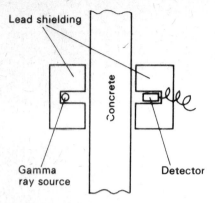

Fig. 1.4 Transmission technique for measurement of the density of concrete using gamma rays

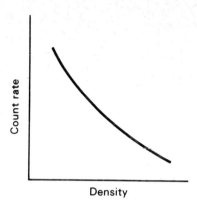

Fig. 1.5 The relation between transmitted intensity of gamma rays and density

atoms) the moderation of fast neutrons will give an indication of moisture content. A generator is placed on the material and a detector positioned near it. The response of the detector will then be dependent on the moisture content of the material. Rapid, *in situ* measurements can be made. For greatest accuracy, calibration graphs may be produced using results obtained by conventional methods. *In situ* measurements can be of great advantage, for example in soil compaction where optimum moisture content depends on the compaction method, so that a small hand-compacted sample may have a different optimum moisture content to the correct value corresponding to compaction by machine. A further application is the measurement of binder content in asphalts, the binder consisting of hydrocarbon and therefore behaving in a manner similar to water.

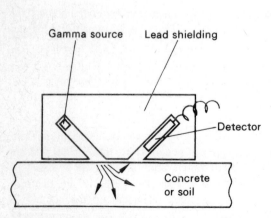

Fig. 1.6 Backscatter method for density measurement using gamma rays

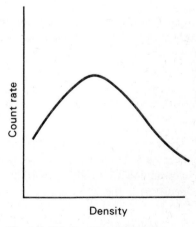

Fig. 1.7 Relationship between back-scattered gamma radiation and density

Half life

The emission of radioactive particles occurs on a statistical basis, and as one particular element decays into another the emission of the former material will decrease, since less of it remains. The relationship is exponential:

$$\frac{dN}{dt} = -\lambda N$$

where N is the number of particles at a time t and λ is a constant. The minus sign signifies that this is a decay process.

Separating variables and integrating:

$$\text{Log}_e N = -\lambda t + C \quad C = \text{constant}$$

If when $t = 0$, $N = N_0$ this gives

$$N = N_0 e^{-\lambda t}$$

The time $t_{1/2}$ at which half the material $\frac{1}{2}N_0$ remains is called its half life.

$$t_{\frac{1}{2}} = \frac{\log_e 2}{\lambda}$$

The term half life gives an idea of the useful life of a particular isotope. The emission of cobalt 60 for example would decrease by 50 per cent over a period of about 5 years—its approximate half life.

Measurement of radioactive radiation

This is normally carried out using a geiger counter. The radiation enters a partially evacuated glass tube containing electrodes at a high d.c. voltage. When a radioactive particle enters the tube, it ionises the gas and causes a pulse of current which may be detected by a loudspeaker or measured using a counter. Neutron detection requires a different technique. Boron trifluoride tubes are commonly used, producing alpha particles when irradiated, according to the equation:

$$_5B^{10} + _0n^1 \rightarrow _3Li^7 + _2H^4$$

boron neutron lithium alpha particle

The alpha particle is detected as previously.

Although the advantages of the above technique are evident, radioactive materials are potentially extremely dangerous, causing burning and destruction of living tissues when excessive doses are received. They should be stored in lead containers (or in paraffin wax or polythene in the case of fast neutron sources), clearly labelled and handled with care, keeping out of direct line with the sources. When used regularly, a badge containing sensitive film should be worn by the operator, being developed periodically. This will give the accumulated radiation received over that period and this should be compared with permissible levels. Badges are, of course, no use in preventing severe exposure due to careless use of radioactive materials. All such sources are dangerous but fast neutrons are particularly harmful.

BONDING OF ATOMS

In order to form a liquid or solid of any tpe, bonding must take place between the atoms of elements. A bond between two atoms will reduce the freedom of each of those atoms, but to produce a solid or liquid, this type of linkage must be formed many times over throughout the mass of the material concerned. This is not to say that in gases there is no inclination to form bonds. This tendency exists to a degree in all elements—even in the inert elements such as helium, which liquefies at a very low temperature. Gases only exist because thermal energy prevents rigid or semi-rigid bonds from forming. Atoms will only bond if, in doing so, the resultant energy of the combination (molecule) is less than that of the constituent atoms. It has already been stated that the lowest energies are associated with complete electron shells, so that most stable compounds can be expected to have achieved this by interaction of the electron 'clouds' of different atoms. All changes take place as a result of a 'chance' encounter of atoms and all chemical reactions are governed by statistical laws. There follows a brief description of the main types of bond; detailed accounts, where appropriate, will be given with specific materials as they are investigated.

Bonds may be subdivided into primary bonds, which are relatively powerful and secondary bonds which are relatively weak.

Primary bonds

The ionic bond. This occurs when, for example, an atom containing a single outer electron encounters another atom with a single electron missing in its outer shell. The electron in the former atom transfers to orbit the nucleus of the other atom. Hence they have empty and complete shells respectively. But the previously uncharged atoms will now be charged and therefore attract one another, coming together until this attraction is balanced by the repulsion of their respective electron clouds. If there are further atoms of each type available, the process will continue and a crystal will form. Common salt is an example (Fig. 1.8)—sodium has a single outer electron and chlorine has seven outer electrons. Similar reactions will take place between divalent elements, for example, calcium and oxygen (CaO) or between divalent and monovalent elements by appropriate proportions; e.g. calcium chloride ($CaCl_2$).

The presence of water reduces the force between the ions so that many ionic compounds dissolve in water producing a dispersion of ions.

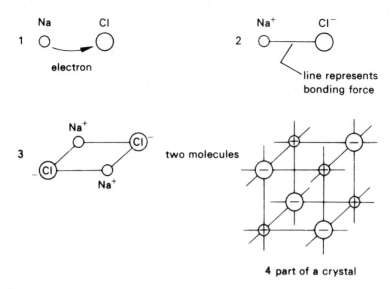

Fig. 1.8 Ionic bonding between sodium and chlorine forming common salt

The covalent bond. This results when certain atoms come together so that one or more electrons orbit both nuclei. In methane, for example, four hydrogen atoms, each having one electron in its shell, approach a carbon atom, having four electrons in the outer shell, and the electrons encompass both nuclei. The arrangement is shown schematically in Fig. 1.9.

Crystals may be formed in this way; for example, carbon forming diamond when the four electrons form symmetrical bonds with one another, and graphite when three electrons combine to produce a flat lattice, the fourth electons forming a metallic bond type and accounting for the electrical conductivity of graphite. Silica (silicon

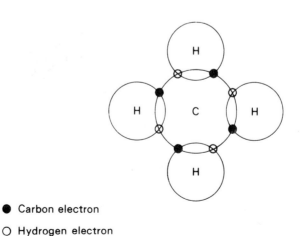

● Carbon electron

○ Hydrogen electron

Fig. 1.9 Covalent bonding between carbon and hydrogen forming methane, CH_4

oxide) forms a similar pattern to Fig. 1.9 and is the basis of sand. The compound also occurs in the non-crystalline form of glass. Groups of three or more different types of atom may be formed by means of covalent bonds, which, being strong and rigid, play an important part in almost every building material. Most gases consist of small groups of atoms bonded in this way, for example, oxygen O_2, nitrogen N_2 and carbon dioxide CO_2. In some materials, notably plastics, the groups are very large and may contain thousands of atoms in long chains (polymers).

It would be misleading to suggest that all bonds are either purely ionic or purely covalent. In fact, many bonds are some combination of these two types. It should be remembered that bonds are formed when electron paths change to encompass one or both nuclei. As well as the possibility of a complete change (ionic bond) or exact sharing (covalent bond), there is the possibility of unequal sharing. Water is an example—it is partially covalent and partially ionic. Furthermore, some molecules may be complex. For example, anhydrous calcium sulphate (the basis of gypsum plaster) consists of a sulphate ion SO_4^{--} in which the sulphur (six outer electrons) shares two of its electrons with each oxygen (each with six outer electrons), the two extra electrons which are necessary being borrowed ionically from the calcium which forms the ion Ca^{++} as in Fig. 1.10.

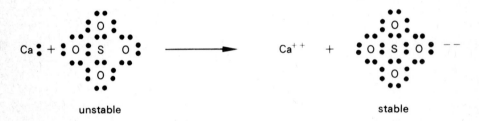

unstable   stable

Fig. 1.10 The formation of calcium sulphate from calcium, sulphur and oxygen

Note that the sharing between the sulphur and oxygen is in one direction only, since with the two ionically borrowed electrons the sulphur has eight electrons and has no need to borrow from the oxygen atoms. Each oxygen on the other hand is two electrons short and therefore must share with the sulphur. Such covalency is known as co-ordinate covalency. The one-way sharing often results in charged dipoles which, as in ionic compounds, tend to cause crystals to grow. Calcium carbonate is an example; it is found in crystalline form such as calcite which occurs in marble.

Some materials crystallise on adding water, which becomes chemically bound. This is the process by which gypsum plaster sets. Various organic compounds formed from covalent bonds are shown in Fig. 1.11.

The metallic bond When atoms of a singe type and containing a few valence electrons approach one another, the electron orbits may change to become of a nondescript nature—they move around the nuclei rather like a gas and cause an overall attraction between the positively charged remainders of the atoms and the electrons themselves

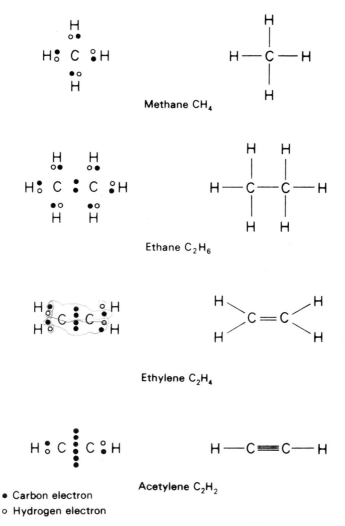

Fig. 1.11 Various ways of representing structure of some organic compounds (i.e. formed from carbon). Note that in each compound hydrogen atoms attain two electrons and carbon atoms attain eight electrons

(Fig. 1.12). Such bonding is clearly undirectional and the atoms therefore pack in tight patterns, resulting in crystals. An electric potential will cause an overall drift of the electron 'gas' through the metal, constituting an electric current—hence metals conduct electricity. Thermal conductivity of metals is also high as electrons carry energy from one point to another by collision. In some circumstances effective bonding may take place between atoms of different types, producing alloys. These are discussed more fully later. A great many elements—some as high in the periodic table as Group IVA, e.g. tin and lead—exhibit metallic behaviour (although tin reverts to a covalent grey powder below 18°C). The metallic bond is weak comparative to ionic or

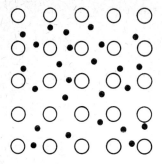

Fig. 1.12 Simple two dimensional representation of a metal showing valence electrons forming a 'cloud' around symmetrically positioned metal ions

covalent bonds but the close packing of atoms results in large numbers of these bonds and hence high strength in the materials as a whole. The close packing means also that density of metals is high relative to most other types of solid, e.g. iron compared to diamond.

Secondary bonds

The van der Waals bond. In the bonds considered so far, the atoms have combined to produce a more stable arrangement by interaction of their electrons. In some cases the materials produced were crystalline and therefore solid; for example, metals, common salt and diamond. In others, a stable arrangement was produced by formation of small groups of atoms; for example, oxygen O_2 or ethylene C_2H_4. It is commonly known, however, that the latter materials may be liquefied or even solidified by lowering the temperature. This can be explained by the van der Waals bond. In any one molecule, the electrons in orbit around it produce small, instantaneous eccentricities of charge which cause neighbouring molecules to be attracted by it. Hence this type of bond is operative between any adjacent molecules and although easily overcome by thermal energy, may produce a solid with a certain amount of strength. The softer plastics are examples of molecular chains made solid in this way. van der Waals bonds also are important in concrete and can be used to explain the phenomenon of creep. Colloidal properties of materials such as clay are similarly explained. The van der Waals bonds are responsible for the solid nature of graphite—they cause attraction between the sheets already described.

Summary of bonding. Bonding takes place between atoms, causing solid materials if the bonding is extended, liquids if the bonding is of short range only and gases when bonding forces are not strong enough to overcome thermal energy. Materials in which the bonding is powerful and extended are strong, durable and have high melting points; for example, silica, diamond and some metals. Other solids may be fibrous, if covalent bonds form long chains, the chains being locked mechanically together or held by van der Waals forces (Fig. 1.13). They may also be plastic; for example, clay, in which groups of covalent bonded atoms are held together by van der Waals forces. In composite materials, the constituents may not be held together by chemical bonding at all. For example, the mortar bond in brickwork is a mechanical key resulting from penetration of mortar into the porous brick surface.

In all states of solid or liquid, the thermal energy of each atom or molecule is governed by statistical laws, hence evaporation may take place when some individual molecules have sufficient thermal energy to overcome bonding forces. This gives rise to vapour pressures. These are very small in most solids, but are significant in liquids and in the case of water lead to the presence of significant quantities of water in the atmosphere and as a result in porous materials, even though these may be protected from moisture in liquid form. The bonding in liquids manifests itself in surface tension (liquid–liquid attraction) and capillarity (liquid–solid attraction). The distinction between liquids and solids is sometimes very difficult to define—glass for example is a

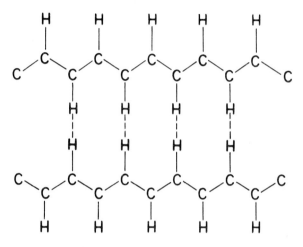

Fig. 1.13 Polyethylene (polythene) chains linked together by van der Waals' bonds (broken)

'supercooled' liquid. Bitumen and cellulose putties exhibit both liquid and solid properties. Even concrete and steel can be plastically deformed. Hence the term liquid or solid is best used arbitrarily in reference to the purpose for which a particular material is intended. Although extending the range of order on a molecular scale will always reduce fluidity, the precise transition from liquid to solid depends on the type and magnitude of the stress applied.

Durability and fire resistance. A material may be said to be durable when it is chemically unaffected by water vapour, gases or radiation in the atmosphere, or solids or liquids around it. Liquids may be responsible for deterioration in porous materials, since they can penetrate units; and in metals because they may contain ions which are chemically reactive.

Gases will tend to react with atoms near the surface of some materials; for example, metals, since the bonding cannot be perfect at the surface, even though the rest of the material might be stable. Radiation gives energy to the surface layers of materials or to the entire thickness of transparent materials—for example, plastics—and generally this causes brittleness. In the extreme case, radiation or heat from another source may cause the material to decompose. This happens at relatively low temperatures with many carbon-based materials which produce flammable gases—gases which react with oxygen with emission of light. Gases may ignite spontaneously if hot enough and heat given out by burning quickly generates more gases from neighbouring material in non-fire resistant materials such as timber. Poor fire resistance may, on the other hand, be due to physical disruption caused by thermal stresses, as for example in glass, or simply due to thermal weakening of bonds with consequent strength reduction as in metals.

Problems

1.1 Give, with reasons, the parts of the atom which are responsible for:
(a) chemical properties; and
(b) radioactive properties.

1.2 Explain why only two electrons are allowed to occupy subshell 2s when six electrons are allowed in the subshell 2p.

1.3 In the periodic table, element 19 (potassium) contains one 4s electron while the 3d shell is empty. Explain the reason for this and name the lightest element which has
(a) a complete 3d subshell;
(b) a complete 5d subshell.
In what way are these two elements similar?

1.4 A gamma ray source used for density measurement has a half life of 5 years. What would its useful life be if a count rate of not less than 25 per cent of the original value is essential for accurate readings?

1.5 The carbon isotope, $_6C^{14}$, produced from carbon in the atmosphere by cosmic rays, has a half life of 5,680 years and is absorbed by living vegetation in which the level remains constant. It decays by beta particle emission. Calculate the age of timber in which the radiation emission has decreased by 5 per cent.

1.6 In the following series, in which uranium I disintegrates into radium, the atomic numbers and atomic masses are shown. What particles are emitted in the five changes?

	Atomic number	Atomic mass
Uranium I	92	238
Uranium X_1	90	234
Uranium X_2	91	234
Uranium II	92	234
Ionium	90	230
Radium	88	226

1.7 What is an ion? Explain why ions of metals have radii smaller than the pure metal atom.

1.8 Explain the meaning of the terms 'atom', 'molecule', 'crystal' and 'polymer'.

1.9 Name two materials in which carbon is found naturally and two synthetic materials in which it occurs. Explain how bonding in these materials leads to their solid/liquid/gaseous nature.

1.10 Arrange in order the melting points of most plastics, ceramics and metals. Explain this in terms of chemical bonds.

1.11 Name two different types of material in which van der Waals bonds are involved; compare their properties and give reasons for similarities and differences.

1.12 Discuss how the chemical bonding in a material affects the following properties:
(a) strength,
(b) ductility,
(c) corrosion resistance,
(d) fire resistance.

1.13 Explain what is meant by disorder, short-range order and long-range order in materials. Classify crystalline solids, amorphous solids, liquids and gases in this way, giving examples of the first two categories.

References

1. R. T. Overman *Basic Concepts of Nuclear Chemistry,* Chapman & Hall.
2. 'Backscattering Method for Density Measurement using Gamma Rays', *Building Science,* Vol. 3, Pergamon, 1968.
3. R. A. Burgess, P. J. Horrobin and J. W. Simpson, eds. *Progress in Constructional Science and Technology* (gamma rays for density measurement), p. 193. Medical & Technical Publishing Co. Ltd.
4. BS 4408, Part 3: 1970, *Gamma Radiography of Concrete.*
5. R. Wormald and A. L. Britch. 'Methods of Measuring Moisture Content Applicable to Building Materials' *Building Science,* Vol. 3 No. 3, Pergamon, 1969.

See also general references.

Chapter 2
SILICACEOUS MATERIALS AND CERAMICS

Silica (SiO_2), an oxide of silicon, is the most common compound in the earth's crust and it is not surprising therefore that it forms the basis of many building materials. Most clays contain a high percentage of silica. Fired clay products are traditionally termed ceramics, although modern use of this term includes many other silicaceous materials with similar properties such as glass and mica as well as some non-silicaceous materials such as metallic oxides used in electrical insulators and glazes.

STRUCTURE OF SILICATES—MINERALS

These are based on the SiO_4 group which in itself is not stable because although the silicon (tetravalent) is satisfied by means of one electron from each oxygen atom making a stable octet in the silicon atom, each oxygen atom has a deficiency of one electron. The situation may be represented in Fig. 2.1. The structure is in fact tetrahedral—that is, each oxygen atom is at the vertex of a pyramid, the silicon being at the centre. Hence four electrons are required and there is a tendency for the silicate units to form ionic bonds with metals by borrowing electrons from them. A large number of metals may combine in many different ways, producing the wide range of minerals which exists in the earth's crust. The silicate itself may form seemingly

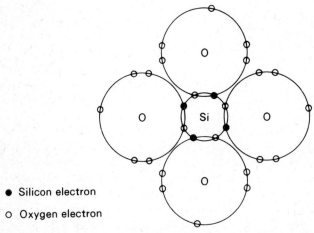

● Silicon electron

○ Oxygen electron

Fig. 2.1 Electron arrangement in the silicate unit. Each oxygen atom has only seven electrons

unrelated types of molecule. If in the tetrahedra of Fig. 2.1 each oxygen atom is joined to another silicon atom and the process is repeated, a diamond type of lattice is produced and the resulting material is pure silica—quartz. Two silicate tetrahedra may be linked by having a base oxygen atom in common. For example, Fig. 2.2 shows the production of a chain in this way. In the repeat distance shown, there are two silicon atoms and six oxygen atoms (four of which require an extra electron). Hence the formula will be in its simplest form, $(SiO_3)^{--}$. The two minus signs represent two ionically borrowed electrons, provided by metals such as magnesium or aluminium which become bonded into the chain. These chains may also be linked by metals to make the ceramic solid. Double chains are possible as in Fig. 2.3. There are four silicon

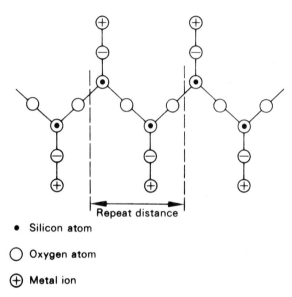

● Silicon atom

○ Oxygen atom

⊕ Metal ion

Fig. 2.2 Silicate chain produced by sharing of base oxygen atoms

atoms and eleven oxygen atoms in the repeat distance, six of which have one electron missing. Hence the formula is $(Si_4O_{11})^{6-}$. These chains may be packed together in regular arrays by means of metal ions, when they produce crystalline forms which occur naturally as minerals. Alternatively, if the fibrous nature is retained, materials such as asbestos result. It is also possible for the silicate unit to form a sheet-like structure as in Fig. 2.4. The various forms of silicates are represented by models in Fig. 2.5.

Another material which is common in minerals is hydrated aluminium oxide (gibbsite) $Al(OH)_3$. In this compound one Al^{+++} ion is ionically bonded to three $(OH)^-$ ions. A sheet structure is again formed, consisting of upper rows of $(OH)^-$ ions, then a layer of Al^{+++} ions (filling $\frac{2}{3}$ of available gaps) and then a lower sheet of $(OH)^-$ ions, similar to the upper sheet, but displaced so that lower $(OH)^-$ ions fit between upper $(OH)^-$ ions (Fig. 2.6). Many minerals are formed when sheets based on silicon and aluminium come together. Each apex oxygen atom of the former replaces one $(OH)^-$

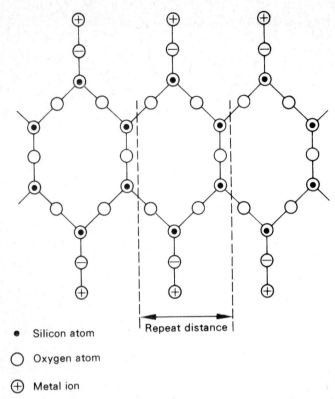

- ● Silicon atom
- ○ Oxygen atom
- ⊕ Metal ion

Fig. 2.3 Formation of a double chain by sharing of base oxygen atoms. Hexagonal shaped patterns are formed. Note that apex oxygen atoms (those above silicon atoms) must be bonded to a metal ion

ion of the latter, producing a stable formation. Kaolinite formula, $Al_2(OH)_4Si_2O_5$, is a simple example (Fig. 2.7). Other minerals may form, for example montmorillonite, when the upper sheet of the gibbsite layer is attached to a silicate sheet in the same way as the lower layer, producing $Al_2(OH)_2 2Si_2O_5$. These sheets tend to pack together by means of van der Waals bonds and may form many layers in some

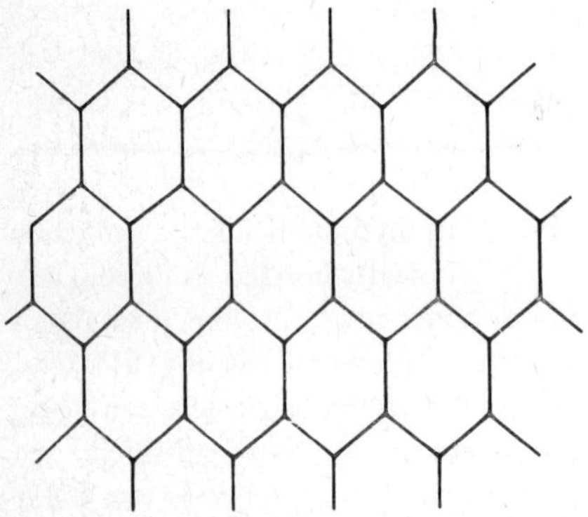

Fig. 2.4 Sheet structure resulting from repetition of the hexagonal-shaped units of Fig. 2.3

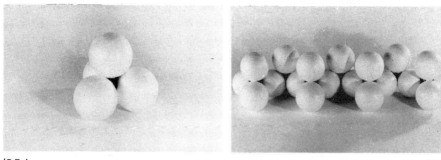

(2.5a)   (2.5b)

(2.5c)

Fig. 2.5(a) Basic silicate unit. Dark sphere—silicon, light spheres—oxygen. All four oxygen atoms require one electron

Fig. 2.5(b) Silicate chain. The apex and side oxygen atoms require one electron

Fig. 2.5(c) Hexagonal silicate unit. This could form a double chain by repeating the hexagons in one direction or a sheet structure by repeating the hexagons in both horizontal directions

(2.6a)   (2.6b)

Fig. 2.6(a) Gibbsite sheet with upper layer of hydroxyl ions (dark), ommitted to show aluminium ions (light) occupying two-thirds of available sites
Fig. 2.6(b) A complete gibbsite sheet showing how upper hydroxyl ions fit between lower ones

(2.7a)   **(2.7b)**

Fig. 2.7(a) Gibbsite sheet with an upper hexagon of hydroxyl, ions removed
Fig. 2.7(b) The apex oxygens of a silicate sheet (Fig. 2.5(c)) fitting into the hexagonal space shown in Fig. 2.7(a) and producing kaolinite

cases. Normally the sheets are very small due to strains imposed by the arrangement of the base oxygen atoms. These strains can be relieved by means of further metal atoms and the sheets then become bigger, forming the mica group of materials.

Properties of the silicates

In all these materials covalent and ionic bonds play an important part. Hence there are no free electrons and the materials are good insulators of heat and electricity. Mechanically, properties depend on the particular structural forms. The crystalline forms, for instance, in minerals, are strong and rigid, but have planes of weakness (cleavage planes) where bond densities are lower. The plate forms, if bonded by van der Waals forces, tend to slip over one another easily, as in clay. They may also tend to absorb moisture. The fibrous forms have tensile strength in the fibrous direction but little strength in other directions. The basic structures of all silicates are very stable, so that they are unaffected by the atmosphere and many acids. This, together with high melting points, makes them a natural choice as building materials.

CLAY AND ITS PROPERTIES

Clay is normally described as a soil of particle size less than 2 μm (cf. 150 μm, the smallest BS sieve size for fine aggregate). Hence clays need not by definition consist of minerals, although most clays do contain a substantial proportion of mineral materials, so that a study of them will lead to an understanding of clay properties. The formation of kaolinite from silica and hydrated aluminium oxide has already been described, this being in fact one of the commonest minerals in clay. There are a number of others and many of these differ from kaolinite only in the arrangement of the silicon and aluminium-based platelets. Many properties of clays derive from the fact that they have a strong affinity for water owing to a negative charge which exists on the surface of clay particles. Possible causes of this are:

1. An aluminium ion (trivalent) occupying the place of a silica ion (tetravelent). The silicate sheet would have one negative charge.

2. A divalent ion, e.g. magnesium, occupying the place of the aluminium ion in the alumina sheet.
3. Broken bonds, as at the edge of a sheet.
4. Adsorption of negative hydroxyl (OH)⁻ ions to the clay surface.

The negative charge causes positive ions in the water to be attracted toward the clay surface and water is bonded to the surface by a bond similar to the van der Waals bond. The water is moveable along the clay surface, but not away from it and these layers may be quite thick. Owing to the very small size of clay particles, agitation easily overcomes the van der Waals bonds when clay is in a very moist condition. Hence it may behave as a liquid on agitation, reverting back to a solid on leaving it for a short time. Clay is said to be colloidal, being known as a 'gel' in the solid state and a 'sol' in the liquid state. Bentonite, a form of montmorillonite, is particularly interesting, since by agitation it may be made sufficiently liquid for pressure grouting. On allowing it to stand for a while, however, it becomes a gel in which the water is ionically bonded so that the material is waterproof. Bentonite therefore has application as a waterproofing or stabilising medium in foundation work.

It is well known that there is an optimum moisture content for compaction of clay. This is evident from the above, since, when large quantities of water are present, the material will behave almost as a liquid, while at low moisture contents bonding increases the stiffness of the clay so that air voids cannot be removed. Furthermore, the fact that the water is adsorbed—held to the clay—makes it difficult to drain saturated clay.

Electro-osmosis

This is a direct consequence of the presence of the negative charges on the surface of clay particles. The gaps between particles in a saturated clay will be filled with water containing positively-charged ions as shown in Fig. 2.8. If a voltage is applied to the

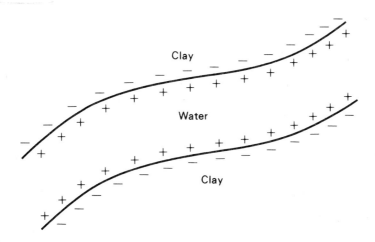

Fig. 2.8 The double layer formed at the surface of clay particles as a result of their negative surface charge

clay by means of electrodes, the positive ions in the water will be drawn to the negative electrode (cathode), carrying moisture with them. This phenomenon is known as electro-osmosis and gives a simple, if expensive, means of draining saturated clay or silty soils. A further effect connected with electro-osmosis in which colloidal particles move in the opposite direction (toward the anode) takes place simultaneously. This is known as electrophoresis and has been used for the injection of bentonite into soils. The bentonite then gels and stabilises the soil, forming a waterproof diaphragm. Alternatively, bentonite may be used in this way to waterproof walls and basements.

CLAY BRICKS

In spite of difficulties associated with high-rise buildings and the expense of a craftsman's skill involved in laying, brickwork is still much in demand, perhaps because it provides, as well as a structural unit, a maintenance-free weathering surface of first-class appearance.

Classification

Bricks may be classified according to clay type, place of manufacture, type of pressing process, type of surface or colour, type of firing process, or use. Typical examples are:

Staffordshire Blue—a type of engineering brick
Dorking Stock—the term 'stock' implies a locally made brick
Fletton—a brick for ordinary or common use.

Manufacture

Clay is a silicaceous material, the particles being in the form of small platelets. These plates attract water to the extent that some clays are as much as 90 per cent water. The water in clay is important in making clay products because it gives the clay sufficient plasticity to enable it to be shaped. Once the product has been made, the moisture content must be reduced, especially if a rapid firing process is used, otherwise considerable distortion of the unit would take place in firing due to the pressure of the water vapour. The object of firing the unit is to cause localised melting or sintering of the clay, so that it becomes a coherent mass. This takes place at temperatures well below the melting point of pure silica due to the presence of metallic oxides in the clay which behave as fluxes. On cooling, the molten material forms a glassy solid enclosing the crystalline particles. Although reducing the original moisture content reduces void spaces, all bricks are nevertheless to some degree porous and absorb water which forces the platelets apart causing expansion. Hence some idea of the durability of a unit (as well as its strength) can often be obtained from a measurement of its density. This may be compared to the density of pure silica (2650 kg/m^3).

Forming the unit

The clay usually occurs in strata, the various types being suitable for different forming and firing processes. After 'winning' the clay, it is crushed and small quantities of salts such as barium carbonate may be added to combat soluble salts. The barium carbonate reacts with soluble sulphates, producing insoluble barium sulphate. There are three main methods of moulding: the semi-dry process, the wire cut process and the soft mud process.

1. *The semi-dry process.* This uses a low moisture content between 10 and 20 per cent, the clays being moulded under high pressure by machine. Drying is not necessary unless firing is extremely rapid. The unit produced is strong and of low porosity. In a slight variant of this called the stiff plastic process, clots are first made, being pressed into shape in the moulds.

[$10 - 20\%$ H_2O]

2. *The wire cut process.* The moisture content is slightly higher than that of (1) (15–25 per cent), producing a softish clay of fine texture. This is extruded complete with perforations and then cut to size by tensioned wires. Such units are easily recognised by the small scores in the cut face, caused by movement of particles under the wire. These units are normally dried before firing and produce a strong unit of reliable dimensional accuracy.

[$15 - 25\%$ H_2O]

3. *The soft mud process.* Clay in a soft plastic form is moulded by machine or by hand, the latter method producing the crease marks which are responsible for the high aesthetic value of hand-made bricks. The moisture content is normally over 20 per cent, hence drying is necessary and the fired product will generally be more variable in dimension than (1) or (2); of lower strength and higher porosity.

[$>20\%$ H_2O]

Firing processes

1. *The car tunnel kiln.* Units are fed, specially stacked on trolleys, into a tunnel about 100 m long and in the course of about a day pass through drying, firing and cooling zones. The kilns are oil or gas fired.

2. *The Hoffman kiln.* The bricks are loaded into a series of chambers normally forming an oval shape. Heat is then supplied in rotation to these chambers through flue ducts. The total firing time is about a week. Heat, traditionally supplied by coke, is now increasingly obtained from gas. Like the car tunnel kiln, this is a continuous kiln since loading, firing and unloading all take place simultaneously in different sections of the kiln. Continuous kilns developed from the Hoffman kiln provide at present the majority of clay bricks.

3. *Clamps.* These are very large formations of bricks built on a breeze base. This, together with fuel included in the bricks, is ignited so that the entire mass becomes red hot. The resulting product is rather variable in shape, colour and strength, but is still used on account of its aesthetic qualities.

Properties of bricks

Although properties could be described under a large number of different headings, perhaps the most important and representative ones are:

1. Strength.
2. Soluble salt content.
3. Water absorption.

Other properties such as dimensions and appearance are also important but these are relatively easily assessed and do not greatly affect the stability of durability of the structure. Bricks are inherently variable due to statistical fluctuations in clay type, moisture content and firing temperature and it is therefore essential that in measuring properties a sufficiently large number of representative samples should be taken.

Compressive strength

Values may vary between 10 N/mm^2 for some common bricks to 100 N/mm^2 or more for engineering bricks.

Soluble salts

These occur in the form of sulphates of calcium, magnesium, potassium and sodium. They may have three effects:

(a) *Crystallisation.* This occurs when, on drying, salts inside the brick crystallise, leading to pressure which may disrupt the surface of the brick. A similar effect occurs when lime particles in the brick expand, flaking off the surface.

(b) *Efflorescence.* This is visible crystallisation of salts on the brick surface, where most evaporation takes place. The salts are often already present in the brick, but they may also have come from the mortar or soil or they may be due to atmospheric pollution. Efflorescence is unsightly but does not cause damage. It is normally most severe on new bricks in exposed positions which dry out after a period of wet weather.

(c) *Sulphate attack on mortar.* Sulphates attack the cement in mortar causing expansion and failure of joints. Sulphates may arise from sources as in (b), but in brick chimneys, where sulphate attack is common, the main source of sulphates is the flue gases. For this reason it is now normal practice to line flues which carry sulphurous gases.

Water absorption

Absorption of water may result in efflorescence, crystallisation, sulphate attack on mortar, frost damage or may in itself be undesirable, for example in solid walls, where it may lead to penetration of dampness. Hence it is a useful test and a better guide to durability than a porosity test, since closed pores are no disadvantage in this respect. The absorption rate as well as the eventual absorption is also important since it will affect the degree of saturation at any one time.

Tests for clay bricks and blocks (BS 3921)

This standard classifies bricks according to durability as of internal quality, ordinary quality or of special quality to be used where severe exposure is likely. Requirements are given, with sampling methods, for dimensions, strength and appearance, for all brick qualities. Ordinary and special qualities have an efflorescence requirement and water absorption is specified for engineering bricks and bricks for damp proof courses, a value of not more than 4·5 per cent being required except for engineering class B bricks (7 per cent). Bricks which in respect of absorption or strength satisfy engineering brick standards are regarded as of special quality, although evidence of frost resistance is recommended on these where necessary. Special qualities of bricks are also subject to soluble salt requirements and should be 'hard fired'. BS 3921 also describes dimensional and strength requirements for hollow clay blocks for partitions, floors and roofs.

Effect of firing temperature

Maximum firing temperatures vary from about 1000°C for common bricks to 1300°C for engineering bricks. Variations in firing temperature or firing time have important effects on the properties of bricks. For satisfactory results, it is important that the temperature should be the same throughout the batch of bricks as they are fired, and that temperature variations from batch to batch should be minimised. Modern tunnel kilns have recording thermometers which monitor temperatures at all parts of the process, thereby providing maximum control. Although properties of particular bricks depend on clay types and method of formation, basic properties are in general affected by temperature as follows:

Strength This increases by sintering of clay constituents which takes place from 700°C upwards. Underfiring produces a soft, weak brick. Overfiring produces over-vitrification causing brittleness and reduced strength due to 'bloating' caused by trapped gases.

Dimensions Bricks expand on heating up to temperatures of about 900°C. Thereafter shrinkage occurs and porosity reduces as vitrification takes place. Overfiring or too rapid firing may cause bloating and irregular shape due to pressures exerted by trapped gases.

Soluble salts. These become fused into the glass fraction of the brick as the temperature rises, hence an underfired brick will contain a high proportion of soluble salts.

Expansion on first wetting. This decreases as the firing temperature of the brick rises. Underfired bricks may have a much larger expansion on first wetting than well-fired bricks.

Refractory bricks

These are used where high temperatures are encountered, such as in furnace linings. They are formed from clays which are mainly silica and alumina, since the presence of metallic oxides found in many clays causes a reduced melting point owing to their action as fluxes.

Calcium silicate bricks

These are made by steam autoclaving, under pressure, a finely divided mixture of sand and lime. A reaction occurs between the surface of the sand particles and the lime, producing a calcium silicate hydrate. The process takes about 12 hours, during which there is no change of size, so that dimensional tolerances are very good comparative to clay bricks. Soluble salts or discoloration are not usually present provided constituent materials are free from clay or organic impurities. Sand lime bricks are covered by BS 187 which classifies strength as for clay bricks with a maximum value of approximately 40 N/mm^2 (comparative to 104 N/mm^2 for class 15, load-bearing clay bricks) and recommends uses for each grade. Hence strengths are in general lower than in clay bricks and the mortar should be adjusted accordingly to avoid cracking of bricks. The moisture movement of sand lime bricks is considerably higher than that of clay bricks, hence they should not be saturated before laying, rendering or plastering. BS 187 gives allowable drying shrinkages which decrease in the higher strength classes. Joints in brickwork are recommended every 7 m or so, and due to differential thermal movement cracking may occur if, in large lengths, they are bonded to clay brickwork. Although calcium silicate bricks are suitable for all normal purposes, their chemical resistance is not as good as that of clay bricks and slight deterioration has been known to occur over periods of years in polluted atmospheres.

Selection of bricks

A brick must be suited to the purpose for which it is intended. Environments may vary between dry, warm air, as in interior use, and permanently damp and possibly aggressive soils when used below damp proof courses or in earth-retaining walls. Even a correctly selected brick may be unsatisfactory if used improperly. For example, calcium silicate bricks, laid wet, will tend to shrink if used internally and may then crack, especially if the mortar used is too strong. Similarly, clay bricks undergo an irreversible expansion on first wetting so that it is bad practice to lay when fresh from the kiln. (Approximately 50 per cent of this expansion occurs in the first 7 days.) Note that concrete structures tend to *shrink* with time, so that brick panels in concrete structures must have movement joints. Otherwise spalling of bricks may occur. In general, as with other materials, bricks should be stored in conditions similar to those of use.

Ideally, in order to ascertain the suitability of a brick for a certain purpose, a panel of brickwork may be constructed and exposed in such conditions for at least 1 year, but failing this, a good guide can be obtained from the tests for special-quality bricks, provided sampling procedures are satisfactory. Variability from batch to batch is important and a rapid assessment of the likely variability of bricks generally could even be obtained by careful length measurements of samples of bricks, since variations in length, as in strength, porosity, etc., will be caused by the same fluctuations, namely variations in clay materials and firing of individual bricks.

Load bearing brickwork

Considerable progress has been made concerning the behaviour of bricks and mortar in brickwork leading to the possibility of multistorey brickwork structures. The main problem is that of testing large units under the various possible stress systems which could be encountered in a wall. What are at the moment necessarily large safety factors in brickwork will reduce as quality control in brick production improves and the nature of loading stresses is increasingly understood.

Larger units

Although experimental variations in size of bricks have not produced a satisfactory appearance, several newer types of unit have been produced, a notable example being perforated or hollow building blocks that obviate the need for a cavity. These give a wall of increased stability and with lower erection costs. The perforations produce similar thermal performance to a cavity brick wall although damp proofing properties are not so good. One disadvantage of such units is that, when used to replace a cavity wall, the whole wall is then of dense clay material being more expensive and of considerably inferior thermal properties to the now established clay brick outer leaf and insulating block inner leaf construction. Experiments have been made with complete brick panels, mortar joints being obtained by pressure grouting of pre-assembled bricks. Such panels, however, are difficult to move unless reinforced and would only be suitable for large-scale modular types of construction.

Other fired clay products

Although the use of pre-formed plastic and concrete units has increased tremendously in recent years, many different types of fired clay products are still used and accepted as first rate materials. They have the advantage that they have been proved by use in buildings over many years. Although only clay roofing tiles and pipes are described here, the range of fired clay products is extensive, including, as well as the above, sanitary ware, glazed porcelain tiles, flooring tiles, terracotta (unglazed clay units used for decorative or architectural purposes) and faience (glazed decorative units). The products to be described are similar in composition and manufacture to clay bricks, though it may be worthwhile to indicate the chief criteria on which individual units may be judged.

Clay tiles for roofing

The first requirement is that of water absorption since units are relatively thin and would tend to become saturated very quickly if absorbent. BS 402, *Clay plain roofing tiles and fittings*, requires a limit of 10·5 per cent for the average absorption of a sample of 25 tiles in each 10,000. Tiles with suitably low absorption will normally have good frost resistance. The standard also requires a minimum transverse strength since tiles must be able to withstand stresses caused by transportation to the site or roof repairs. The curvature of each tile is also important since this prevents capillarity between tiles. The durability of a tiled roof will generally increase as the pitch becomes steeper, since the tiles retain less water in this case. Some machine-made tiles have a shorter life than hand-made tiles, since there is a tendency for laminations which occur in them to reduce their frost resistance.

Clay pipes

The continued use of clay pipes, perhaps like tiles, reflects their proved reliability in use. Modern plastic jointing methods have reduced fixing costs and allow greater movement of pipes. Salt glazing has been largely replaced by ceramic glazing or by vitrifying pipes, since, during the salt glazing process, hydrochloric acid is emitted in gaseous form into the atmosphere, causing pollution. The British Standards for clay pipes (BS 65 and 540) do not require any type of glazing and this is due to the comparatively smooth abrasion-resistant surface which is produced by modern manufacturing methods. Water absorption is of little consequence except where aggressive fluids are encountered since pipes are not normally subject to frost attack.

BS 65 and 540 give dimensional tolerances and loads for 'standard' strength, and 'extra' strength pipes. A pressure test is specified, with two classes, corresponding to surface and underground pipes. The latter also require an impermeability test. Alkali and acid resistance are also specified.

STONES FOR BUILDING

These may be natural stones or reconstructed stone. Since the latter involves use of an artificial binder, it will be described under the heading of concrete. While the use of stone as a structural material has decreased in recent years, wide use still is made of it as a decorative finish in flooring and cladding. A stone which is suited to its purpose and correctly formed and applied achieves extremely good effect and durability. Natural stones may be broadly classified according to origin.

Igneous

This is rock which is formed from the molten state. Those formed by the earth's crust are coarse grained with large crystals of minerals such as felspar, as in granite. Rapid cooling, as for example when volcano lava solidifies, produces a finer structure such as basalt. Both granite and basalt are very hard with no natural bedding planes and are hence difficult to work, but when used for simple shapes, e.g. kerb stones, have produced units of excellent durability. Porosity and moisture movement are negligible due to the crystalline forms of these stones. Their high silica content also means that they are unaffected by environmental pollution. These properties, together with advances in mechanical cutting and finishing, make granite a popular material for use in thin sections in cladding of buildings. Other modern applications of granite include use as an aggregate for high strength concrete and in ground form in abrasion-resistant surfaces. There are granite quarries in most parts of Britain, with the exception of the South East, where sedimentary rocks predominate.

Sedimentary

These consist of small particles of either igneous rocks such as quartz or felspar, or fragments of decayed animal or vegetable matter, cemented together by materials such as silica, calcium carbonate, clay or iron oxide. They may be broadly classified as sandstones or limestones corresponding to grains of silica and calcium carbonate respectively. Sedimentary stones have natural bedding planes which, on exposure, tend to admit water causing flaking. Hence the bedding planes are best laid horizontal. This is quite possible where load bearing stone blocks are used, but may be impossible where thin sections are required as in cladding. For this reason, the use of sedimentary stones for cladding is relatively uncommon.

Sandstones. The silica—often pure quartz—is cemented together with iron oxide, clay or calcium carbonate. The iron oxide is responsible for the brown colour of some sandstones. The best type of sandstone is that which is cemented by silica, the resulting product being strong and durable; for example, Dunhouse stone from Durham. Calcareous sandstones are strong but less resistant to atmospheric pollution. Clay cemented sandstones are of low durability. Most sandstones are found in North England and Scotland, where they are used extensively as aggregates for concrete.

Limestones. These are based on calcium carbonate. This may occur in the form of a sediment deposited by living matter. It is then fine grained, as for example in chalk, where the calcium carbonate is present as the crystalline form calcite, finely divided to give a soft rock in South England, but more crystalline to give a hard limestone in North England, Ireland and Scotland. Alternatively it may consist of a precipitate from solution or of marine life cemented together. In some cases, the sediment occurs in the form of rounded grains—oolites; for example, Ancaster stone and Portland stone. Portland stone is oolitic but also contains large fossils. As would be expected with any massive occurrence of sedimentary rock, the properties of the stone vary with depth. One particular feature of limestones is their low coefficient of thermal expansion—approximately $4 \times 10^{-6}/°C$, compared with granite, which has a coefficient of expansion of $11 \times 10^{-6}/°C$. Some limestones contain significant quantities of dolomite which has the formula $CaCO_3MgCO_3$. Such stones are known as magnesian limestones.

Metamorphic stone

This is a rock or clay whose structure has been changed by heat or pressure, increasing its crystallinity. There are two important types used in building: marble which is normally imported, and slate—found mainly in North Wales, Northern Ireland and Northern Scotland.

Marble. This can be considered as recrystallised limestone with various other materials based on iron incorporated, the latter giving rise to the attractive colouring of the stone. Although more resistant varieties may be used externally, as a limestone it has poor resistance to atmospheric pollution and soon loses its polish so that it is used mainly as a decorative material for internal uses.

Slate. This is caused by modification of clay by pressure to shale and then by heat, into slate. The stone has pronounced thin laminations which are responsible for its use as a roofing material. Being derived from minerals found in clay, slates have extremely good resistance to weathering and pollution. Over a period of time however delamination takes place causing disintegration. This may occur in less than 10 years with some imported slates. Some Lake District 'slates' are in fact obtained from sedimentary rocks with thin bedding planes. Slates have also been used successfully as damp proof courses. Roofing slates are covered by BS 680, which specifies an absorption of not more than 0·3 per cent after 48 hours' boiling, together with a wetting and drying test. Slates to be used in conditions of severe exposure to atmospheric pollution should satisfy a sulphuric acid resistance test.

Selection of stones for building

When used internally, selection may be based primarily on aesthetic effects, although ease of cleaning and abrasion resistance will also be important, especially for flooring. Externally, some types of stone can be so expensive to maintain in polluted city atmospheres that their use is restricted to 'prestige' building. Some varieties of stone—especially limestone—have, to some degree, a self-cleaning effect due to dissolution of the surface by water. The effect is, however, not always satisfactory, since over a period of time considerable erosion can take place and sheltered parts of the building are not cleaned in this way. Granites stay clean for longer periods of time but are more difficult to clean once dirt has accumulated. Limestones form hard resistant films on exposure, although this film may flake off due to differential thermal movement with the background or by crystallisation of salts underneath it. Care should be taken when using stones of different types. Sandstone in particular may be affected by sulphate solutions produced by the effect of pollution on limestone or cast stone. Since even stone from the same quarry may vary as new beds are uncovered, the assessment of the suitability of a stone should be based on weathering tests on newly quarried samples. When severe exposure is anticipated, for example as in copings, freezing tests are essential. Further tests on the effect of salts present in background brickwork or atmosphere should also be carried out, although it is now common practice to coat the back of stone with bitumen if the stone is to be used against brick or concrete. Table 2.1 shows some well-known stones which are representative of their type, together with properties.

GLASS

Modern scientific progress has brought with it new materials and methods, but as a glazing material glass has remained unchallenged and seems likely to continue to dominate this field into the foreseeable future. Raw materials are plentiful and cheap

Table 2.1

Properties of some typical natural building stones

Group	Type	Name	Compressive Strength (N/mm²)	Density (kg/m³)	Absptn (per cent)	Example
Igneous	Granite	Dartmoor Granite	130	2650	0·1%	Waterloo Bridge
Sedimentary	Oolitic	Portland Stone	40	2200	4%	St. Paul's Cathedral
	Magnesian	Anston	30	2100	7%	Houses of Parliament
	Sandstone	Woolton	60	2400	5%	Anglican Cathedral, Liverpool
Metamorphic	Slate	Kirkstone Slate	130	2700	0·1%	Lake District villages

and glass has unrivalled abrasion resistance, light-transmission properties and resistance to weathering or chemical attack.

The basic component of glass is silica, in the form of a supercooled liquid at room temperature. This amorphous structure is formed rather than a crystal structure since the rate of cooling is too rapid to allow crystals to form (a crystalline form would have neither the strength nor the optical properties of glass). Glass can indeed be made to crystallise by heating to a temperature at which crystallisation (devitrification) takes place or by mechanical vibration or impact, or by ageing over a long period.

Pure silica is not satisfactory for glass manufacture since it has too high a melting point (approximately 1700°C). Sodium carbonate is therefore added, forming sodium oxide on heating which results in ionic bonds in the material, reducing its melting point. The material formed however is soluble in water so that calcium carbonate must be added to stabilise the glass. The approximate composition of a typical soda-lime glass is:

$$SiO_2 \qquad 75 \text{ per cent}$$
$$Na_2CO_3 \qquad 15 \text{ per cent}$$
$$CaCO_3 \qquad 10 \text{ per cent}$$

Smaller amounts of other materials may be added—for example, manganese dioxide—to remove coloration due to iron in the sand, or borax, which produces borosilicate glass with low thermal expansion.

Manufacture of glass

A quantity of 'cullet'—scrap glass—is mixed with the right quantities of raw materials and heated to about 1500°C. The materials fuse together and react chemically and the liquid is then cooled until, at a temperature of about 1000–1200°C, it is ready for forming. The most important processes are:

The flat drawn process. The glass is drawn upwards on a metal grille known as a bait, the sheet engaging with rollers which prevent it waisting. The glass is annealed to relieve cooling stresses and then cut to size. This type of glass contains slight ripples but is economical and is commonly used in domestic dwellings, offices and factories.

Rolled glass. The glass is drawn off in a horizontal ribbon on rollers and is then annealed. Such glasses do not give clear vision but can be given textured or patterned finishes. Wire may be incorporated, producing 'Georgian glass', a material with higher fire resistance and increased safety against injury from impact.

Float glass. This glass is optically flat and is produced by drawing the glass along the surface of molten tin in a bath. It is used for mirrors, shop windows and other situations where clear, undistorted vision is essential.

Toughened glass. Although glass may have a very high tensile strength—above that of cold drawn steel wire—its strength is normally limited by the presence of microscopic surface cracks. These flaws could be removed chemically, but toughening can also be carried out by heat treatment. Sheet glass is heated uniformly until just plastic and then cooled by air jets. The outer layers contract and solidify, and then as inner layers try to follow they throw the outer layers into compression, tending to close the microscopic cracks. In this way, the strength of the glass overall can be increased several times and impact strength may increase sevenfold. Figure 2.9 shows the approximate stress distribution in a sheet of toughened glass. On bending, the compressive stress on one face reduces and failure occurs only when this has been reversed to the normal tensile limit. If the surface is broken, the stress distribution

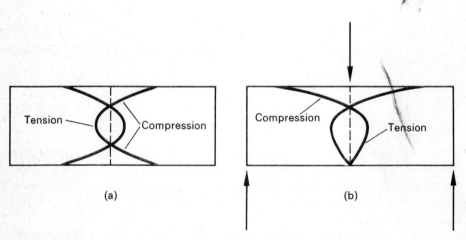

(a)   (b)

Fig. 2.9 Simple representation of the stresses in a sheet of toughened glass. (a) The stresses in a sheet with no external load. (b) The stresses in a sheet under loading indicated. Failure does not occur until the tensile strength at the lower surface is exceeded

becomes unbalanced and the material shatters into fragments. Hence cutting or edge working are not possible and it must be ordered to size. Toughened glass has widened the application of glass to include solid glass doors, large windows and suspended glass curtains. Very large areas of glass are more conveniently suspended from a structural frame, since in this case the weight of glass itself contributes considerably towards stability. Large sheets may be joined by square metal plates at their corners, gaps being filled with transparent plastic material. Additional stability may be achieved by means of stiffening fins which may also be of glass. Such glass curtains are themselves an architectural feature and have been used as complete faces of two-storey buildings.

Thickness and weight

Although the thickness of ordinary glass was traditionally measured in terms of its mass per unit area, thickness is now given directly, the common sizes being 3 and 4 mm thick. The thickness of glass for ordinary glazing should increase with wind load and glass area. Square sheets should be thicker in general than rectangular sheets, since for a given area there is less restraint at the centre of a square sheet of glass. The thickness of toughened glass also depends on other factors such as the impact loading it is likely to have to withstand.

Thermal conductivity—double glazing

Glass, being largely silica, has a thermal conductivity similar to a dense clay brick (approximately $1 \cdot 0$ W/m°C). The resistance of single glazing to heat loss is due to the surface resistances of the glass rather than to its own ability to restrict heat flow. Double glazing similarly depends on the four surface resistances of the two glass sheets. The most efficient types of thermal double glazing are those in which the cavity is factory sealed, either by doubling up and sealing the sheet of glass itself or by using plastic sealing strips between two sheets. These types reduce greatly the risk of condensation in the cavity. A thermal double glazing unit need not have a large cavity to be effective; a 5-mm cavity is satisfactory and cavities larger than 20 mm tend to increase heat losses since they allow air circulation within them. Vertical single glazing in conditions of average exposure will have a 'U' value of approximately 5 W/m² °C while that of double glazing with a 5-mm cavity would be about 3 W/m² °C, cf., $1 \cdot 7$ W/m² °C for a 280 mm cavity brick wall.

Thermal movement

This varies between $5 \cdot 6 \times 10^{-6}$/°C for high silica glasses such as borosilicates to 9×10^{-6}/°C for lead crystal. The former will therefore be more resistant to thermal shock. Thermal movement takes place in glazing, and glazing compounds should have the ability to allow this movement. Fracture of windows often follows when fixing tacks contact the edge of the glass. In a suspended glass assembly, the sheets expand downwards so that a flexible jointing material should be provided at the base and around door frames. Damage may also result from solar radiation which produces differential movement between the centre of the glass and its perimeter which is shaded from the sunlight by the glazing compound. This is particularly true with heat-absorbing glasses. The stresses which result are most likely to cause failure when the edge cover is about 30 mm, since smaller cover reduces the differential and larger cover increases the area of cool edge-glass to meet the tensile stress produced. Risk is minimised by reducing edge cover as far as possible; using dark, heat-absorbing frames; by avoiding insulating materials in direct contact with the glass in the case of cladding and by avoiding edge flaws in the glass which usually initiate fracture. Toughened glass has, of course, greater resistance to damage by solar radiation. Coloured toughened glass panels are available with a layer of Fibreglass and a vapour barrier bonded directly behind them, giving a 'U' value of about $1 \cdot 0$ W/m^2 $^\circ$C.

Light and heat transmission

The direct transmission of light depends on the angle of incidence as well as the glass thickness, but a maximum value of 90 per cent may be assumed in normal glazing. Glass tends to absorb infra red radiation so that corresponding heat transmission is about 80 per cent. Thin metallic layers can be included in the glass during manufacture and these reduce the transmitted heat by some 30 per cent, though the light transmission properties are also affected. Such glasses are useful where solar radiation is a problem, as in roof lights or large areas of glazing. In air conditioned buildings, they reduce the cooling requirement and hence the plant size, and in other buildings they improve standards of thermal comfort.

Durability

Glass is unaffected by the atmosphere and by most acids with the exception of hydrofluoric acid. Alkalis, as occur in cement or chemical paint strippers, attack glass and destroy the smooth surface and light transmission properties.

Sound insulation

The sound reduction properties of glazing are typical of those of a thin panel or membrane. Resonances occur at low frequencies, the insulation improving towards

Table 2.2
Sound level reduction in single and double glazing
(openable windows)

Type and thickness of glazing	Reduction (dB)
3-mm single glazing	20
12-mm single glazing	22
3- and 4-mm double glazed window with absorbent in 200-mm cavity	31

high frequencies. High-frequency insulation is however reduced by the 'coincidence effect'. In double glazing, the cavity size required for effective and sound reduction is about 200 mm; much larger than that for best thermal insulation properties. To be satisfactory, it is extremely important that air paths through glazing should be prevented. The use of different thicknesses of glass in the two sheets and an absorbent material in the cavity increases the sound insulation. Typical sound-reduction values at medium frequencies for opening windows are given in Table 2.2.

ASBESTOS

Asbestos exists in many different forms but is a silicaceous material with the fibrous molecular structure already described. It is, in fact, the only naturally occurring inorganic fibre. Being a mineral, it has extremely good durability and chemical resistance and can be heated to high temperatures without melting or burning. Most uses derive from these properties, together with its high strength in the fibre direction. An unfortunate disadvantage is that fine asbestos particles, as produced by cutting, have a harmful effect on the lungs so that precautions are necessary when working it. Special saws and drills with exhaust ventilation units are obtainable, but failing this damping of work helps to reduce dust levels.

Asbestos occurs in the seams of some types of rock, found chiefly in Canada and South Africa. The most widely used form of asbestos is chrysotile, which has the basic formula $Mg_3Si_2O_5(OH)_4$ together with small amounts of aluminium, iron and sodium. The fibres are variable in length, being on average about 10 mm long and have high tensile strength—approximately 500 N/mm^2. Crocidolite and amosite are two other types and these contain larger quantities of iron than chrysotile. Crocidolite is the strongest of the three and has greatest acid resistance, while amosite contains relatively long, stiff fibres. These properties make amosite particularly suitable for use in lightweight insulating boards. The other varieties are commonly used in asbestos cement. Alkali resistance of all types is good. Degradation of asbestos commences at 700-1000°C while fusion is complete by 2000-2500°C.

The chief products of asbestos in construction are as follows:

Asbestos cement

This material is formed from a mixture of short fibres, Portland cement and water, built up in layers to form sheets which are moulded and cured. Alternatively, silica may be added during manufacture, the mix being steam autoclaved. Such types are also covered by British Standards given below. It is used to form many products, many of which are used externally, having a life of at least 40 years. During this time, however, impact strength decreases due to embrittlement (which also produces an *increase* in flexural strength). Some softening of the surface may also occur due to the action of pollution on the cement. Life can be prolonged by painting, an alkali-resistant primer being essential. Since products are brittle, fixings must allow a certain amount of movement and must not cause localised stresses around them. Asbestos cement is commonly used in rainwater goods, many types of pipe, cisterns, conduits and troughs. In sheet form the following types are available:

1. *Fully compressed sheets.* (BS 4036 and BS 690 Part 2). These sheets have a fine dense surface and are useful for infill panels for curtain walling, balconies and also in shuttering for concrete. (When used in shuttering, a waterproof membrane is essential since asbestos cement may absorb up to 25 per cent by dry weight of water.) Where greater flexibility is required, these sheets are available with increased fibre content, being suitable for use as lining for ceilings, walls, doors and partitions. Factory-applied painted or metallic finishes are obtainable. Similar sheets have been produced by extrusion and this process may lead to the introduction of asbestos cement products with more complex shapes.

2. *Semi-compressed sheets.* (BS 690). These do not have as good a surface finish or impact resistance as fully compressed sheets although their thermal conductivity is lower so that for a given thickness of sheet the thermal insulation is slightly better. They are used extensively in roofing when the sheets are corrugated. When such roofing is subjected to the external fire exposure test of BS 476, it is given the maximum rating 'Ext.S.AA'. This implies no penetration in one hour and no spread of flame. However, as indicated, in C.P. 143 Part 6, 'Sheet roof and wall coverings', there is a tendency for asbestos cement to shatter under the intense heat of an internal fire. Extra protection is therefore necessary and this could be in the form of a sprayed asbestos inner lining. A great reduction in heat losses is obtained by use of double sheets containing Fibreglass infill. Special shaped sheets may be used in decking with spans up to 3 m (BS 3717).

3. *Low-density boards.* (BS 3536). These may be of asbestos cement, or, alternatively, an autoclaved mixture of asbestos, lime, sand and water, the hardening process in the latter case being the same as that for calcium silicate bricks. They have a density between 900 and 1400 kg/m^3 compared with at least 1600 kg/m^3 for fully compressed sheets, with thermal conductivity correspondingly lower—between 0·12 W/m °C and 0·25 W/m °C. They are used as wallboards, for insulation purposes, and are also suitable for encasing columns and beams to improve resistance. When used in external walls or roofing for insulation purposes, a vapour barrier may be necessary to prevent condensation.

Sprayed asbestos (BS 3590)

If a mixture of cement, water and asbestos is sprayed on to a surface, it forms a material having a very low thermal conductivity due to entrapped air, and hence excellent resistance to fire. The material is commonly used for protection of structural steelwork and concrete. For bonding to metal, a priming coat of resin or bituminous paint is necessary although sprayed asbestos may be used direct on porous materials such as concrete. As an illustration of the effectiveness of sprayed asbestos for improving fire resistance, the resistance of a 90-mm thick concrete floor is increased from half an hour to 4 hours by a 25-mm coating of sprayed asbestos.

The material also has excellent heat insulation properties, a 25-mm coating decreasing the 'U' value of corrugated steel roofing from 8·5 W/m^2 °C to 1·5

W/m^2 °C. Sprayed asbestos will absorb a certain amount of condensation, but where long periods of high humidity are likely a vapour barrier may be necessary to prevent saturation. Sprayed asbestos, being sound absorbent, is also used for acoustic purposes and has the advantage that it can be used to coat irregular-shaped objects.

THE MECHANICAL PROPERTIES OF CERAMICS AND OTHER RIGID SILICATES

Ceramics normally fail in a brittle manner, since there is no possibility of substantial plastic movement where the materials have been hardened so that van der Waals bonds are replaced by ionic or covalent bonds. If distortion above a certain point takes place, positive ions become adjacent (Fig. 2.10) and hence complete bond failure is caused rather than slip along planes. Furthermore, especially where tensile stresses occur, the

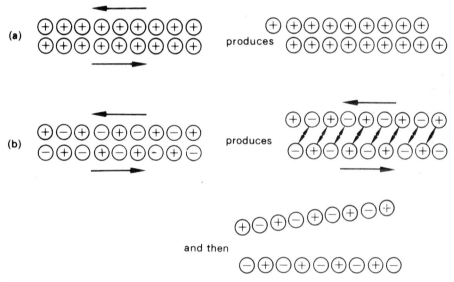

Fig. 2.10 Comparison of the effect of shear stress on metal and ceramic crystals. (a) Metal. Plastic flow does not damage the crystal. (b) Ceramic. Strong repulsion of similarly charged ions causes high internal stresses and eventual failure.

release of elastic energy on breakage of a single bond will very rapidly provide energy to rupture neighbouring bonds, causing rapid crack propagation. Pure compression can only reinforce bonding although in practice there is always a shear stress corresponding to a compressive load (of maximum value equal to half the compressive stress and inclined at 45° to it) and failure may take place in this way. Compressive stresses also induce tensile stresses according to the Poisson ratio of the material and there is a body of opinion which considers that these induced tensile stresses are actually responsible for failure in a large number of cases. Theoretically, tensile strengths could be very high since ionic and covalent bonds are powerful, but microscopic cracks are often present in ceramic materials due to thermal or shrinkage stresses and these would, of course, be extremely sensitive to applied tensile stresses. Further evidence in support of this argument is that perfectly formed fibres of material such as glass, or etching to remove surface defects, may produce very high tensile strengths.

Problems

2.1 Describe how their basic molecular shape is responsible for properties of pure silica, mica, clays and asbestos.

2.2 Explain the following properties of clays:
  (a) their slippery nature when wet,
  (b) their cohesive nature when uniformly damp,
  (c) the tendency to compact most efficiently at a certain moisture content,
  (d) their shrinkage and increased strength on drying,
  (e) the difficulty involved in draining them.

2.3 Tests carried out on a certain type of brick of average length 220 mm and average width 106 mm showed that its average compressive load was 1830 kN. After 5 hours boiling in water, the average mass increased from 2·94 to 3·05 kg. Use BS 3921 to classify the brick.

2.4 A brick is required for use in a parapet wall where appearance is important and where severe exposure is likely. Describe some simple tests which could be made to ascertain its suitability.

2.5 What do you consider to be the prospects of brickwork in the future? Give suggestions as to what developments will be necessary to ensure maximum potential.

2.6 Suggest possible modes of failure in a brick wall or pier. Explain why the mortar does not have to be as strong as the bricks themselves. (See also Chapter 3).

2.7 Give four possible sources of sulphates in brickwork and explain how they may affect
  (a) the bricks,
  (b) the mortar.

2.8 Discuss the deterioration of building fabrics due to crystallisation.

2.9 Discuss the relative properties and uses of limestone and granite.

2.10 What properties of glass cause it to be regarded as a supercooled liquid? Describe the inherent weakness in glass and explain how *it* may be overcome.

2.11 Discuss how the structure of asbestos is responsible for the following properties:
  (a) tensile strength;
  (b) resistance to fire;
  (c) resistance to heat conduction.
  Give applications of the material based on each property.

2.12 Describe how, by appropriate design and use of glass and asbestos, a timber-framed glazed door could be made resistant to radiant heat and flame penetration.

References

1. Herman Salmang. *Ceramics,* Butterworths, 1961.
2. R. N. Young and B. P Warkentin. *Introduction to Soil Behaviour,* Macmillan, 1966.
3. *Fullers' Earth Products,* Fullers' Earth Union Ltd., Redhill, Surrey.
4. L. Casagrande. *The Application of Electro-osmosis to Practical Problems in Foundations and Earthworks,* H.M.S.O., 1947 (Paper No. 30).
5. National Brick Advisory Council, H.M.S.O., 1950 (Paper No. 5).
6. *Selection of Clay Bricks,* B.R.S. Digests, Nos. 65 and 66.
7. H. O'Neill. *Stones for Building,* Heinemann, 1965.
8. D. B. Honeybourne. *Laboratory Freezing Test for Natural Building Stone,* B.R.S. Miscellaneous Papers No.3, 1965.
9. *Glass,* Technical information from Pilkington Bros. Ltd St. Helens.
10. Asbestos, Technical information from Turner Asbestos Cement Ltd.

Relevant British Standards

BS 65 & 540: Part I: 1971. *Clay drain and sewer pipes including surface water pipes and fittings.*

BS 187: Part II: 1970. *Calcium silicate (sandlime and flint lime bricks).*

BS 402: Part II: 1970. *Clay plain roofing tiles and fittings.*

BS 680: Part II: 1970. *Roofing slates.*

BS 690 1962. *Asbestos cement slates, corrugated sheets and semi-compressed flat sheets.*

BS 3536. *Asbestos insulating boards and asbestos wallboards.*

BS 3590: 1970. *Sprayed asbestos insulation.*

BS 3717: 1964. *Asbestos cement decking.*

BS 3921: Part II: 1969. *Bricks and blocks of fired brickearth, clay or shale.*

BS 4036. *Asbestos cement fully compressed flat sheets.*

Chapter 3
CEMENT AND CONCRETE

Concrete is a mixture of aggregates, cement and water. On mixing, the latter materials form a matrix which encloses and fixes the aggregate, producing strength. Other materials may be used instead of, or as well as, the above (e.g. additives—substances added during manufacture of cement, or admixtures—substances added during mixing of the concrete). It is important that properties of all constituent materials are understood in order to predict the likely performance of hardened concrete. Hence these materials will be discussed first.

CEMENTS

The vast majority of cements used for concrete are hydraulic, that is, they set solely by chemical reaction with water. Portland cements are most widely used, although two other types, high alumina and supersulphated cement, are also worthy of mention.

Portland cements

These were first so named owing to the similarity of concretes made with them to Portland stone. There are many types of Portland cement produced by variants in raw materials or in the manufacturing process. The most common type is known as 'Ordinary Portland Cement'.

Manufacture of ordinary Portland cement

The basic raw materials for ordinary Portland cement are clay or shale and calcium carbonate, in the form of chalk or limestone. (Most clays consist chiefly of silica, SiO_2, abbreviated 'S', alumina, Al_2O_3, abbreviated 'A' and some iron oxide, Fe_2O_3, abbreviated 'F'.) The materials, in approximate proportions 80 per cent calcium carbonate and 20 per cent clay or shale, are finely ground, mixed and heated together to a temperature of about $1350°C$ in a rotary kiln, which is inclined slightly so that on rotation the material passes gradually from one end to the other. The kiln is heated by powdered coal, injected at the lower end. As the constituents pass down the kiln, the temperature rises, causing dehydration of raw materials by $400°C$. The calcium carbonate decomposes to form calcium oxide (abbreviated 'C') by about $900°C$, and as the temperature increases further the compounds dicalcium silicate (C_2S), tricalcium aluminate (C_3A) and tetracalcium alumino ferrite (C_4AF) are formed. The latter materials fuse together and further reaction between them, C_2S and free lime produces a fourth compound, tricalcium silicate (C_3S). Hence in the cement, the C_3A and C_4AF form the matrix and the other two compounds occur as crystals within the matrix. On cooling, a clinker is formed. Figure 3.1 shows a sample of such clinker,

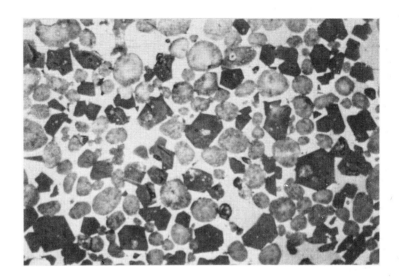

Fig. 3.1 Magnified view of etched polished section of Portland cement clinker. The dark angular material is tricalcium silicate, the rounded lighter material dicalcium silicate and the lighter background tricalcium aluminate. Some darker background material is visible. This is tetracalcium aluminoferrite

ground, polished and etched, crystals of C_2S and C_3S being visible against the glassy background of C_3A and C_4AF. About 5 per cent of gypsum is added ground with the clinker to form a fine powder which is Portland cement. The properties of the four chief compounds in cement are as follows:

Tricalcium aluminate (C_3A). This is chiefly responsible for the initial setting of the cement. It combines rapidly with water, disintegrating into a powder. Gypsum is added to retard this reaction. Considerable heat is evolved on setting (870 J/g) and resistance to sulphates is low. It has little value as a cementitious material, but behaves as a flux during manufacture, enabling C_2S and C_3S to form at lower temperatures. It constitutes about 10 per cent of ordinary Portland cement.

Tetracalcium aluminoferrite (C_4AF). This is the only compound in cement containing iron. Hence the quantity produced depends only on the iron content of the clay. Ordinary Portland cement contains about 10 per cent of C_4AF. The compound sets quickly and is controlled, like the C_3A, by the added gypsum. Also, as with C_3A it behaves as a flux during manufacture of the cement. The material contributes little to the ultimate strength of cements but is expensive to remove. It is responsible for the grey colour of Portland cements.

Tricalcium silicate (C_3S). This hydrates quickly on adding water with high heat evolution (500 J/g). It occupies between 30 and 60 per cent by weight of Portland cement. It is mainly responsible for early strength (for example at 7 days).

Dicalcium silicate (C_2S). This hydrates slowly with a heat evolution of 260 J/g. It occupies between 15 and 35 per cent of ordinary Portland cement. It is largely responsible for the ultimate strength of the cement.

Factors affecting the properties of Portland cement (BS 12)

Modern construction methods often involve exacting specifications for concrete and it is therefore of prime importance that the properties of the cement used be known and that they be as consistent as possible. The nature of the raw materials for cement (including coal used for firing) are such that there is an inherent difficulty in producing uniform quality, since variations are bound to occur to some degree from day to day as well as on a long term basis. However, a considerable amount can be done to minimise variations in cement properties and when these do occur it is usually possible to ascertain them either by private testing or by contacting the cement manufacturer on a day-to-day basis, if necessary. The properties of cement are affected chiefly by its chemical composition and its fineness.

1. *Chemical composition.* The relative proportions of the four compounds already described depend on the relative proportions of the four constituent compounds, calcium oxide, silica, alumina and ferrite, which in turn depend on the relative proportions of clay and limestone and the balance of minerals within the clay. Bogue has produced equations which enable the quantities of the four compounds to be calculated:

$$\text{per cent } C_4AF = 3.04 \text{ (per cent F)}$$
$$\text{per cent } C_3A = 2.65 \text{ (per cent A)} - 1.69 \text{ (per cent F)}$$
$$\text{per cent } C_2S = 8.60 \text{ (per cent S)} - 3.07 \text{ (per cent C)} + 5.10 \text{ (per cent A)} + 1.08 \text{ (per cent F)}$$
$$\text{per cent } C_3S = 4.07 \text{ (per cent C)} - 7.60 \text{ (per cent S)} - 1.43 \text{ (per cent F)} - 6.72 \text{ (per cent A)}$$

Note that the C_4AF, the only compound containing iron, is determined completely by the percentage of F. The percentage of C_3A is determined by the alumina content but with a deduction due to the alumina taken up by the C_4AF. The C_2S and the C_3S equations are more complex but note that on adding the equations:

$$\text{per cent } C_4AF + \text{per cent } C_3A + \text{per cent } C_2S + \text{per cent } C_3S =$$
$$\text{per cent } F + \text{per cent } A + \text{per cent } S + \text{per cent } C \text{ (approximately)}$$

The Bogue equations are useful since the results of a normal chemical analysis of cements give the percentages of calcium oxide, silica, alumina and ferrite. They also enable the effect of variations in the relative proportions of limestone and clay to be determined. For example, if the calcium oxide content increases by 1 per cent, silica would decrease by about 0.7 per cent, alumina by 0.2 per cent and ferrite by 0.1 per cent, so that the change in C_2S is $8.60 \times (-0.7) - 3.07 \times (1) + 5.10 \times (-0.2) + 1.08$ $(-0.1) = -10.2$ per cent. A similar increase of C_3S occurs and these changes will have a significant effect on the properties of the cement. Hence it is essential that the balance between limestone and clay must be very carefully controlled.

Other methods of chemical analysis such as microscopic examination of etched, polished sections of cement clinker enable the compounds in cement to be measured directly.

BS 12 lays down limits for the proportion of calcium oxide to the silica, alumina and ferrite; for combustible or acid soluble impurities and magnesia (magnesium oxide) which may cause expansion (unsoundness) of cement paste on hydration. If free lime in crystallised form in the cement clinker is present, this could also lead to unsoundness and since this is not easy to distinguish from the large quantity of chemically combined lime in cement, a separate soundness test for it is required by BS 12. The expansion of a pat of hydrated cement after a period of boiling is measured, boiling being essential to accelerate hydration of the lime. (This test does not detect magnesia—hence the separate requirement for the latter.) An excess of gypsum could also cause unsoundness, so that BS 12 specifies limits for this, depending on the percentage of tricalcium aluminate present.

The chemical composition of cement affects also the setting time and strength of cements, but, since other factors also are involved, BS 12 measures these properties directly rather than in terms of the four main compounds described above. (In any case, results using the Bogue equations, which are based on equilibrium between the four compounds in crystallised form, are subject to errors, since the compounds C_3A and C_4AF, which were formerly liquid, do not crystallise completely; there is always a proportion of 'glass' in the cement clinker and this affects the proportions of C_2S and C_3S.) An initial and final setting time are defined empirically using a cement paste of standard consistency. The initial setting time should not be less than 45 minutes for ordinary Portland or rapid-hardening Portland cement, a period related to the time after mixing required for placing, compaction and finishing of concrete. The final setting time should not be more than 10 hours. Strength tests on mortar cubes in compression or mortar briquettes in tension are described. Alternatively, if suitable aggregates are available, 100-mm concrete cubes may be used for the compression test.

2. *Fineness.* The hydration of cement is a process which involves penetration of water into cement particles to produce a cement 'gel'. Hence a finer ground cement will hydrate more quickly and produce earlier strength. At the same time, more gypsum is essential to combat the extra C_3A revealed by the greater surface area of cement particles. Since, on drying, cement gel shrinks, finer cements will correspondingly exhibit greater initial drying shrinkage at an early age. Final strength and shrinkage values are, however, similar to those of ordinary Portland cement. Fineness is measured by the term 'specific surface'—the average surface area of cement in m^2/kg. It is obtained according to BS 12 by measurements of the permeability to air of a compacted cement bed of standard thickness, a finer cement being less permeable. Ordinary Portland cement is required to have a specific surface of not less than 225 m^2/kg; rapid hardening Portland cement, not less than 325 m^2/kg.

Other types of Portland cement

Rapid hardening Portland cement. This is covered by BS 12, being essentially different to ordinary Portland cement only in respect of fineness and strength requirements. It attains a strength approximately 50 per cent higher than ordinary Portland cement at three days, though long-term strengths are similar. Accompanying the rapid early strength gain is a considerable evolution of heat so that rapid hardening Portland cement is often used in cold weather to assist in development of maturity. However, on the same account it should not be used in mass concrete, where the heat concentrations would cause a reduction in strength due to thermal stresses.

Ultra-rapid hardening cements which are very finely ground are also on the market, the same arguments as above applying but to a greater degree.

Extra rapid hardening Portland cement. This consists of rapid hardening Portland cement with approximately 2 per cent by weight of calcium chloride. (For the effect of this, see 'admixtures'.) Unlike rapid hardening Portland cement, the setting time is considerably reduced. Note that finer cements and especially extra rapid hardening Portland cement are particularly prone to deterioration if stored in damp atmospheres so that they must be kept dry, and used when reasonably fresh.

Low heat cement (BS 1370). This contains relatively small percentages of the compounds C_3S and C_3A which have the greatest heat evolution. BS 1370 requires a heat output of not more than 250 J/g by 7 days and 290 J/g by 28 days. The rate of gain of strength is lower but this cement has an ultimate strength similar to that of ordinary Portland cement and is suitable for mass construction where heat concentration must be avoided. Its fineness as required by BS 1370 must not be less than 320 m^2/kg in order to ensure satisfactory strength development. Note that due to the small amount of C_3A sulphate resistance of this cement is greater than that of ordinary Portland cement.

Sulphate-resisting Portland cement (BS 4027). Sulphate attack is due primarily to the effect of sulphates in solution on C_3A. (See 'hydration of cement'.) Hence the sulphate resistance of a cement will improve as the quantity of C_3A decreases. This can be achieved by addition of iron ore to the raw materials so that more C_4AF is produced and the alumina is used up in this way instead of forming C_3A. In other respects sulphate-resisting cement is similar to ordinary Portland cement. Note that even concrete made with sulphate-resisting Portland cement may be attacked physically by sulphates if porous, since, on drying, crystallisation will take place inside the concrete, causing expansion and disruption. Hence the use of sulphate-resisting cement is no substitute for production of dense, non-porous concrete.

Portland blast furnace cement (BS 146). This consists of Portland cement clinker and gypsum ground together with up to 65 per cent of quenched blast furnace slag which contains lime, silica and alumina. The hydration of the Portland cement initiates that of the latter, producing a strength progression similar to that of ordinary Portland cement, though early strengths may be lower, so that adequate curing is essential.

Portland blast furnace cement has a higher sulphate resistance than ordinary Portland cement, hence its use in sulphate soils and for construction in or near the sea. A low heat form of Portland blast furnace cement is available and is covered by BS 4246. The heat output and strength development are similar to those of low heat Portland cement.

White cement. This is made using china clay, which contains very little iron, the latter being responsible for the grey colour of ordinary cement. White Portland cement is one of the most expensive Portland cements, since there are few geographic locations where china clay is found.

Hydrophobic Portland cement. This is ordinary Portland cement to which a small percentage of a water repellent such as oleic acid is added. Such cements can be stored for a considerable time in damp atmospheres without subsequent deterioration. On mixing, the acid coating breaks down and behaves as an air entraining agent but mixing time should normally be about 25 per cent longer than for ordinary Portland cement. Early strength development of concretes using such cements is slightly reduced.

Cements other than Portland cements

High alumina cement (BS 915). This is made by heating a mixture of limestone or chalk and bauxite (aluminium ore) in a special furnace, heated by powdered coal to a temperature of about $1600°C$. This causes complete fusion of materials. Cooling produces a clinker which is ground to give a cement having a similar specific surface to that of ordinary Portland cement.

The predominant compound in high alumina cements is CA (monocalcium aluminate), though compounds with other proportions of calcium oxide and alumina also exist, together with small proportions of iron, silicon, titanium and magnesium oxides.

On hydration of the cement, the chief compound produced is calcium aluminate decahydrate, CAH_{10}. Setting is not rapid (BS 915 requires an initial setting time of not less than two hours); however, once setting commences, strength development is much quicker than Portland cements, the final set being not more than two hours after the initial set and the required strength of mortar cubes at 24 hours being $41 \ N/mm^2$ minimum. Figure 3.2 shows comparative strength developments of a 1 : 2 : 4 concrete mix using various Portland cements and high alumina cement at a water cement ratio of 0·6. There is considerable heat evolution so that wet curing is essential during the first 24 hours. If the temperature of high alumina cement hydrate is allowed to rise above about $25°C$ in the presence of high humidity, the CAH_{10} becomes unstable, changing gradually into C_3AH_6 (tricalcium aluminate hexahydrate) and AH_3 (aluminium hydroxide) and this process may occur at any stage in its life. These changes are accompanied by the formation of small pores in the cement so that the resulting hydrate has consequently decreased strength and increased permeability. The process is known as conversion but the reduction in strength can be avoided if some unhydrated cement is still present during conditions of conversion, so that pores are filled with new hydrates as they are formed. For this reason, it is common practice to use mixes with low water/cement ratios and these are best compacted by vibration. Although high alumina cement requires a water/cement ratio of about 0·5 for complete hydration, values below this do not lead to reduced strength since there is chemical bonding between hydrated and unhydrated parts of cement grains.

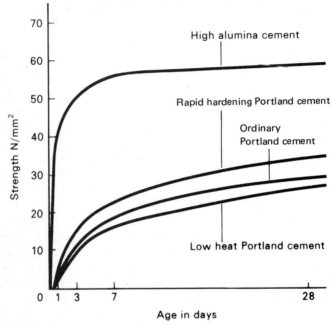

Fig. 3.2 Strength development of 1 : 2 : 4 concretes using various cements at a water–cement ratio of 0·6

The other product of conversion—AH_3, which is also present in normal hydrated cements—contributes to the chemical resistance of high alumina cement concrete which in any case is superior to that of ordinary Portland cement.

A further important use of high alumina cement is as a refractory cement, since on desiccation by heat a good bond is retained up to temperatures of 1600°C. The cement is used in lightweight concretes for flue linings.

Mixtures of high alumina cement and ordinary Portland cement. The setting time of such mixtures is reduced to a degree dependent on their proportions, a very rapid 'flash set' taking place when between 30 per cent and 80 per cent high alumina cement is used. This is thought to be due to rapid setting of the Portland cement fraction owing to chemical combination of its retarder, gypsum, with calcium aluminate hydrates from the high alumina cement. The ultimate strength of such pastes increases with the percentage of high alumina cement used but ultimate strengths are lower than those of ordinary Portland cement unless at least 75 per cent high alumina cement is used. Mixtures may be useful when a very rapid set is required, for example, in sealing leaks, but mixing of these cements is not generally recommended.

Super sulphated cement (BS 4248). This is made from granulated blast furnace slag, calcium sulphate (hence the name) and a small percentage of Portland cement clinker which behaves as an activator. The cement is highly resistant to sulphates and has a low heat output so that it may be used in mass concrete even in tropical conditions. The ultimate strength is similar to that of ordinary Portland cement. Water/cement ratios less than 0·50 should not be used since the cement has a high water requirement. Richer mixes than would be required by ordinary Portland cement are essential, therefore, for a given strength and workability. Super sulphated cement is not suitable for steam curing since this retards its strength development.

Pozzolanic cements. These are cements which, on mixing with Portland cements, react with the lime they liberate on hydration. The active ingredient is a form of silica which occurs in the residue of many combustion processes; for example, pulverised fuel ash. The properties of the latter vary considerably according to source but it is often used in partial replacement of cement in amounts up to 50 per cent by weight, giving increased plasticity, slow gain of strength, low heat output and good chemical resistance at reduced cost.

Hydration of Portland cement

This is a complex and gradual process, involving reaction of water first with the surface regions of the cement particles forming hydrated cement and then penetration of further water through the pores in the already formed hydrate, to react with remaining uncombined cement. The hydrated cement 'grows' from the surface of the particle, gradually occupying some or all of the space occupied by the water, depending on the water/cement ratio. The chief compounds which contribute to strength in Portland cements are C_2S and C_3S. They combine with water as follows:

$$2(2CaOSiO_2) + 4H_2O \rightarrow 3CaO \cdot 2SiO_2 \cdot 3H_2O + Ca(OH)_2$$
$$\text{tobermorite gel}$$
and
$$2(3CaOSiO_2) + 6H_2O \rightarrow 3CaO \cdot 2SiO_2 \cdot 3H_2O + 3Ca(OH)_2$$

(In these equations the full formula for calcium silicates has been used to enable the equations to be balanced.) Note that calcium hydroxide is produced in each case—in the form of crystals. It would be wrong to regard these reactions as a complete description of hydration of the calcium silicates. Various compounds in the C-S-H system are possible depending on ratios of constituents, prevailing conditions and time, the various products possibly having quite different crystal structures. The products exist in the form of extremely small crystals connected together to form a solid matrix and known as a 'gel', implying that there is no long range order as in, say, metallic crystals. The actual form of the gel depends on the water/cement ratio; it occurs mainly in thin plates at low water/cement ratios (e.g. 0·25) and in the form of fibres at high water/cement ratios (e.g. 1·0). In each case, the dimensions are very small and a characteristic of cement gel is its consequent very high specific surface (over 100,000 m^2/kg compared with approximately 300 m^2/kg for unhydrated ordinary Portland cement). The term 'tobermorite gel' has been used to describe the calcium silicate hydrates since tobermorite is the nearest natural occurring mineral to cement gel but in general it would be inaccurate to use this term as a description of hydrated calcium silicates owing to the various forms of the latter.

The hydration of C_3A is modified by the gypsum added during manufacture. Calcium sulphoaluminate (ettringite), which has a high sulphate content, is first formed but as more C_3A dissolves the concentration of the sulphate radical decreases and eventually a calcium aluminate monosulphate hydrate is formed. There may, in fact, be a sudden emission of heat some hours after hydration begins if, when all the gypsum is consumed, there is some remaining tricalcium aluminate which will hdyrate quickly. The monosulphate will revert to ettringite in the presence of sulphates, causing expansion and disruption of the hardened cement.

C_4AF also forms a calcium aluminate hydrate, the iron forming a separate compound.

Water in hydrated cement

It is clear from the above that water exists, chemically bound in hydrated cement, in the form mainly of calcium silicate and calcium aluminate hydrates. However, this is not the only water involved with the cement gel since the latter, owing to its very high specific surface, adsorbs water strongly. The spaces in which this water exists are known as 'gel pores' and occupy about 28 per cent of the total gel volume. Hence although in theory a given mass of cement requires only approximately 25 per cent of its mass of water for complete hydration, in practice, adsorbed water in the gel is not available for hydration and fully hydrated cement gel corresponds to a water/cement ratio of about 0·42. Therefore, at low water/cement ratios hydration can never fully occur. This is however not necessarily a disadvantage from a strength point of view, since the bonding in unhydrated cement particles is more powerful than that in the cement gel and there is also strong bonding between hydrated and unhydrated parts of a cement particle such that, in normal concrete, strength increases even as water/cement ratios decrease to values as low as 0·25. It might be thought at first that in saturated concrete low water/cement ratio cement pastes would be able to hydrate using 'external' water, available during curing but this may not be possible since cement hydrate expands by about 114 per cent of its former volume—hence it must occupy at least some of the space previously occupied by the water and there may therefore be insufficient room for the hydration products when low water/cement ratios are used. For example, 1 g of cement (specific gravity = 3·15) occupies about 0·318 ml before hydration and therefore after hydration approximately

$$0·318 + 0·318 \times \frac{114}{100} = 0·68 \text{ ml}$$

Therefore 0·362 ml of water corresponding to a water/cement ratio of 0·36 will be required to provide the space for expansion (though this is insufficient to cause complete hydration). At water/cement ratios over 0·36 correspondingly there will be extra space around the cement gel, known as capillary pores, and it is through these that water for further hydration passes. Capillary pores must contain water if hydration is to continue and since a 0·42 water/cement ratio paste will contain capillary pores, complete hydration cannot take place unless extra water is available during curing to fill them. Full hydration, in fact, requires a water/cement ratio of about 0·5 or greater.

The rate of hydration of cement decreases exponentially with time and, even in the presence of ample water, it is doubtful whether the process ever reaches completion, since continued hydration depends on penetration of ions through the hydrated gel to the unhydrated cement kernel. At water/cement ratios of about 0·7, depending on the fineness of the cement, the capillary pores remain interconnected and continuous even in fully hydrated cement, so that the resulting concrete is porous. At a water/cement ratio of 0·4, on the other hand, the cement becomes largely non-porous at an age of about 3 days. The effect of water/cement ratio may be summarised as follows:

water/cement ratio below 0·23: insufficient water for complete chemical combination.
water/cement ratio 0·23–0·36: sufficient water for chemical combination but hydration does not take place fully because:

(i) there is insufficient water for gel pores to fill (unless further water is available during curing); and
(ii) there is insufficient space for the cement gel.

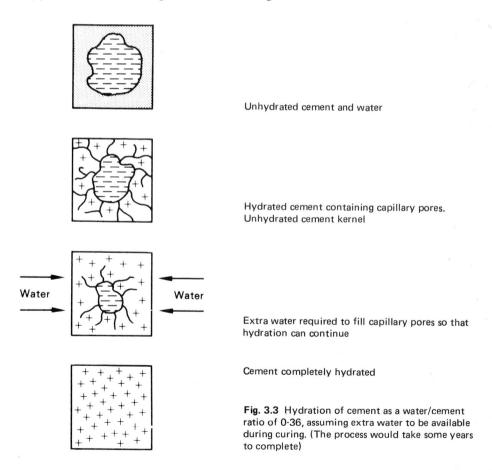

Unhydrated cement and water

Hydrated cement containing capillary pores. Unhydrated cement kernel

Extra water required to fill capillary pores so that hydration can continue

Cement completely hydrated

Fig. 3.3 Hydration of cement as a water/cement ratio of 0·36, assuming extra water to be available during curing. (The process would take some years to complete)

water/cement ratio 0·36–0·42: hydration may take place completely only if extra water is available during curing (see Fig. 3.3).

water/cement ratio 0·42: there is sufficient water for hydration and gel pore water, but in practice, since capillary pores must contain water for the hydration process to continue a value of 0·5 is necessary unless water is available during curing. At water/cement ratios over 0·7, the cement paste remains porous indefinitely.

The strength of hardened cement

The atoms within each platelet or fibre of cement gel are, of course, bonded by covalent or ionic bonds as in clay platelets. For the cement to have strength, however, these platelets themselves must be bonded together. The bonding here is thought to be of two types—van der Waals bonds, due to the very small distances between platelets or fibres and further 'primary' bonds also. The former are responsible for the strong adsorption of water and the latter are essential to limit the swelling of hardened cement paste which tends to occur on adsorption of water. Without the existence of these primary inter-particle bonds, cement would disintegrate like clay on soaking in water. The primary bonds are responsible to a large degree for the strength of cement paste but the van der Waals bonds are important in explaining moisture movement, thermal movement, shrinkage and creep.

The low tensile strength of cement paste relative to its compressive strength is explained using the same arguments as in the case of ceramics, together with the fact that in the damp or wet state the internal pressure exerted by adsorbed water tends to assist tensile stresses and oppose compressive stresses. As a consequence, the tensile strength of cement products is lower when they are wet.

AGGREGATES FOR CONCRETE BS 812 AND 882

Aggregates are used in almost all concretes chiefly because they reduce the cost of the material considerably but also because they often result in an improved product; for example, shrinkage and thermal movement of most concretes are less than those of neat cement pastes and properties such as abrasion resistance are often better. In a typical 1 : 2 : 4 mix using aggregates of specific gravity approximately 2·5, about 75 per cent of the total volume is occupied by fine and coarse aggregates and in lean mix concrete this figure may be as high as 85 per cent.

Aggregate size

Aggregates are classified as coarse aggregate if they are largely retained on a 5-mm mesh sieve and fine aggregate if they largely pass a 5-mm sieve. The term 'sand' is normally reserved for fine aggregate resulting from the natural disintegration of rock. The maximum size of aggregate to be used in concrete is governed mainly by the dimensions of the structure for which it is required. As a general rule, the largest size of aggregate should not exceed 25 per cent of the minimum dimension in the structure, particular care being taken with heavily reinforced concrete. In most constructional engineering and building applications, the normal maximum aggregate size is 20 mm, while in roads it may be 40 mm, and larger still in mass construction such as dams. In the latter, occasional large lumps of rock or masonry known as 'plums' are used, though these should not occupy more than about 30 per cent of the total volume of concrete. Since increasing maximum aggregate size reduces the surface area of aggregate to be bonded in a given volume, the cement and water requirement for a given strength may be reduced, producing a more economical mix. In mass concrete, this will reduce the heat production of the concrete, though above about 40 mm maximum size concretes tend to become weaker, due to failure of the now heavily stressed bonds between aggregate and cement paste. The fine aggregate should also be 'matched' to the maximum size of coarse aggregate; for example, a fine aggregate with fine grading combined with a large coarse aggregate may lead to a concrete of low cohesion.

Types of aggregate

The great majority of aggregates used for concrete are obtained from natural sources, either in the form of rock which is crushed, or gravel which may be crushed or simply screened (i.e. large sizes removed) before use. In any particular area, only one type of aggregate usually occurs locally and, due to high costs of transportation of aggregate, normal concrete will be made with this type of aggregate.

Aggregate properties and their effect on the properties of concrete

Shape. This may vary between 'rounded' (implying water-worn material) to 'angular' (material with clearly defined edges, produced by crushing). Particles between these extremes would be classed as 'irregular'; that is, having rounded edges. In normal concretes, angular material tends to produce concrete of lower workability but higher strength for a given water/cement ratio. In high strength concrete, workability is not affected in this way—some angular aggregates may produce higher workabilities than rounded aggregates. Other possible shapes include 'flaky' and 'elongated' but the non-isotropic and relatively high specific surface of these detracts from their value as aggregates for concrete.

Surface texture. The two extremes are 'rough' or 'honeycombed' surfaces which will provide an extremely good key to cement, and 'glassy' surfaces which do not form a strong bond with cement. Intermediate possibilities are 'smooth' or 'granular'. Although rougher surfaces will tend to reduce workability, they also tend to result in increased strength—subject of course to the aggregate itself being satisfactory in other respects.

Crushing strength. There is little advantage in using rich concrete mixes containing weak aggregates, since clearly the latter, which generally have low 'E' values, will take only a small stress under load, the cement paste therefore being overstressed and failing at low loads. Similarly, a high strength aggregate such as crushed granite would be best utilised where a high strength concrete is required; the extra cost of such materials would be of little benefit in the medium strength range. A guide to the suitability of a particular aggregate from the strength point of view may be obtained by inspection of crushed concrete cubes made with that aggregate. If a significant number of fractured aggregate particles (say more than about 25 per cent) is visible, then it is likely that improved strength would be obtained with stronger aggregate. In practice, there is, of course, the question of availability of stronger material and it may be more economical to provide more cement per unit volume in a mix than to transport stronger aggregates over considerable distances.

Grading. This term is used to describe the relative proportions of various particle sizes between the nominal maximum aggregate size and the smallest material present, which passes a 150-mm sieve. The object of grading aggregates is to produce concrete with satisfactory plastic properties (workability, cohesion and resistance to bleeding) as well as satisfactory hardened properties (strength, voids content, durability and surface finish) using as little cement as possible. The importance of grading may be illustrated by referring to an opposite extreme, for example, concrete made with marbles of a single size. If marbles were packed perfectly into a given volume, they would occupy a maximum of 74 per cent of the total volume. Supposing such a figure to be unlikely in practice, take a value of 70 per cent. This would imply voids of 30 per cent requiring this total percentage of water and cement to occupy them. Assuming a water/cement ratio of 0·5 and specific gravities of 1 and 3 respectively, 0·33 parts by volume of cement would occupy 0·5 + 0·33 = 0·83 parts by volume of void space. Hence the percentage cement and water to occupy, say, 30 parts of void would be

$$30 \times \frac{0\cdot33}{0\cdot83} = 11\cdot9 \text{ parts cement and } 18\cdot1 \text{ parts water}$$

By volume the mix would be

$$70 : 11\cdot9 : 18\cdot1$$
aggregate cement water

By mass the mix would be approximately

$$175 : 35\cdot7 : 18\cdot1 \text{ assuming specific gravity of aggregate} = 2\cdot5$$

This implies an aggregate/cement ratio of about 5 : 1 which does not represent an extremely rich mix and, assuming the cement fully hydrates, this should produce a non-porous concrete. Such a mix would, however, be totally unsuitable for concrete because:

(a) The cement paste would bleed (that is the cement particles would settle out of the water due to their relatively high specific gravity)
(b) it would be impossible to obtain a finish on the concrete,
(c) the large areas of neat aggregate and cement would cause severe shrinkage, movement and loading stresses at interfaces.

A graded aggregate will tend to overcome these problems to a degree dependent on the type of grading. Hence a well graded aggregate will, by ensuring that there are no large volumes of neat cement paste, produce a cohesive but workable concrete resistant to bleeding and with satisfactory strength. In a well graded aggregate, the voids between particles of a given size are filled by particles which are slightly smaller, voids left by these being filled in the same way until the smallest sized particles are reached. The absence of an intermediate size will tend to mean that for a given strength and workability more finer material than necessary will be required with consequent increase in cement and water contents to coat the extra surface. Perhaps the exception here occurs with 10- and 5-mm sizes which may be omitted if a larger percentage of sand is used, the aggregate being 'gap graded' in this case. If, however, there is an excess of intermediate sizes such as these, the mix will tend to be 'harsh' with increased friction, lower workability and increased air voids due to insufficient finer material to fill the voids they create. Figure 3.4 shows four grading curves for 20-mm

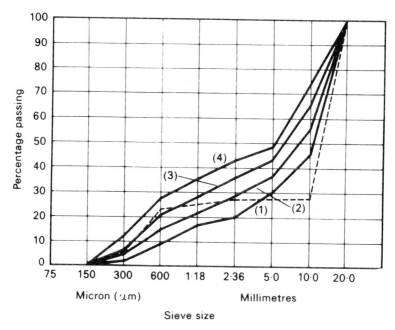

Fig. 3.4 Four grading curves for 20-mm aggregates, given in Road Note 4, together with a 'gap graded' curve (indicated by the dotted line)

aggregates as found in Road Note 4 which, from experience, have been found to produce satisfactory concrete, together with a typical 'gap graded' curve. The upper curves correspond to finer gradings which therefore require more cement for a given strength. The lower curves are coarser and therefore cheaper but with an increased tendency to segregation, especially with lean, wet mixes. Segregation is the term used to describe settlement of coarse material to the bottom of the concrete, the mortar and laitence (cement paste) being towards the top.

From the above, it is apparent that close control over aggregate grading is essential if best use is to be made of material and it is now common practice to obtain aggregates in two or more sizes rather than in 'all in' form. The latter may be of use in low strength concretes but wherever concrete of consistent strength durability, colour and texture is required, use of two or more sizes is a major contribution, provided gradings are checked periodically. Use, for example, of 20–10 mm; 10–5 mm aggregates and fine aggregate means that size proportions from 20–5 mm are closely controlled and of constant ratio to fine aggregate. Materials in this form will be more expensive, require separate stockpiles and extra supervision and testing, but for a given characteristic ('minimum') strength a lower average strength of concrete should be acceptable so that the concrete is more economical. BS 812 gives the grading requirements of all the forms of aggregates given above. Figure 3.5 shows the four 'zones' into which fine

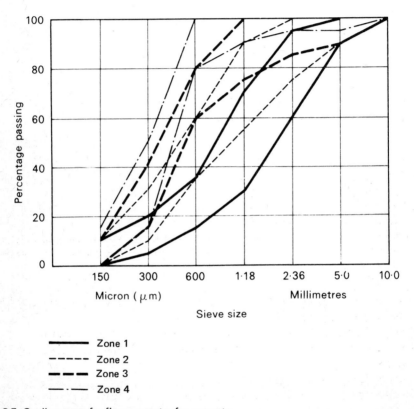

Fig. 3.5 Grading zones for fine aggregates for concrete

aggregates may be classified. Zone 1 is the coarsest. Owing to the high specific surface of Zone 4, sand (into which zone 'builders' or 'soft sands' often fit), BS 812 suggests that trial concrete mixes should be made to ascertain suitability. Similar arguments apply to the coarser Zone 1 sands.

Quality. This term manifests itself primarily in two ways:

1. *Silt.* This may be defined as material composed of particles between the sizes 60 μm and 2 μm. Owing to its high specific surface, its presence requires additional water for a given workability. Also, since such materials are often of a clayey nature, they decrease the bond between aggregate and cement, reducing the strength of concrete.

2. *Organic impurities.* Such materials, being acidic, reduce the alkalinity of cement paste which is essential for its hydration, thereby affecting setting time and strength.

Moisture. Almost all aggregates contain some moisture, although the important requirement for batching of aggregates for concrete is to know whether this moisture will contribute to that required by the mix as calculated or whether extra water will be needed due to absorption of aggregates. There are four different states which an aggregate may be in (Fig. 3.6).

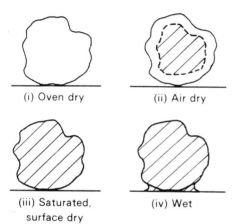

(i) Oven dry

(ii) Air dry

(iii) Saturated, surface dry

(iv) Wet

Fig. 3.6 The possible states that an aggregate may be in with respect to moisture content

1. *Oven dry:* implying that on heating to 105°C there would be no loss of weight. This state rarely occurs in practice.
2. *Air dry:* there is no free moisture, and surface layers of aggregate are dry.
3. *Saturated surface dry:* this is the 'ideal' state for an aggregate for concrete since it requires no alteration to mixing water.
4. *Wet:* surplus moisture is present.

(1) and (2) will require extra water to be added at the mixer especially in the case of lightweight aggregate concretes since these aggregates are highly absorbent. (4) will require a deduction of water at the mixer equal to the total free moisture present in the batch of aggregate. Fine aggregate normally holds greater amounts of free moisture than coarse aggregate, since in a given mass there are more points of contact between the larger numbers of particles involved. Water is held at these points by capillarity.

DESIGN AND SPECIFICATION OF CONCRETE MIXES

The object of mix design is, by systematic analysis of materials' properties and knowledge of how they affect concrete properties, to produce batch quantities for a given volume of concrete such that the properties of both the fresh and hardened materials are as required for the specific purpose, as economically as possible. The most important properties of fresh concrete are workability and cohesiveness, while those of hardened concrete may include strength, durability, colour, surface texture, density or other properties. It must be emphasised that the materials for concrete are such that mix design methods rarely produce the exact properties required of the concrete, and trial mixes should be made in all cases in order to obtain best performance of materials. Best results will be obtained by a combination of both techniques, the design stage being used to give an indication of batch quantities. Results of trial mixes may also be extremely useful for future purposes as they provide information and the effect of variation of batch proportions on the concrete. Mix design, implying step by step determinaton of ratios or batch quantities for a specific purpose, is still relatively uncommon in this country. More common and widely used by the ready mixed concrete industry are standard or 'prescribed' mixes, that is, mixes in which cement, aggregate and possibly water content are specified for each volume required. Such mixes may be satisfactory for many purposes provided a sufficient range is available. Many companies rely partly on the skill of the batcher-man to judge correct workability, so that water figures where given are not always adhered to—especially where moisture is present in aggregates. Table 3.1 shows some prescribed mixes in the BS Unified Code of Practice 110 *The Structural Use of Concrete* (replacing Codes 114, 115 and 116). Such mixes are often used for 'normal' concretes since they obviate the need for design while still allowing some prediction of strength and durability. A step further still from designed mixes are nominal mixes (e.g. '1 : 2 : 4; medium workability') in which no characteristic strength is specified and quality control is minimal. Such mixes are only suitable for small quantities of slightly stressed concrete such as footings or raft foundations in domestic buildings. It will be apparent therefore that designed concrete mixes will be used either where carefully controlled or special properties in the concrete are required or where large quantities of concrete will be used. In the latter, the cost of mix design and quality control will be regained by the more economical mix specifications they lead to.

Mix design procedure.   Selection of materials.

This must be a compromise between what is ideal for the particular purpose, what is readily available and relative costs. For example, there is a wide range of cements on the market and although ordinary Portland cement is the cheapest, there may well be a reason for using a 'special' cement, perhaps if early or very early strength is required, where ordinary Portland cement would induce thermal stresses, or where extra heat would be advantageous such as in winter concreting. On the other hand, it may be worth considering the use of a modified ordinary Portland cement mix as an alternative to special cements. There is often little choice in selection of aggregates since locally available materials are usually far cheaper than 'imported' aggregates. However, the use of lightweight aggregates is increasing and their use may be considered. Admixtures may also be of benefit in particular situations, although a very wide range of concrete mixes can be produced without them and their use constitutes another possible source of error, particularly in view of the small quantities normally required.

Preliminary tests on materials

1 *Cements.* Ordinary and rapid hardening Portland cements are covered by BS 12, which is the basis of design graphs, so that cement testing is not normally necessary unless a higher strength performance than that given in BS 12 is required. Even when this is the case, a knowledge of the compressive strength of the cement is not essential since the performance of cement would be reflected in trial mix properties. Cement testing is extremely important however as a part of quality control, although the tests of BS 12 are not site tests and require skilled personnel for their execution. Cement manufacturers are however normally willing to supply details of their cement properties.

2. *Aggregates.* The following tests are essential, the first three acting as a guide to the overall suitability of a given aggregate and the fourth enabling the water content of the mix to be accurately calculated. The latter test should also be carried out regularly during production and the other tests at intervals or when there is cause for doubt. Specific gravities of aggregates and bulk density of coarse aggregate may be required by some design methods. BS 812 describes methods for these.

Grading. A grading curve for the aggregate is obtained using the BS standard sieves ranging from the nominal maximum size of the aggregate to 150 μm. It is essential to obtain a representative sample of aggregate—a poorly produced stockpile may itself contain segregated sizes, larger sizes tending to be at the bottom. Several samples should be taken and mixed and then divided either by quartering or by a riffle box to give a quantity suitable for sieving. The aggregate should be dry, and too large a quantity will give false analysis due to 'blinding' of sieve apertures by particles. Table 3.2 shows gradings of a typical fine and 20-mm coarse aggregate, the method for calculating fineness modulus being indicated. Figures 3.7 and 3.8 show the Road Note 4 and Cement and Concrete Association methods of proportioning these aggregates, to give the grading curves of Road Note 4. The Road Note 4 method is convenient for two aggregate sizes: gradings of available materials are represented on the two vertical axes, respective sieve sizes being joined by lines and then the gradings from Fig. 3.4 indicated. The grading which fits best can be ascertained, bearing in mind the properties of these gradings already described. It is rare (and also unnecessary) for gradings to conform exactly to 'ideal' gradings and it is always possible to adjust mix proportions if gradings do not match closely those required. The grading shown by way of example is intentionally a rather poor fit. A ratio of 30 : 70, fine : coarse aggregate has been chosen, though this is slightly richer in fine particles and will tend to lead to a lower workability mix. If this proves to be the case in a trial mix, the problem could be remedied by slightly increasing water and cement contents, while keeping the water/cement ratio constant. The alternative method of combining aggregates is shown (Fig. 3.8) and this is particularly useful where three sizes of aggregate are to be combined (e.g. when the coarse aggregate is obtained in single sizes) since proportions of fine, medium and coarse material can be read off directly from intercepts on the vertical axis. It is advisable, however, to calculate obtained gradings using the ratios obtained in order to compare with that required. If a mix is lean, or

Table 3.1

Prescribed mixes for ordinary structural concrete (C.P. 110). Weights of cement and total dry aggregates in kg to produce approximately 1 m³ of fully compacted concrete together with the percentages by weight of fine aggregate in total dry aggregates. The grades represent characteristic 28-day cube strengths (five per cent failures), though cube testing is not required for prescribed mixes

Concrete grade		Nominal max. size of aggregate (mm) 40		20		14		10	
	Workability	Medium	High	Medium	High	Medium	High	Medium	High
	Limits to slump that may be expected (mm)	50–100	100–150	25–75	75–125	10–50	50–100	10–25	25–50
7	Cement (kg)	180	200	210	230	—	—	—	—
	Total aggregate (kg)	1950	1850	1900	1800	—	—	—	—
	Fine aggregate (per cent)	30–45	30–45	35–50	35–50	—	—	—	—
10	Cement (kg)	210	230	240	260	—	—	—	—
	Total aggregate (kg)	1900	1850	1850	1800	—	—	—	—
	Fine aggregate (per cent)	30–45	30–45	35–50	35–50	—	—	—	—
15	Cement (kg)	250	270	280	310	—	—	—	—
	Total aggregate (kg)	1850	1800	1800	1750	—	—	—	—
	Fine aggregate (per cent)	30–45	30–45	35–50	35–50	—	—	—	—

Grade									
20	Cement (kg)	300	320	320	350	340	380	360	410
	Total aggregate (kg)	1850	1750	1800	1750	1750	1700	1750	1650
	Sand*								
	Zone 1 (per cent)	35	40	40	45	45	50	50	55
	Zone 2 (per cent)	30	35	35	40	40	45	45	50
	Zone 3 (per cent)	30	30	30	35	35	40	40	45
25	Cement (kg)	340	360	360	390	380	420	400	450
	Total aggregate (kg)	1800	1750	1750	1700	1700	1650	1700	1600
	Sand*								
	Zone 1 (per cent)	35	40	40	45	45	50	50	55
	Zone 2 (per cent)	30	35	35	40	40	45	45	50
	Zone 3 (per cent)	30	30	30	35	35	40	40	45
30	Cement (kg)	370	390	400	430	430	470	460	510
	Total aggregate (kg)	1750	1700	1700	1650	1700	1600	1650	1550
	Sand*								
	Zone 1 (per cent)	35	40	40	45	45	50	50	55
	Zone 2 (per cent)	30	35	35	40	40	45	45	50
	Zone 3 (per cent)	30	30	30	35	35	40	40	45

*'All in' aggregate may be used in grades 7, 10 and 15. In other grades coarse and fine aggregates must be used

likely to segregate, it is better to use more fine aggregate to decrease the possibility of undersanded parts in the mix. Yet another alternative is to calculate the quantity of fine aggregate required as a part of the mix design procedure, using its fineness modulus (see below), though this has the disadvantage that the aggregate grading cannot be fully described by any single number.

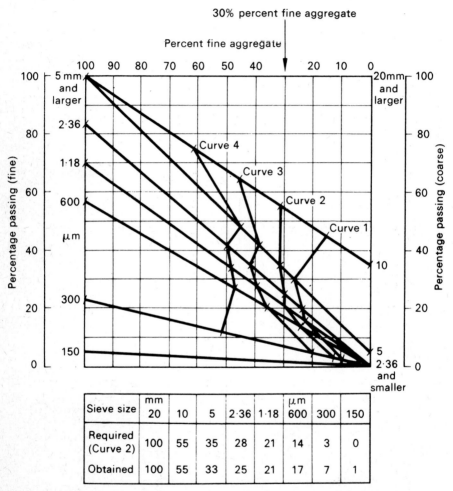

Sieve size	mm 20	10	5	2·36	1·18	μm 600	300	150
Required (Curve 2)	100	55	35	28	21	14	3	0
Obtained	100	55	33	25	21	17	7	1

Fig. 3.7 Road Note 4 method of combining fine and coarse aggregates to conform to a given grading curve. In this case, curve 2 of Fig. 3.4 has been used, resulting in 30 per cent aggregate being required

Silt test. This is mainly a problem in relation to fine aggregate and a rapid assessment of silt content can be obtained by a field settling test. A sample of aggregate is shaken in a measuring cylinder containing salt solution. On allowing it to stand, the silt settles slowly as a distinct layer above the aggregate, the salt in solution helping to flocculate silt particles which might otherwise stay in suspension. If the result is greater than 8 per cent by volume, the material is suspect. BS 812 describes a more accurate method for determination of silt content by weight and this should be used if in doubt. Where excessive silt is present the aggregate should be rejected, or if this is not possible, cement content should be adjusted and trial mixes made to test suitability of the concrete.

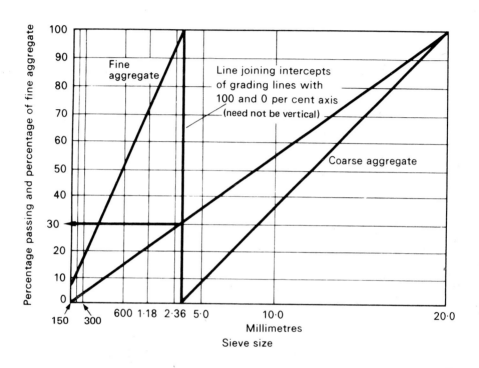

Sieve size	mm 20	10	5	2.36	1.18	μm 600	300	150
coarse	100	35	5	0	0	0	0	0
fine	100	100	100	83	70	57	23	5
70% coarse	70	24·5	3·5	0	0	0	0	0
30% fine	30	30	30	24·9	21·0	17·1	6·9	1·5
obtained	100	54·5	33·5	25	21	17	7	1
required (curve 2)	100	55	35	28	21	14	3	0

Fig. 3.8 Cement and Concrete Association method of proportioning aggregates. The sieve size scale is obtained from the percentage passing data of the required grading, working backwards from the diagonal line which then represents the required grading. To obtain straight lines for gradings of given aggregates, draw the steepest reasonable lines

Table 3.2a

Details of a sieve analysis of 0·5 kg of a fine aggregate. Comparison of the per cent passing column with Fig. 3.5 shows that the aggregate is a zone 2 aggregate. From below, the fineness modulus = 2·62

Sieve size	Amount retained (g)	Cumulative amount retained (g)	Per cent retained	Per cent passing
10·0 mm	0	0	0	100
5·0 mm	0	0	0	100
2·36 mm	85	85	17	83
1·18 mm	65	150	30	70
600 μm	65	215	43	57
300 μm	170	385	77	23
150 μm	90	475	95	5

Sum of percentages retained = 262.

Table 3.2b

Details of a sieve analysis of 5 kg of 20-mm coarse aggregate. The sum of percentages retained is equal to 260 and this together with the four smaller sieve sizes not used here makes the total percentage retained for fineness modulus calculations = 660. Hence fineness modulus = 6.60

Sieve size (mm)	Amount retained (kg)	Cumulative amount retained (kg)	Per cent retained	Per cent passing
40	0	0	0	100
20	0	0	0	100
10	3·25	3·25	65	35
5	1·50	4·75	95	5
2·36	0·25	5·00	100	0

Organic impurities. The test described in BS 812 is based on the effect of organic impurities on the pH value of a standard cement paste. Almost immediately after mixing, the calcium hydroxide liberated in solution in concrete raises its pH to a strongly alkaline value (12·40 or above in the case of the standard mortar paste). On the pH scale, 0 is concentrated acid, 7 neutral and 14 concentrated alkali. Organic impurities, for example topsoil, if present in significant quantities, will reduce the pH value of the concrete and hence affect setting and strength properties. In the test described in BS 812, the cement is first checked with a standard sand, first clean, then contaminated to ensure that the particular cement in use gives the pH value required with the clean sand and then a sufficient reduction on contamination. In the 1973 edition of BS 882, the BS 812 test is not required as evidence of quality. When in doubt, concrete cubes should be made.

Moisture content

In the case of aggregates containing free moisture, it is the *free moisture only* which is required, since absorbed water will not affect the properties of the concrete. This is determined most commonly by one of the following methods:

(a) *Oven drying method.* This is a direct and simple way of determining moisture content. Results may be determined very quickly by use of microwave ovens. These would give total moisture content since microwave ovens cause evaporation of absorbed as well as surface moisture.

(b) *Siphon can* (BS 812). This is based on the principle that a given mass of aggregate containing free water will occupy a larger volume than a dry aggregate. The volume of each is obtained by displacement of water in a specially designed can, suitable for site use. A sample of dried material is, however, necessary. If the free moisture content of the aggregate is required, this sample should be surface dry only. If the total moisture content is required, it should be oven dry. This test relies heavily upon constant specific gravity of material from sample to sample.

(c) *Chemical method.* A rapid value can be obtained by mixing a sample of the damp aggregate with an excess of calcium carbide in a pressure vessel. The calcium carbide reacts with the moisture producing a gas whose pressure is proportional to the quantity of moisture present. The moisture content reading will correspond to a value somewhere between the free and total moisture content, depending on the degree of crushing of the material.

It is most important to note that moisture contents often vary from one part of an aggregate stockpile to another, as well as with time. Great care should be taken in obtaining a representative sample, especially when the final sample is small as in method (c).

In the case of absorptive aggregates, the absorption coefficient would also be required.

Example of calculations

Non-absorptive aggregates. Calculate corrected batch masses of aggregate and water for a concrete mix if given quantities are:

$$
\begin{array}{lcl}
\text{coarse aggregate} & - & 1300 \text{ kg} \\
\text{fine aggregate} & - & 500 \text{ kg} \\
\text{water} & - & 100 \text{ kg}
\end{array}
$$

and the fine and coarse aggregates content 5 per cent and 3 per cent moisture based on wet weight respectively.

1300 kg of coarse aggregate contains $3/100 \times 1300 = 39$ kg water and therefore only 1261 of coarse aggregate. Hence use $1300 \times 1300/1261 = 1340$ kg of coarse aggregate.

500 kg of fine aggregate contains $5/100 \times 500 = 25$ kg water and therefore only

475 of fine aggregate. Hence 500 x (500/475) = 526 of fine aggregate. These contain 1340 x 3/100 + 526 x 5/100 = 40 + 26 = 66 kg water. Therefore water to be added at the mixer = 100 − 66 = 34 kg.

Repeat the above example assuming the aggregates have absorption coefficients of 5 per cent and 10 per cent by weight of dry material, fine and coarse respectively.

The masses of aggregates required are as above.

In 1340 kg of coarse aggregate there are 1300 kg of dry material which will absorb 130 kg of water.

In 526 kg of fine aggregate there are 500 kg of dry material which will absorb 25 kg of water. Therefore

total water capable of being absorbed	=	155 kg
water already present	=	66 kg
net addition required	=	89 kg

Therefore water to be added at mixer = 100 + 89 = 189 kg.

3. *The quality of water for concrete (BS 3148).* This is important since contaminated water may lead to impaired performance of the hardened concrete. As a general rule, if water is suitable for drinking, then it is likely to be suitable for making concrete. If there is any doubt, it is advisable to carry out the setting time and strength tests of BS 12 using samples of the water in question and also distilled water for comparison.

Although sea water is suitable for ordinary concrete, since the effect of salt in the normal concentrations found is slight, it is not recommended for reinforced concrete, owing to the increased corrosion risk, or for high alumina cement concretes.

Determination of batch quantities

This is based on the required properties in relation to the results of preliminary tests on, or assumed properties of, materials. There are four quantities which must be determined for a given volume of concrete; those of water, cement, coarse aggregate and fine aggregate. These quantities are designed to give an average strength which will be higher than the characteristic strength by a margin that depends on the quality control and other factors (see 'Statistical analysis').

It is widely acknowledged that the strength of fully compacted concrete in the strength range 20–50 N/mm^2, as measured by concrete cube tests, is determined largely by the water/cement ratio; that is, by the quantity of free water in the mix relative to that of cement, by weight. Figure 3.9 shows typical strength/water/cement ratio curves for ordinary Portland cement and rapid hardening Portland cement at different ages, based on Road Note 4, though modern cements normally give rather better performance than these curves indicate. Results are also found to depend on aggregate type. It is possible, as has already been mentioned, that high water/cement ratio concretes tend to be porous, so that the ratio may be more restricted on account of durability of the concrete than strength. Table 3.3 shows typical maximum values. In addition, as in C.P. 110, a minimum cement content may be specified.

The workability of a concrete mix will be dictated by the method of compaction, which will in turn depend on the use of the concrete. Values may vary between 'high'

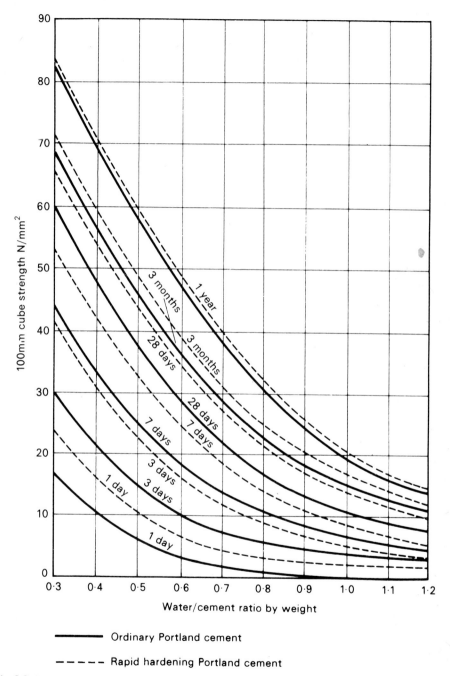

Fig. 3.9 Relationship between water/cement ratio, age and strength for ordinary Portland and rapid hardening Portland cements. (Road Note 4)

Table 3.3
Maximum water/cement ratios for concrete to be durable in various types of structure and environment

Type of construction	Climate	
	Severe	Normal
Bridge decks	0·45	0·50
Thin sections in air exposed to weather	0·50	0·55
Moderate sections; road slabs	0·55	0·60
Concrete protected from weather	–	–

for sections with congested reinforcement to very low—for example, in the case of road bases compacted by vibrating rollers. The workability of a mix is chiefly determined by its water content, for a given aggregate size, shape and grading.

This fact forms the basis of the American Concrete Institute design method, typical tables being shown in Table 3.4. The workability will in practice also be affected by the quantity of cement but this may be corrected in trial mixes, if necessary. Road Note 4 effectively fixes water content by specifying a certain aggregate/cement ratio for a given workability, aggregate grading and water/cement ratio.

Table 3.4
The water content required for a given workability of concretes, air entrained and non air entrained (American Concrete Institute)

	Water requirement in kg per m^3 of concrete					
	Non air entrained			Air entrained		
Slump in mm	10-mm agg.	20-mm agg.	40-mm agg.	10-mm agg.	20-mm agg.	40-mm agg.
25–50	208	183	163	183	163	143
75–100	228	203	178	203	178	158
150–175	242	212	188	212	188	168
Approx. entrapped air (per cent)	3	2	1	–	–	–
Approx. Entrained air (per cent)	–	–	–	8	6	4·5

To this point, water and cement contents are both specified or, if Road Note 4 is used, the ratios of water/cement/aggregate are obtained.

To obtain batch quantities per cubic metre, either the density of the concrete must be predicted or it may be calculated from absolute volumes of constituent materials. Hence there are three possible alternatives:

(a) Obtain water and cement contents and assuming a density for the concrete, find the total weight of aggregate by subtraction. Combine coarse and fine aggregates by grading curves.

(b) Obtain water and cement contents as above and by empirical tables and the results of aggregate tests, obtain the quantities of coarse aggregate required for a cubic metre of concrete. The American Concrete Institute method is an example of this and Table 3.5 shows how the absolute bulk volume of coarse aggregate per cubic metre is

Table 3.5

The relationship between bulk volume of rodded coarse aggregate and the volume of concrete produced as a function of maximum size of coarse aggregate and fineness modulus of fine aggregate

Maximum size of aggregate (mm)	Ratio $\dfrac{\text{bulk volume of rodded coarse aggregate}}{\text{volume of concrete produced}}$			
	Fineness mod. fine agg. = 2·4	Fineness mod. fine agg. = 2·6	Fineness mod. fine agg. = 2·8	Fineness mod. fine agg. = 3·0
10	0·46	0·44	0·42	0·40
20	0·65	0·63	0·61	0·59
40	0·76	0·74	0·72	0·70

obtained from the fineness modulus of the fine aggregate and the maximum aggregate size. The table is based on the fact that a finer aggregate will tend to occupy mainly void spaces so that the fraction

$$\frac{\text{bulk volume of coarse aggregate}}{\text{volume of concrete produced}}$$

tends to unity. A large aggregate also assists in this trend. The fine aggregate per cubic metre is found finally by calculating the absolute volumes of materials using specific gravities and subtracting volumes from 1 m³. The density of the fresh concrete will also be obtained. (The proportioning of materials by volume contribution is now increasingly used since, having determined water/cement ratio from strength and durability requirements, the remaining problem is essentially, by measurements of shape, size and grading of the solid material in the concrete, to proportion these to give satisfactory workability and cohesion, and minimum air voids using as little cement as possible. This is a study in volume packing modified by friction and these parameters depend mainly on the *geometry* of the materials.)

(c) Batch quantities for a cubic metre can be easily found if the water/cement ratio and aggregate/cement ratio are known, as by Road Note 4 method, together with a knowledge of the approximate density of the concrete. If this is not known, it may be determined from specific gravities as in (b).

A number of other methods exist but the above illustrate the main arguments involved in mix design. An illustration of the above methods follows:

Calculate batch masses for a cubic metre of concrete to have 25–50 mm slump and an average strength of 30 N/mm^2 at 28 days using ordinary Portland cement. The coarse aggregate is 20 mm max. size; of irregular shape and the fine aggregate is natural sand. The aggregates have gradings as in Table 3.2 and specific gravities of 2·60 and 2·50; coarse and fine respectively. The coarse aggregate has a bulk density of 1650 kg/m^3 and the density of the fresh fully compacted concrete, if required, may be assumed to be 2300 kg/m^3.

Method (a)

From Table 3.4 water content = 183 kg/m^3

From Fig. 3.9 for ordinary Portland cement, water/cement ratio = 0·58

Hence cement content = $\frac{183}{0·58}$ = 316 kg/m^3

Therefore aggregate content = $2300 - (316 + 183) = 1801$ kg/m^3

Figs. 3.7 and 3.8 show that 30 per cent fine aggregate may be used, hence

fine aggregate content   = 30 per cent x 1801 = 540 kg/m^3

coarse aggregate content = 70 per cent x 1801 = 1261 kg/m^3

Method (b)

Water and cement contents are found as in Method (a).

From Table 3.5 the bulk volume of coarse aggregate in m^3 per m^3 of concrete = 0·63

Therefore mass of coarse aggregate = 0·63 x 1650 = 1040 kg/m^3 of concrete.

To find volume of fine aggregate, add together volumes of all materials and deduct from 1 m^3.

Volume of materials so far:

$$= \frac{183}{1000} + \frac{3·16}{3·15 \times 1000} + \frac{1040}{2·6 \times 1000} + 0·02$$

    (water)   (cement)   (coarse   (entrapped air)
                                 agg.)   Table 3.4

$$= 0·183 + 0·100 + 0·400 + 0·020$$

$$= 0·703 \ m^3$$

Therefore volume of fine aggregate = $1·000 - 0·703 = 0·297$ m^3 per m^3 of concrete

Therefore mass of fine aggregate = 0·297 x 2500 = 745 kg/m^3

The density of concrete predicted by this method = 183 + 316 + 745 + 1040

= 2284 kg/m^3

Method (c) (see Road Note 4)

Road Note 4 classifies 25–50 mm slump as 'low workability'.

As in Method (a), water/cement ratio = 0·58

From Road Note 4, the aggregate/cement ratio for a water/cement ratio of 0·58,

20 mm aggregate of irregular shape, low workability is 6·6 : 1 using grading curve 2 of Fig. 3.4.

Fine aggregate/cement ratio = 30 per cent x 6·6 = 1·98

Coarse aggregate/cement ratio = 70 per cent x 6·6 = 4·62

Therefore ratios are   1   : 1·98   :   4·62   / 0·58

                     cement   fine agg. coarse agg. water

Hence 1 kg of cement gives $1 + 1·98 + 4·62 + 0·58 = 8·18$ kg of concrete.

Assuming a density of 2300 kg/m^3; 2300 kg of concrete are required.

Therefore quantity of cement $= \frac{2300}{8·18}$ $= \underline{281 \text{ kg/m}^3}$ of fresh concrete.

Quantity of water $= 0·58 \times 281 = \underline{163 \text{ kg/m}^3}$

Quantity of fine aggregate $= 1·98 \times 281 = \underline{556 \text{ kg/m}^3}$

Quantity of coarse aggregate $= 4·62 \times 281 = \underline{1300 \text{ kg/m}^3}$

Check; total quantity of materials $= \underline{2300 \text{ kg/m}^3}$

Comments on the above results

Apart from water/cement ratio requirements, which are all based on the same graph, batch quantities as predicted by different methods show quite large differences in some cases.

Methods (a) and (b) require 35 kg more cement per cubic metre of concrete than method (c), which will make them considerably more expensive. This is due to the larger water requirement (183 kg/m^3 compared to 163 kg/m^3) of the former mixes. The figure 183 kg/m^3 of water, obtained from the American Concrete Institute (Table 3.4), is in fact rather large for the relatively low sand content of method (a) and will lead to a higher workability and harshness than method (b) proportions, where a high percentage of fine aggregate is obtained. General conclusions are therefore that method (a) in this case will probably give a rather expensive harsh and wet mix, inclined to segregation; method (b), although also expensive, gives a more cohesive concrete, probably correct workability, capable of giving a good surface finish, method (c) gives a relatively inexpensive concrete with satisfactory workability and fairly good cohesion. In order to arrive at final batch masses, trial mixes using each set of values should be made and properties compared. Cube strengths obtained from the above are likely to be generally higher than the target average strengths since the water/cement ratio–strength curves of Road Note 4 (Fig. 3.9) are based on cements which are of lower quality than most cements in use today. For example, the 'Rapid Hardening Portland Cement' curve will, if used in conjunction with ordinary Portland cement, give a nearer approximation to the required strength than the 'Ordinary Portland Cement' curve.

Trial mixes

These are a most important part of the mix design procedure. Initial trial mixes may be made in small quantities; for example, using a 20-kg sample of concrete. Water should be added until by visual inspection the workability is correct. The workability and cohesion should then be determined and adjustments made as necessary. For example, if the workability is correct, but the mix is harsh, the proportion of fine aggregate should be increased, decreasing the aggregate/cement ratio to maintain workability. If, on the other hand, the cohesion is good but the workability is too high, then the water content should be reduced and the cement content reduced such that the water/cement ratio remains constant. An increase in the mass of fine aggregate, such that its volume increase is equal to the volume reduction of cement, could then be made to maintain cohesion. Cubes should also be made to check the strength of the mix. Having corrected proportions, a full size trial mix could be made, placed and compacted, using plant and techniques to be employed in production, since these inevitably affect the properties and performance of concrete. A density determination of this concrete would then give an accurate indication of the volume yield of the mix. This mix could be used for a temporary structure or perhaps as foundation concrete.

Modern trends in mix design procedures

The above methods of mix design contain a number of inherent disadvantages. For example, the water/cement ratio, as determined by strength requirements, depends on the type of coarse and fine aggregate used and errors introduced by use of standard graphs as Fig. 3.9 can be considerable. Again, it has been shown that satisfactory concrete can be made without aggregates having to conform to grading curves as in Fig. 3.4 and fineness modulus also is an insufficient description of the grading properties of fine aggregate. These problems all relate to aggregates and in practice it may take time to apply effectively general rules for design, to particular aggregates. Since, in a given district, aggregates are obtained from a small number of sources, a logical approach to mix design might be to produce design graphs for a particular aggregate type and workability, enabling batch quantities per cubic metre to be read off directly. Such design graphs would take time to produce but, once in existence, would obviate the need for the above, more approximate methods of mix design. A typical graph by P. L. Owens is shown in Fig. 3.10. Trial mixes will still be necessary, as cement and aggregate properties may vary, but results obtained should be closer to those required, without extensive testing of aggregates and time spent on 'rational' methods of mix design. There will always be a place for such techniques but they could be employed in the production of such graphs for each aggregate type, so that time taken by the engineers in designing mixes is minimised. Such schemes have already been used but the main problem in adopting them for general use in the establishment of a suitable commercial basis for their operation.

TESTS ON FRESH CONCRETE

It should be appreciated that the properties of hardened concrete are closely related to those of the freshly mixed, plastic material, so that it is of great importance to be able to measure and control the latter. Furthermore, if, by means of tests, the concrete is found to be unsuitable for its purpose, it is far easier to reject a mix before it has set and hardened and easier still if the failure can be detected by tests before placing. Perhaps the most important term relating to properties of fresh concrete is 'workability'. Also of importance, however, is a means of measuring entrapped or entrained

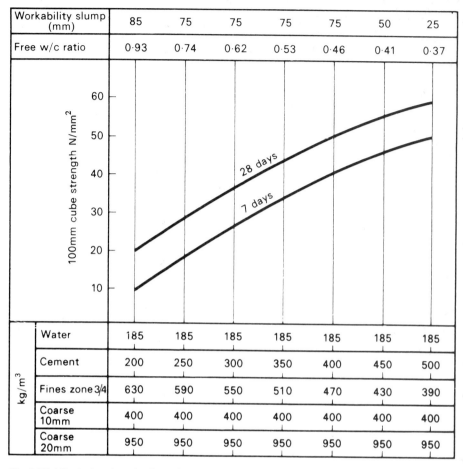

Workability slump (mm)	85	75	75	75	75	50	25
Free w/c ratio	0·93	0·74	0·62	0·53	0·46	0·41	0·37

		Water	185	185	185	185	185	185	185
kg/m³		Cement	200	250	300	350	400	450	500
		Fines zone 3/4	630	590	550	510	470	430	390
		Coarse 10mm	400	400	400	400	400	400	400
		Coarse 20mm	950	950	950	950	950	950	950

Fig. 3.10 Mix design chart, by P. L. Owens, for concrete of medium workability using 20-mm quartzite aggregate. Note that quantities of water; 10-mm and 20-mm aggregate are constant. As the cement content increases, the sand content decreases such that the total volume of materials remains constant. The strength graphs are obtained experimentally

air in concrete and a technique which is becoming more widespread—the analysis of fresh concrete.

Workability

Workability may be defined as that property of concrete which determines its ability to be placed, compacted and finished. If one of these terms is particularly important it must be that of compaction, since a poorly compacted concrete will contain entrapped air with disastrous effects on strength. For example, 5 per cent of entrapped air would, on average, produce a strength reduction of about 30 per cent. Hence the workability of a concrete must be matched to the compaction technique used (as well as to placing and finishing methods). If the workability of a mix is correct, then the density of that concrete should be the maximum possible. If the workability were too low, the density would be low, due to entrapped air; if the workability were too high, the density would be too low, due to the excess of water, with its relatively low specific gravity. Workability is a complex property involving interplay between the quantity of water in the mix, the weight of constituents and internal friction due to particle abrasion. Hence its measurement must be made empirically and, in practice, mixes of different proportions but of similar workability, may give different results to a particular test. The workability categories, extremely low, very low, low, medium and high, can only act as a guide when specifying concrete and some reliance must be placed upon trial mixes. During production, however, workability tests provide a simple means of quality control. A further point is that, due to absorption of water by cement (and aggregates, if absorbent), workability may decrease rapidly after mixing. To compare results, therefore, tests should be carried out at equal times after addition of the water and preferably just before placing.

The slump test

This is still the most widely used test, due to its simplicity and convenience. Concrete is placed and compacted in four layers by tamping rod, in a firmly held slump cone (Fig. 3.11). On removal of the cone, the difference in height between the uppermost

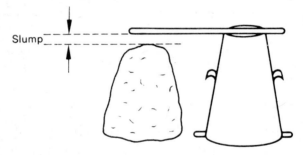

Fig. 3.11 The slump test

part of the slumped concrete and the cone is recorded in mm, as the slump. Less cohesive mixes, for example lean mixes, tend to give a greater or even collapsed slump and aggregate type also affects the result at given workability, so that allowances may have to be made. Dry mixes often give no slump at all and in this case another test should be used.

Compacting factor test

A sample of the mix is allowed to fall through two hoppers into a cylinder, thereby compacting itself to a degree dependent on its workability. The contents of the cylinder are weighed and then the same volume of fully compacted concrete is weighed. The compacting factor is then calculated from:

$$\text{Compacting factor} = \frac{\text{weight of partially compacted concrete}}{\text{weight of fully compacted concrete}}$$

A value near unity indicates a workable mix, while a value of, for example, 0·70 would indicate a dry mix. The compacting factor test is useful for drier mixes, although these tend to hang up in the hoppers. The problem of richness also applies, richer mixes compacting more easily for a given compacting factor. The apparatus is also more bulky than the slump test apparatus and most forms require separate weighing equipment, so that it is not as commonly used as the slump test.

Vebe consistometer

A slump test is first carried out using a slump cone fixed on to a small portable vibration table. Then a weighted transparent plastic disc, held in a vertical guide, is allowed to rest on the surface of the slumped concrete. The vibrator, in the form of an electrically operated eccentric rotor under the table, is then operated and the time in seconds for the disc to fall, such that the concrete wets its whole circumference, is recorded. This is then the consistence of the concrete in 'Vebe degrees'. The Vebe test is suitable for dry mixes and particularly those which are to be compacted by vibration, since the test itself involves vibration of the concrete. A possible disadvantage of the Vebe apparatus is that it requires an electric power supply (normally 3 phase).

Comparative results of the above workability tests are shown in Fig. 3.12. The approximate form only is indicated, that actually obtained being dependent on

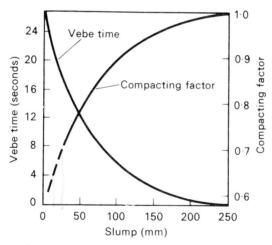

Fig. 3.12 The Vebe result is seen to be very sensitive to dry mixes; the compacting factor is suitable for mixes of low or medium workability and the slump test for medium or high workabilities

richness of mix and type and grading of aggregate. The graph indicates, however, the reasons for the suitability of each test as given above. In practice, having decided from the above arguments which type of test is to be used, it is normal to use that method only, since it is not easy to correlate results from different methods and, in any case, these do not assist in quality control—an important use of workability tests.

Entrapped or entrained air in concrete

The former term refers to air voids present due to insufficient compaction and the latter to air intentionally included in the form of very small air bubbles, as a workability aid or to improve frost resistance. The total air content of a fresh mix can easily be obtained by an apparatus based on Boyle's law and shown in Fig. 3.13. A

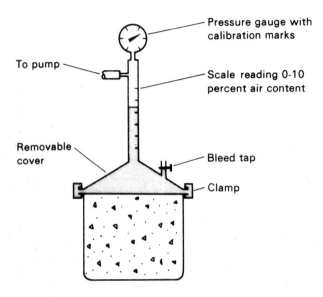

Fig. 3.13 An apparatus for measurement of the quantity of air in freshly mixed concrete

sealed vessel containing a sample of the compacted concrete is pressurised to a standard pressure, normally about 2 atm. The air in the concrete is the only compressible medium and the percentage of air in the contents, measured by the reduction in the volume, can be read off directly from a calibrated scale. It is important to attempt to simulate the compaction of the concrete in the actual structure when using this test. This method also fails to detect water-filled voids in the concrete which, on drying out, would become air voids. The presence of such voids could be detected by density methods—from cubes (although, again, compaction as in the structure is not likely) or by *in situ* methods—for example, radioactive techniques.

Analysis of fresh concrete

An apparatus to analyse concrete mixes accurately and quickly—preferably within a few minutes—would be of great benefit in many aspects of concrete production. It would detect errors in batching equipment or in its operation; detect segregation or simply act as a further means of control, allowing steps to be taken, if necessary, before placing. The main problem is that of obtaining sufficient accuracy quickly. Figure 3.14 shows a typical scheme. The water content of the mix, if required, may be

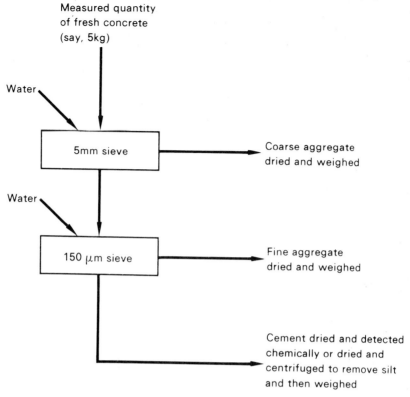

Fig. 3.14 A typical scheme for analysis of fresh concrete

determined by subtraction of coarse and fine aggregate and cement quantities from the original weight of concrete. Results are normally inaccurate, due to errors such as absorption of water by aggregates, but this is of little consequence, since workability tests should detect errors in water content. The chief object of the method is to obtain the aggregate/cement ratio and this has been achieved to within 2 or 3 per cent.

CURING CONCRETE

This is the process in which, by means of moisture in the concrete, the material matures, increasing in strength and decreasing in porosity. This process is in no way dependent on air, so that, once setting is complete, ideal curing conditions are those in which the concrete is completely saturated. Temperature is also important; hydration of cement occurs more quickly at higher temperatures, provided the concrete remains moist and will not proceed at all below freezing point of water. Curing should continue until the material has sufficient strength to resist shrinkage cracking. Thin sections in particular tend to dry out very quickly as soon as protection is removed. Even in mass concrete, a short curing period may cause problems since, on exposure, surface layers may dry and shrink while inner layers continue to hydrate, resulting in surface cracking. It is clear from the above that the curing method and precise curing period will depend on the type of structure and its situation but, ideally, the concrete should be kept moist, if necessary by artificial means, for at least seven days and, after this, thermal shock or rapid drying due to, for example, solar heat, should be avoided. In the case of concrete slabs, curing may be achieved by covering with sacking which should be kept damp, or with polythene sheeting which is effective in retaining moisture. Concrete road bases are effectively sealed by plastic sheeting or by coating with bitumen emulsion or aluminium curing compound, although cracking may still occur, due to temperature variations. Formwork for structural concrete protects it from temperature changes and drying and should be left in position as long as possible. Cements with a high heat output present a problem, since temperatures within formwork may rise 20°C or more above the ambient temperature. The use of low heat cements is recommended where this is likely to happen but, in any case, if formwork is left in position as long as possible sudden stresses due to cooling and evaporation will be minimised. There is often a temptation to spray a surface found to be warm, on removal of formwork, with cold water but this may be disastrous, due to the thermal shock and consequent surface stresses it produces.

Curing in hot weather

Hot weather will exaggerate some of the problems already mentioned. Owing to evaporation, the quantity of mixing water may have to be increased to produce the required workability at the time of placing, which may have to be carried out more quickly, due to more rapid hydration of cement with consequently decreased setting time. A warm, dry atmosphere may cause plastic cracking, due to surface evaporation. Such cracks may be retrowelled but steps must then be taken to conserve all possible moisture in the concrete. The use of a low heat cement or lean mixes will reduce the extra heat due to hydration. Aggregates form the main bulk of the concrete, so that, if these are stored in large stockpiles, the diurnal temperature variation in them and hence the concrete, will be minimised. In general, concreting thin, exposed sections above about 30°C in low humidities should be avoided.

Curing in cold weather

Freezing of concrete before it is fully cured may result in a substantial reduction in strength and durability and, if freezing occurs before it sets, concrete is rendered virtually useless. The term maturity has been adopted to give an indication of the minimum period which should elapse under given conditions before concrete is exposed to frost. Maturity is defined as

$(t + 10) \times$ age (hours) (t is the average temperature of concrete in °C)

and units are in °C hours.

The temperature effect is that already mentioned, the additional 10°C being included as a result of experimental investigations. The age is measured from the time of stiffening of the concrete. As concrete matures, water which was formerly 'free' water will become chemically bound as gel water and therefore unaffected by frost. Hence at a certain maturity, dependent on the water/cement ratio, concrete will become resistant to frost damage, provided capillary pores and voids in the concrete are not saturated. The graph in Fig. 3.15 shows the approximate relationship between the characteristic 28-day strength of concretes and maturity required before exposure to frost, using ordinary Portland cement. Slightly lower maturities may be acceptable when using rapid hardening cements. If concrete is likely to be saturated, a larger value is necessary—such that the capillary pores are no longer interconnected. This may require a maturity double that required above and concretes with water/cement ratios above 0·7 will never be suitable for such conditions, since capillary pores in these are

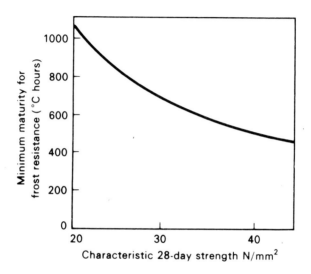

Fig. 3.15 Relationship between characteristic 28-day strength and minimum maturity for frost resistance

always interconnected. In all types of concrete, full compaction is necessary if maximum frost resistance is to be provided. When concreting is being carried out in cold weather, measurements of concrete temperature, using a thermometer in the concrete, protected by a metal sheath, should be made periodically, so that maturity can be calculated. The following steps will assist in obtaining the required maturity:

1. Use a rapid hardening or high alumina cement, an admixture such as calcium chloride or use a higher strength mix requiring lower maturity before exposure.
2. Heat the aggregates and/or water to increase the initial temperature of the concrete.
3. Use insulated formwork. The best insulator is a layer of trapped air. This may be obtained by, for example, tarpaulin over an airspace on slabs, or formwork with a backing of an insulating material.
4. Enclose the structure in a temporary heated covering; for example, polythene sheeting on scaffolding.

If the concrete relies on its own heat, together with insulated formwork for protection, thin sections will be far more difficult to deal with satisfactorily since they are, in general, of greater surface area for unit mass. Such types of construction should be avoided in very cold weather unless satisfactory maturity before freezing can be ensured.

TESTS ON HARDENED CONCRETE

The majority of tests are carried out on concrete at an early age and are concerned with the rheology of the concrete (that is, its behaviour under load) with a view to assessing development or variation of strength and durability. Tests may be classified as destructive and non-destructive.

Destructive testing of concrete (BS 1881)

The cube test. This is the most common type of destructive test for concrete owing to the comparative simplicity of manufacture of cubes and the cheapness of cube moulds. Carefully selected samples of the concrete mix are placed and compacted in steel moulds, the inner surfaces of which are coated with a release agent. The surface of the cube is covered with a rubber mat with identification marks, or the entire mould sealed and, after 24 hours, the cube is removed and cured under water at about 15°C, until testing. The cube is then placed between the platens of a compression testing machine, trowelled face sideways and the load is applied such that the stress increases at a given constant rate until failure. The maximum load is recorded. The compressive strength of concrete, as recorded by the cube test, may be affected by the following factors:

1. The size of the cube. 150-mm cubes (which would be required if 40-mm aggregate were used) tend to fail at slightly lower stresses than 100-mm cubes made from the same mix, possibly connected with the fact that 100-mm cubes have a higher surface area per unit volume than 150-mm cubes.
2. Cubes should be tested when wet, since drier cubes give higher readings.
3. Decreasing the loading rate gives lower cube strengths, due to the increased contribution of creep to failure.
4. Low results will be obtained if there are stress concentrations at the surface of the cube. These may be due to particles of loose material on the cube surface or irregularities in the surfaces of the loading platens, due to wear. The machine must stress all parts of the cube surface equally. To this end it is most important that the upper platen of the testing machine, which is located on a ball seating, should lock on loading, so that the concrete cube is evenly stressed, even if its elastic modulus varies from place to place or if the cube is not exactly centrally placed. Failure to lock would result in preliminary failure of the weaker or most heavily stressed areas of the concrete cube. It is found that best results are obtained if the ball seating of the testing machine is not lubricated. Correct and incorrect failure of concrete cubes is illustrated in Fig. 3.16. The ability of the machine to load correctly can be ascertained by use of, for example, a rectangular aluminium prism, with strain gauges attached to its four faces. On stressing such a prism in the machine, equal stresses should occur on the four faces. The concrete cube should, of course, be centred in the machine to minimise eccentricities in loading arrangement.

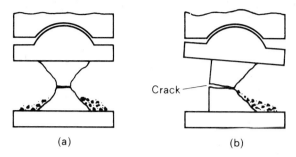

Fig. 3.16 Possible modes of failure of a concrete cube. (a) is correct and (b) is incorrect

The machine itself should also be checked for accuracy in calibration of loading.

The existing British Standard for testing machines deals with load calibration but does not cover possible eccentricities in loading, such that a 'Grade A' machine may still be unsatisfactory in this respect. A standard which covers this important requirement is essential if a meaningful description of a machine's accuracy is to be obtained.

If expensive in terms of pessimistic results, it is perhaps fortunate that inaccurate testing machines nearly always give readings which are too low.

Nature of failure and significance of cube test results. A suggested explanation of cube failures is that they fail along 45° planes due to shear, these planes being planes of maximum shear stress under a uniaxial loading arrangement, hence the appearance of the failed cube as in Fig. 3.16. However, the stresses in the cube are not uniaxial since the platen surfaces themselves provide considerable frictional lateral restraint to the cubes as illustrated in Fig. 3.17. This is confirmed by the decrease in cube strength obtained by inserting rubber pads above and below the cube, thereby decreasing restraint.

If this is the case, the pyramid shapes could correspond to the regions of influence of the platen restraint, actual failure being in tension as a result of stresses induced in

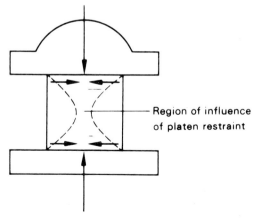

Fig. 3.17 Stresses caused by platen restraint on a cube during testing

the remainder of the cube, according to the Poisson's ratio of the concrete. In any case, the observed compressive strength of concrete has been estimated to be as much as double that in the actual structure for this and other reasons; for example, curing conditions. Hence it is very difficult to correlate closely cube strength to structure strength. The use of prisms or cylinders (as in the U.S.A.) would reduce the effect of platen restraint but such shapes are more costly to produce. The main value of the cube test is *not* in attempting to obtain directly the strength of the structure. The test may be useful in the following ways:

1. As a means of quality control. Assuming cubes are reliably made, cured and tested, cube variations will be indicative of variations in the concrete from which they are sampled. Hence they provide a means of detection of changes in materials or errors in methods.
2. A minimum or 'characteristic' cube strength is the normal way of specifying concrete strength, rather than attempting *in situ* measurements on the structure itself. The required cube strength for a given structure is decided upon by experience or from codes of practice.

Tensile testing of concrete

The BS test in tension currently operating is the cylinder splitting test, in which 300-mm long, 150-mm diameter cylinders, placed on edge, are loaded gradually in compression on a diametric plane parallel to the axis of the cylinders, stress concentrations at the surfaces being avoided by means of thin hardboard strips (Fig. 3.18). By the Poisson ratio effect, tensile stresses induced in the vertical plane produce

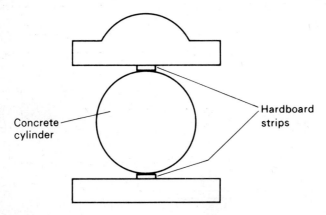

Fig. 3.18 The cylinder-splitting test for measurement of the tensile strength of concrete

failure in this plane and splitting of the cylinder. The tensile strength f_T is calculated from the formula:

$$f_T = \frac{2P}{\pi DL} \quad \text{where} \quad P = \text{load at failure}$$
$$D = \text{diameter of cylinder}$$
$$L = \text{length of cylinder}$$

The tensile strength of concrete, so measured, is normally about 10 per cent of its compressive strength. The test may be useful where the concrete is required to take a tensile stress but problems have been experienced with the above method of test, since the hardboard loading strips, which are essential to produce uniform loading along the cylinder, offer some restraint to lateral movement of the cylinder, producing rather optimistic results. The test is required for concrete to be used in road carriageways.

Flexural strength

This may be used in preference to the cube test as a strength criterion, especially where the concrete may have to withstand a flexural stress, as for example, in roads. The test described in BS 1881 uses a two-point loading system on a 100 x 100 mm or 150 x 150 mm beam, as shown in Fig. 3.19, which produces a constant bending

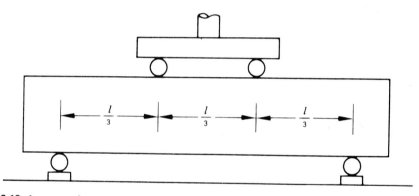

Fig. 3.19 Apparatus for measurement of flexural strength of concrete, showing two-point loading system

moment between loading rollers. Assuming that normal bending theory applies, the extreme fibre stress at failure is given by

$$f = \frac{Wl}{bd^2}$$ where l = length of beam between supporting rollers
W = load at failure
b = breadth
d = depth

provided failure occurs between the loading rollers. BS 1881 also describes an 'equivalent cube' test which can be carried out on the broken ends of the beam after failure. These ends, which are not damaged in the flexural test, are loaded in compression between auxiliary platens 100 or 150 mm square, appropriate to the width of the beam and give an indication of the cube strength of the concrete (Fig. 3.20). Results are normally about 5 per cent higher than a normal cube test result due to the contribution to strength of the concrete outside the auxiliary platens.

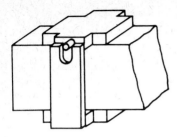

Fig. 3.20 Equivalent cube test for measurement of 'cube strength' of a broken part of a concrete beam

Compressive testing of cores drilled from the concrete

Cores, although expensive to obtain, allow visible examination of concrete for segregation or voids and also an estimate of the strength of the *in situ* concrete. Cores are provided with a moulded capping before crushing, normally of a high alumina cement mortar. The maximum load is then multiplied by a constant dependent on the length/diameter ratio to produce the equivalent strength of a core in which this ratio is 2 : 1. To compare with cube results, a further factor of 1·25 is used, since cores, like prisms, fail at reduced loads, due to decreased platen restraint in the region of failure.

Non-destructive testing

Where these methods of testing are required to indicate crushing strength, they must do so by means of some other property such as hardness or modulus of elasticity. Therefore, caution should be taken that readings obtained are correctly correlated to crushing strength and this correlation will in general be different for different types of aggregate.

The Schmidt rebound hammer. This is a small, portable instrument containing a spring loaded plunger. On pressing against a well-restrained concrete surface, the plunger is forced into the instrument, loading a spring to a point when a mass is released and, under the energy of the spring, hits the end of the plunger. The mass rebounds to a distance depending on the hardness of the material the plunger rests against. The rebound distance is recorded by a marker and may be correlated to strength for a given material by means of cube results. The distance of rebound depends on the inclination of the hammer, use on soffits, for example, giving higher readings due to the assistance of gravity on the rebound. Since the area of contact of the plunger with the surface is only a few square millimetres, a large number of readings (for example, twenty) is essential to average out local variations in the concrete. The simplicity and convenience of the instrument makes it a useful means of checking the strength of *in situ* concrete.

Electrodynamic method. This is based on the principle that the resonant frequency of a concrete beam depends on the velocity of compression waves through it, which, in turn, depends on the modulus of elasticity of the concrete. The simplest form of resonance, shown in Fig. 3.21, occurs when the wavelength (λ) equals twice the length

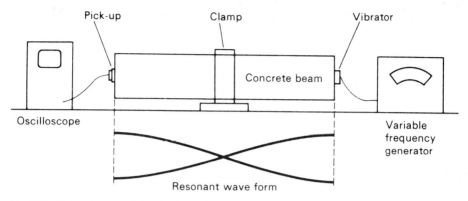

Fig. 3.21 Determination of the elastic modulus of concrete by an electrodynamic method

of the beam (*l*). If the frequency (*f*) of applied mechanical vibrations is varied until the pick-up response is a maximum, then the velocity *v* of the waves is given by:

$$v = f\lambda$$
$$= 2\,fl$$

If the beam is assumed to approximate to an infinitely long, thin rod, then *v* is related to *E*, the elastic modulus by the equation:

$$v = \sqrt{\frac{E}{\rho}} \quad \text{where } \rho = \text{the density of the concrete}$$

Therefore $E = 4f^2 l^2 \rho$

Ultrasonic pulse velocity method. Pulses of high frequency sound, usually about 150 kHz, are passed through a concrete cube or beam and, by means of electronic circuitry, an accurate indication of the time taken is obtained. However, the formula $v = \sqrt{E/\rho}$ cannot be used as with the electrodynamic method, since there is much more scope for lateral movement of waves in this c se, the waves being of much lower wavelength. Hence the above formula, which applied only to infinitely long, thin rods, must be replaced by one involving Poisson's ratio σ:

$$v^2 = \frac{E}{\rho} \frac{(1-\sigma)}{(1+\sigma)(1-2\sigma)} \left(\text{Poisson's ratio} = \frac{\text{induced lateral strain}}{\text{applied axial strain}} \right)$$

This limits the usefulness of the pulse velocity method for absolute determination of the elastic modulus of concrete, since Poisson's ratio tends to vary for different concretes. (Values range between 0·15 and 0·20.) Furthermore, the effects of accelerators or moisture content changes on pulse velocity are not in proportion to their effects on cube strength. The test is therefore mainly used in quality control in relation to one type of mix. It is also useful for the detection of cracks or voids since these affect the readings considerably.

The value of *E* obtained from the electrodynamic method as well as the ultrasonic pulse method is higher than that obtained by static measurements, since the latter are obtained by application of relatively high loads which will introduce a creep component into the strain as well as the elastic·component detected by dynamic methods.

Use of the covermeter for location of reinforcement

Since reinforcement depends for its protection on the alkaline environment of the concrete, it is important that it be at a sufficient depth below the surface, particularly where the concrete is subject to wetting and drying. Over a period of time surface layers 'carbonate'; that is, calcium hydroxide in the concrete reacts with carbon dioxide in the atmosphere producing calcium carbonate. This reaction decreases the alkalinity of surface layers and corrosion of the steel could ensue if carbonation reached the reinforcement. The operation of the covermeter depends on the magnetic effect of steel (Fig. 3.22) and enables the depth of reinforcement to be determined to

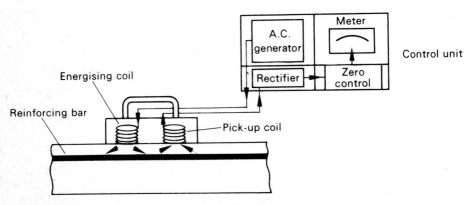

Fig. 3.22 Covermeter for location of the depth of reinforcement

within about 20 per cent accuracy for a range of sizes of reinforcement. The thickness of cover necessary depends on the grade of concrete and the severity of exposure. C.P. 110 requires cover of not less than 15 mm for high grades and this value increases for lower grades or severe exposure, being 50 mm for grade 25 concrete in concretes exposed to sea or moorland water.

The extent of testing of concrete

As with other aspects of quality control, the extent of testing of concrete depends on the quality and quantity of concrete to be produced. When small quantities of concrete only are produced, it may be considered better to provide an extra safety margin in terms of cement content rather than worry about testing. Such practice is, however, open to grave errors which may pass unnoticed unless some check on quality is made and, in any case, many specifications require a certain cube strength so that cubes must be made. If a detailed check on strength development is required, E values by the electrodynamic or pulse velocity methods may be obtained at frequent intervals, being correlated with cube strengths periodically. Such methods may also be used to predict likely strengths at 7 and 28 days. Alternatively, accelerated curing techniques enable prediction of these strengths within 24 hours of placing of the concrete.

Other tests described may be useful if for any reason the quality of concrete is in doubt. If, for example, cube test results are unsatisfactory, rebound hammer readings could be taken in the *in situ* concrete (provided, of course, the hammer is calibrated), and if this also gives unsatisfactory results a final decision on removal of concrete could be taken after cutting and testing cores.

STATISTICAL ANALYSIS AS AN AID TO QUALITY CONTROL AND DESIGN

It is now widely accepted that statistical techniques are necessary to rationalise design of building elements since any one component will have inherent variations of a statistical nature, so that one can never be absolutely certain of its ability to perform its task. Instead, an acceptable probability of failure is decided upon and, as far as possible, components are designed upon such a basis. In this way, safety margins for different types of component can be matched, bearing in mind the importance of that component, so that economic designs are produced without undue danger of 'weak links' in the chain. Such methods also may be applied to other materials, for example, steel, timber and bricks.

Graphical evaluation of cube results

If a graph relating to the frequency of a certain cube strength occurring to cube strength is plotted, for concrete of a particular type the graph obtained will be of the form shown in Fig. 3.23. The average strength is obtained by dividing the area in half by a vertical line and it will normally be close to the peak of the graph. The variability of the cube results is represented by the width of the graph. Graph B clearly represents concrete which is more variable than that of Graph A. Variability is normally measured by the term standard deviation, s. For a set of n results, of values $x_1, x_2, \ldots,$ $x_i, \ldots, x_n$ of average value $\bar{x}$, s is given by

$$s = \sqrt{\frac{\Sigma(x_i - \bar{x})^2}{n - 1}}$$

Also, since in some cases, larger results may be expected to have larger variations, the coefficient of variation v is defined

$$v = \frac{100s}{\bar{x}}$$

Hence, if for a given type of measurement, s is proportional to $\bar{x}$, then v will be constant.

If, as indicated above, a characteristic strength is specified for a concrete, implying a certain probability of failures or, in the case of cube results, a certain percentage of failures, then the average of cube strengths is not the only information of importance.

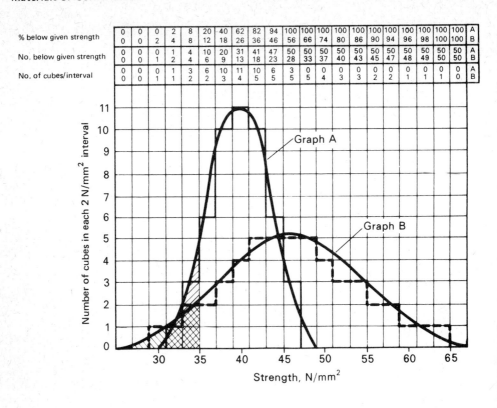

% below given strength	0	0	0	2	8	20	40	62	82	94	100	100	100	100	100	100	100	100	100	100	100	A
	0	0	2	4	8	12	18	26	36	46	56	66	74	80	86	90	94	96	98	100	100	B
No. below given strength	0	0	0	1	4	10	20	31	41	47	50	50	50	50	50	50	50	50	50	50	50	A
	0	0	1	2	4	6	9	13	18	23	28	33	37	40	43	45	47	48	49	50	50	B
No. of cubes/interval	0	0	0	1	3	6	10	11	10	6	3	0	0	0	0	0	0	0	0	0	0	A
	0	0	1	1	2	2	3	4	5	5	5	5	4	3	3	2	2	1	1	1	0	B

Fig. 3.23 Histograms drawn from the results of two sets of fifty concrete cube tests. Graph A represents good quality control and Graph B poor quality control. The total area under each graph is the same. Also, the area under each curve to the left of the 35 N/mm² line is the same, implying equal numbers of results beneath this stremgth. Curve B is, however, indicative of a greater probability of very low cube results than curve A

In Fig. 3.23 the area to the left of a given line relative to the whole area indicates the proportion of results below that strength level. The total areas of Graphs A and B are equal since 100 per cent of results must lie somewhere. The two curves have been drawn such that the areas below a strength of 35 N/mm² are equal and such that the probability of finding a cube result below this strength is in each case 8 per cent; that is,

$$\frac{\text{area of graph below 35 N/mm}^2}{\text{area of graph above 35 N/mm}^2} \times 100 = 8 \text{ per cent}$$

Note, however, that Graph A achieves this probability with:

(a) a lower average strength than Graph B (40 N/mm² compared to 46 N/mm²);
(b) fewer very low cube results than Graph B.

'A' represents better quality control than 'B' and this will cost more but the concrete producing Graph A will require less cement than that produced by Graph B, so that provided sufficient quantities of mix A are used, the reduction in the cost of cement will more than offset the extra cost of better quality control. Furthermore, a structure made with mix A will be safer than that made with mix B because the probability of very low cube results is lower.

It is clear from the above that an assessment of probability of results below a certain value depends on the areas of the histogram type of graph shown. The process can be simplified by plotting the percentages of results falling below each strength on a special non-linear scale against strength. The result is a straight line graph (see Fig. 3.24). Having drawn the graph, the percentage of results falling below any strength can be read off directly.

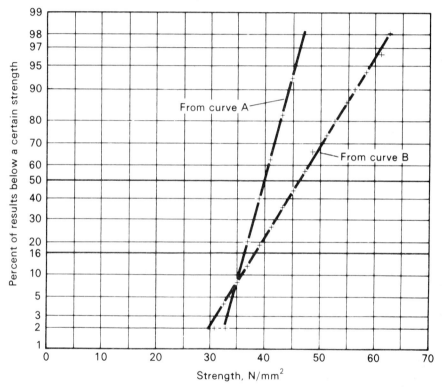

Fig. 3.24 The results of Fig. 3.23 plotted such that a straight line graph is obtained. In each case, the standard deviation can be obtained by subtracting strengths corresponding to the 50 per cent and 16 per cent lines. For example, Graph A corresponds to a standard deviation of 40·0−36·5 = 3·5 N/mm2

Alternatively, if the standard deviation and average of results are known, the (characteristic) strength below which a percentage of results falls can be assessed from a 'k factor' given by:

$$A \quad = \quad C \quad + \quad k \quad s$$

| average strength | characteristic strength | k factor | standard deviation |

A table of k factors for various percentage failures is shown in Table 3.6. For example, the mix of Graph A has an average strength of 40 N/mm^2 and $s = 3\cdot5$ N/mm^2. To find the strength below which 5 per cent failures occur, use $k = 1\cdot64$. Hence:

$$C = A - 1\cdot64s$$
$$= 40 - 1\cdot64 \times 3\cdot5 = 40 - 5\cdot74$$
$$= 34\cdot26\,(34\cdot3)\ \text{N/mm}^2$$

This value can be checked from the 5 per cent line on the graph.

This type of technique enables a target mean strength (T) to be established when designing a concrete mix, based on a required characteristic strength C, with a given failure rate defining a certain value of k. Some idea of the standard deviation is essential in order to find T in the equation $T = C + ks$. In the case of new plants, this may be made suitably large, and then reduced when cube results give a direct value of s.

Table 3.6

A table of k values for various values of percentage failures

Number of failures permitted	k factor
16	1·00
10	1·28
5	1·64
2	2·05
1	2·33

The initial value of s chosen normally depends on the strength of concrete being produced. To some degree, stronger concretes are likely to have higher standard deviations since it is impossible to obtain negative cube strengths (that is, the coefficient of variation, v, is constant). On the other hand, high-strength concrete mixes normally require careful control and, in any case, cube results above the ceiling strength for a given aggregate type are extremely unlikely. Hence, standard deviations may decrease at high strengths. These arguments are reflected by C.P. 110 recommendations for initial ks values. For grades 7, 10 and 15, the margin is taken to be two-thirds of the characteristic strength, hence, the margin increases with strength. For grades 20, 25 and 30 concretes, a margin of 15 N/mm^2 is specified, and for high-grade concretes a lower margin (not less than 7·5 N/mm^2) may be used. High- or low-strength concretes often give skew distribution curves for the reasons given above so that characteristic strengths obtained by the use of formula may not correspond to those measured directly from graphs of the type given in Fig. 3.23. Generally, calculations result in low values of characteristic strength for low-strength concretes and high values for high-strength concretes.

A simple means of calculating the target mean strength is provided by Road Note 4. The characteristic strength is multiplied by a factor which increases for low degrees of control. This results in an increment which is proportional to strength. At high strengths, however, the increment tends to be excessive, even with 'very good control'.

Statistical methods are of greatest value when large quantities of concrete are being continuously produced, as on large sites or in the case of ready mixed concrete. In these situations, it is an advantage to monitor continuously the concrete using cube tests, results of such tests being plotted so as to make clear the trends in average strength and standard deviation as soon as possible. A simple way of achieving this is to plot results on a graph, as shown in Fig. 3.25. Control limits of $T \pm ks$ are included

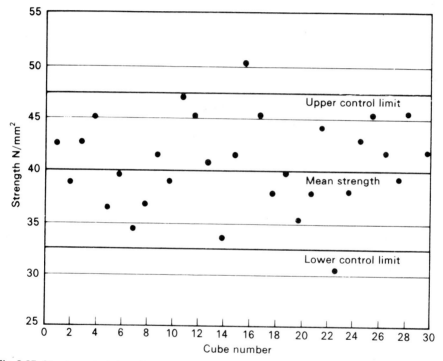

Fig. 3.25 Simple control chart for monitoring progress during production of concrete. The target strength in this case is 40 N/mm² and the anticipated standard deviation is 4·5 N/mm² with a permissible failure rate of 5 per cent. The first thirty cube results are shown and these indicate satisfactory performance since only one result is below the lower control limit and there are approximately equal numbers of cubes on each side of the mean strength line

and, as well as the general trend of results, low or high results are immediately apparent. A more sophisticated method is the use of cumulative sum techniques. For example, if the target mean strength is 35 N/mm² and cube results are 31, 39, 32, 34, 37 N/mm², the differences are −4, +4, −3, −1, +2 and the cumulative difference is −2 N/mm², which means that the average strength as given by the above five results is slightly below that required. By means of a continuous plot of this value as new results are obtained, steps can be taken to rectify any sudden change in average strength.

Similar procedures can also be used with standard deviation values, differences between the results being compared to the average expectable difference for the given s value. If accelerated curing techniques are being used to predict twenty-eight-day strength, a similar graph can be drawn for accumulated differences in corresponding cube results, changes being made in the correlation graphs as necessary.

If, for any reason, a change in mix proportions is found to be necessary, this can be effected by altering cement content using a graph which relates strength to cement content, or, if such a graph is not available, by altering the cement content on the basis that an increase of 6 kg of cement per cubic metre will increase the average strength by about 1 N/mm^2 and vice versa. If the standard deviation alters, the change should be multiplied by the k factor concerned and the cement content then changed as above. For example, if, with a k factor of 2·0, the standard deviation increases to 4·5 from 4·0, the average strength must be increased by $2 \times 0·5 = 1$ N/mm^2, requiring 6 kg extra cement per cubic metre. In all cases, the cause of changes should be investigated and if necessary remedial measures taken. A very high cube result should be regarded with suspicion—it increases the standard deviation and hence causes a *reduction* in characteristic strength. The question may well be asked, 'Why aren't all the cube results as good as this?'

OTHER TYPES OF CONCRETE

High-strength concrete

Contents of high strength are now widely used in a number of applications; for example, precast products or prestressed members. Using methods already described, it is quite possible to obtain cube strengths as high as 50 N/mm^2 at 28 days. Higher values can be obtained, however, by appropriate selection of materials and slight modification of these methods, giving 28-day strengths of up to 80 N/mm^2, which may be regarded as the 'ceiling strength' for concretes using ordinary Portland cement. Rapid hardening Portland cement may give strengths up to 90 N/mm^2 at 28 days but the long-term strength will be similar to that of ordinary Portland cement.

Aggregates for high-strength concrete should be strong—for example, granite or flint and preferably of angular shape with rough or granular surface texture, as is obtained by crushing natural rock. Hence crushed granite is commonly used. Crushed flint, on the other hand, is not as suitable, since crushing produces smooth, glassy surfaces which do not key well to cement paste.

It is well known that the water/cement ratio is the most important factor in determining strength of concrete. Therefore, to make high-strength concrete, the water/cement ratio should be low—in the range of 0·30 to 0·45. However, the effects of aggregate type and workability on strength at a given water/cement ratio are more pronounced than at medium strengths, so that a design code must include all three parameters in obtaining a certain strength. To illustrate the effect of workability, it is almost impossible to obtain strengths over about 65 N/mm^2 at 28 days at medium workability. Decreasing the workability, at constant water/cement ratio, hence making the mix leaner (and cheaper), will increase this figure towards those given above, provided compaction can be achieved at the very low workabilities that ensue. The reason for this perhaps rather surprising fact is probably that in leaner mixes of a given water/cement ratio, there is less excess moisture in a given volume, hence fewer potential voids with the associated strength reduction.

High alumina cement. The chief value of high alumina cement lies in its rapid strength development. This cement develops 70–90 per cent of its long term strength within 24 hours of mixing, hence it is useful where very tight schedules have to be kept, or in repairs where disruption is involved. The high cost of this cement is, however, a disadvantage. Design of mixes may be carried out as with Portland cements, the resulting concrete being slightly more workable, due to the lower specific surface of high alumina cement.

Failure of the concretes mentioned above is due to cracking in the cement mortar at places where the stresses are most concentrated—perhaps where aggregate particles are closest, since there is no chemical bonding between aggregate and cement. Much higher strengths may therefore be obtained by using unground cement clinker instead of aggregate, since, as already stated, there is a chemical bond between hydrated and unhydrated parts of cement particles. Hence, if cement is mixed with its clinker at a very low water/cement ratio, perhaps 0·1, the whole mixture will become chemically bonded. Compaction under high pressure is essential for such dry mixes but strengths of over 300 N/mm^2 have been obtained in this way. The less hydrated cement, the stronger will be the product, since the 'aggregate' has an E value about four times higher than the hydrated cement. High alumina cement is used in this way, producing a concrete which is very expensive but with high abrasion and chemical resistance as required, for example, for some types of floor surface. The use of high alumina cement in structural concrete is now controlled by Building Regulations owing to the effects of conversion.

Lean concrete

Sometimes known as dry-lean concrete, this material may contain as little as 5 per cent cement by weight. It is normally used for road bases, being compacted by heavy or vibrating rollers, so that workabilities may be much lower than is normally possible for concrete. In fact, the correct water content of lean mix concretes is obtained by compaction tests at various values as for soils, the optimum moisture content (i.e. moisture content at which density is a maximum) being used. For gravel aggregates, the value is 6 per cent by weight of dry materials. The water/cement ratio so obtained is on average higher than that used in normal concrete and may be over 1·0. Since the moisture content is fixed, a given water/cement ratio will determine the cement content of the mix and hence the aggregate/cement ratio. Mixes may be designed easily from the graph shown in Fig. 3.26. The fine aggregate content used is normally between 35 and 40 per cent of the total aggregate. This is perhaps higher than usual but is essential to avoid the possibility of undersanded parts of the mix with consequent segregation and to obtain a sealed surface. The maximum aggregate size may be 20 or 40 mm. The Ministry of Transport specification for Roads and Bridges (1969) effectively requires an average strength of approximately 14 N/mm^2 at 28 days for lean mix concrete to be used in road bases.

This strength, however, relates to cubes compacted to refusal and in practice there will normally be a density shortfall on concrete which is site compacted, with

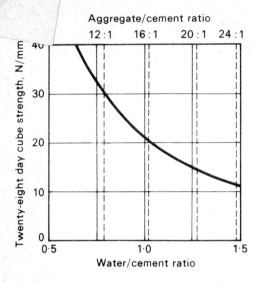

Fig. 3.26 Design graph for lean concrete mixes. The aggregate/cement ratios given correspond to a moisture content of 6 per cent by weight of dry materials in the fresh concrete

consequent strength reduction. The M.O.T. specification limits this density reduction to 5 per cent of the theoretical density (densities measured 'dry' in each case). It also requires aggregate/cement ratios to be between 15 : 1 and 20 : 1. The former figure is given because experience has shown that richer mixes tend to result in large cracks in the road base.

Lightweight concretes

These may have dry densities between 400 kg/m^3 (aerated) and 1800 kg/m^3 (structural lightweight concretes) compared to 2200–2600 kg/m^3 for normal concrete. They may have the following advantages:

1. They produce lower foundation loads and are particularly useful in upper storeys of tall buildings.
2. They may be placed in higher lifts than dense concrete.
3. They improve the thermal performance of buildings by reducing their thermal inertia.
4. They have better fire resistance than dense concrete.
5. Lightweight aggregates are often produced from waste products, hence they are cheap.

As concrete densities decrease, strengths follow a similar pattern, though actual values depend on aggregate type and shape. This is due to the reduction in E values of aggregate caused by air voids in them, or due to voids in the concrete. The low E values of lightweight aggregates also result in lower shrinkage restraint by them, hence there is higher shrinkage and creep in these concretes. Lightweight concrete may be broadly classified into three types—'no fines', lightweight aggregate and aerated concretes.

No fines concrete

As the term implies, this type of concrete contains only coarse aggregate. The material produced has an open texture such that, when used in walling, a good key is provided for plastering internally. Externally, no fines concrete is normally protected by rendering. The upper strength limit is about 15 N/mm^2 but the shrinkage and moisture movement are considerably less than those of normal concrete due to the discontinuous nature of the cement paste. No fines concrete may be made using natural or lightweight aggregates, the former being stronger but denser. Correct batch quantities are best obtained by trial mixes, the water content being chosen such that each particle of aggregate is well coated with cement grout. Too little water reduces cohesion and too much causes the cement grout to segregate at the base. Wetting aggregates before use is the best way of obtaining a consistent water content.

Lightweight aggregate concrete

Although naturally occurring lightweight aggregates have been used (e.g. volcanic cinders and sawdust), the majority of aggregates are manufactured from denser materials such as clay or slate. They are covered by BS 3797. Some examples are as follows:

Foamed slag. This is blast furnace slag, cooled quickly by using water. On crushing, an angular, rough material is produced giving concrete of strength up to 40 N/mm^2 at 28 days.

Expanded clay, shale or slate. This process is based on the fact, already mentioned under 'Bricks', that rapid heating of clay causes bloating due to expansion of trapped gases. The clay is heated in the form of small rolled lumps, the basic shape being retained after firing. Alternatively, a mixture of clay and colliery shale is heated, ignition taking place and producing a fused clinker. Crushing the clinker produces an angular material. These aggregates may be used to give strengths up to about 45 N/mm^2 at 28 days.

Expanded pulverised fuel ash (p.f.a.). The ash, which is obtained as a waste product from power stations, is mixed with water and powdered coal to form nodules. Sintering causes ignition and the nodules expand into hard, spherical particles. The material produces concretes of high strength/density ratio with strengths of up to 55 N/mm^2 and low shrinkage.

Design of lightweight concrete mixes

The method of absolute volumes is not easy to apply, since aggregates are highly absorbent. For a given aggregate type, however, there is a fairly well defined relation between water/cement ratio and strengths. Ratios are often quoted in volumes for lightweight materials, masses for weight batching being obtained from bulk densities. Water added at the mixer should be corrected according to:

1. the absorbed water in aggregates (deduct value); and
2. the absorption of the aggregates (add on value).

There is more justification in lightweight concrete for final correction of water at the mixer to produce correct workability than for dense concrete, since the above corrections are substantial and may vary considerably from batch to batch. Natural fine aggregate used in place of lightweight fine aggregate increases strength and workability and reduces shrinkage but also increases the density of the concrete. Lightweight concretes made with lightweight aggregates in general shrink about 50 per cent more than dense concrete. This fact, combined with the relatively low tensile strength of lightweight concretes, means that adequate movement joints should be provided in continuous lengths of lightweight concrete structures.

Aerated concrete

This is concrete containing bubbles of gas, produced either by means of an air-entraining agent or chemically; for example, by aluminium powder. If fine sand only is used as an aggregate, concretes of extremely low densities (for example, 400 kg/m^3) may be produced. The material, however, behaves rather like ordinary concrete of high cement content, having high shrinkage and moisture movement. These may be reduced by high pressure steam curing so that this material is used mainly for precast blocks and partitions where the very low densities and thermal conductivities obtainable are beneficial.

ADMIXTURES FOR CONCRETE

The term admixture defines a material added at the mixer, rather than one included in the cement during manufacture (additive). There is a large number of admixtures on the market which play a significant role in concrete production, but they must not be regarded as substitutes for good design and production techniques.

Only very small quantities of admixtures are normally required, so that great care should be taken to ensure uniform distribution throughout the concrete mix. Admixtures should be added to the mixing water and thoroughly dispersed before use. A number of the more commonly used admixtures is described.

Accelerators

By far the most common of these is calcium chloride, $CaCl_2$. Extra rapid hardening Portland cement already contains about 2 per cent calcium chloride. The chemical does not affect the ultimate strength of concrete but it accelerates the strength development, 2 per cent calcium chloride by weight of ordinary Portland cement giving concrete of double the strength of ordinary Portland cement when about 3 days old. The increased heat output also helps counteract the possibility of frost damage when concreting in cold weather. Calcium chloride tends to accelerate corrosion of reinforcement so that it is not normally used with reinforced concrete, particularly if it contains thin pre-stressing wires. In any case, the content should not exceed 3 per cent by weight of the cement. Calcium chloride should not be used with sulphate-resisting Portland cement, since it decreases its chemical resistance; or with high alumina cements. The latter have admirable setting and hardening properties without need for admixtures.

Set retarders

These are used in hot weather where early stiffening may affect concrete properties. They are normally based on organic materials such as sugars, tartaric acid and ligno-sulphonates. Quantities required are very small, hence they should be measured carefully. Ready-mixed-concrete vehicles often carry a quantity of molasses which will prevent the concrete setting in the event of non-delivery.

Workability aids

The commonest of these are ligno-sulphonates, which tend to reduce temporarily the water absorption of cement particles so that more water is available for workability. Hydration may be retarded so that accelerators are often added to counteract their effect on strength. At constant workability, the use of a workability aid will enable the water in a given mix to be reduced, producing a 10–20 per cent increase in strength of the concrete at 28 days. Alternatively, the same strength of mix may be produced with a saving in cement of about 5 per cent.

Water-reducing agents are widely used in the ready-mixed concrete industry and are an example of the successful use which can be made of admixtures, provided adequate control measures exist.

Air entraining agents

The most common are those based on vinsol resin—a type of soap obtained from wood resins which produces stable air bubbles in the cement paste. They may be used for the following reasons:

1. To act as a workability aid and to prevent bleeding or segregation. The very small air bubbles (less than 1 mm in diameter) act as a low friction 'aggregate') improving the workability and cohesiveness of the mix. In fact, it is normal to reduce the fine aggregate content of an air entrained mix. In some cases, the workability may be so much improved that the better compaction thus possible increases the strength of the concrete in spite of the presence of air in it (normally about 5 per cent by volume for 20-mm aggregate). Since the air affects primarily the properties of the mortar, concretes made with larger aggregates require less air. Also, since each air bubble is enclosed in a film of moisture, drier mixes or finer cements or aggregates will tend to result in less air for a given quantity of air entraining agent, since there is less free water in such mixes. Air entraining agents are often used in mortars and to improve the properties of the plastic concrete for pumping purposes.

2. To increase resistance to frost and de-icing salts. Provided sufficient small air bubbles are included, frost resistance of air entrained concrete is much better than that

of ordinary concrete. As ice crystals form in the capillary pores in the concrete, excess water is driven into the voids where it remains until the concrete thaws, when it returns. Entrapped air does not have this effect since there are fewer, larger voids so that large volumes of cement paste will have no means of stress relief in this way. Concrete for major road surfaces is now required to be air-entrained.

3. To produce aerated concretes. Lightweight forms of these may contain up to 90 per cent of air, produced by vigorous agitation of mixes containing much larger quantities of air entraining agent than for the above purposes.

Water repelling agents

The use of these must not be regarded as a substitute for the production of dense plain concrete. They may, however, be useful for reducing water absorption and hence discoloration of decorative finishes for a limited period of time. They impart an electrostatic charge to the capillary pores in the cement paste causing water to be repelled. Typical agents are aluminium and calcium stearates.

THE PROPERTIES AND DURABILITY OF HARDENED CONCRETE

These may be described under the headings of shrinkage and moisture movement; creep; thermal properties and fire resistance; resistance to chemical attack.

Shrinkage and moisture movement

Shrinkage may be divided into two types; irreversible shrinkage on first drying and consequent reversible shrinkage or moisture movement. Figure 3.27 shows a typical movement curve of concrete during moisture content changes. The cement gel, which

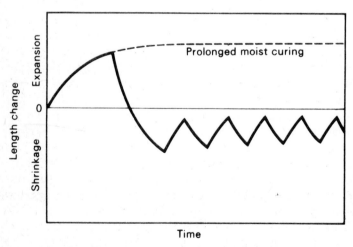

Fig. 3.27 Length changes caused in concrete by repeated wetting and drying. The first expansion occurs during moist curing, the first drying shrinkage occurring next. Subsequent wettings are indicated by upward-sloping lines and drying periods by downward-sloping lines

has a very high specific surface, adsorbs water very strongly to its surface. However, since capillary pores are very small—the order of 1·5 μm in diameter—the amount of water the gel can absorb is restricted, such that more water tries to force its way into the pores to increase the quantity adsorbed. This leads to a 'disjoining' pressure and a compressive stress in the water with consequent expansion of the cement paste and the concrete. When the concrete dries for the first time, the water is partly removed, hence the internal pressure falls and the capillary pores reduce in size with a corresponding reduction in the volume of the concrete. At the same time, new bonds form in the cement paste, increasing its rigidity, so that the next wetting does not produce an expansion equal to the original shrinkage. As time continues, moisture changes produce progressively less change of length owing to the gradually increasing stiffness of the cement gel. Hence the form of Fig. 3.27. Note that the concrete, on hydration, expands to a degree dependent on water/cement ratio of the concrete. It will be apparent that the concretes most susceptible to shrinkage are those with high cement contents, high water/cement ratios exaggerating the effect. For this reason C.P. 110 specifies a maximum value of 550 kg of cement per cubic metre of concrete. The effect of curing time on shrinkage is complex since, although in well-cured concrete there is more cement gel to resist the tensile stresses produced as it shrinks around aggregate particles, there is less scope for stress reduction by creep. Hence cracking may occur after a short or long curing period. (Observed shrinkage in well-cured concrete is less, due to aggregate restraint, but this does not mean that cracking is less likely.)

Carbonation shrinkage

This is not a true shrinkage since it occurs when calcium hydroxide crystals in the cement near the surface of the concrete, which are stressed due to cement shrinkage, dissolve in carbonic acid, which is present due to carbon dioxide in the atmosphere and water in the concrete. Calcium carbonate is formed, crystals being deposited in pores so that the compressive stress formerly acting on the calcium hydroxide crystals is now relieved with corresponding reduction in volume. Carbonation shrinkage requires moisture and therefore increases to some degree at higher humidities. At humidities above about 50 per cent, however, carbonation cannot continue beneath the surface of the concrete since the pores are blocked by moisture. Therefore, at high humidities, carbonation shrinkage falls off.

Creep in concrete

This must not be confused with the time dependent strains which may occur in metals. The nature of the solid constitutents of cement paste is such that plastic movement without damage is not possible. The origin of creep is the same as that of shrinkage—the water in the cement paste. When concrete is stressed, the energy balance between gel and water is disturbed, so that water slowly diffuses to regions of lower energy. This movement relieves the stress but, as in moisture changes, is accompanied by strain in the concrete. A typical graph of creep against time is shown in Fig. 3.28. From the above explanation, it is clear that removal of stress will induce similar unbalances in the water equilibrium so that recovery will also be dependent on time, hence the form of the curve on reduction of stress. It may be surprising that the movement of water which is responsible for creep may take several months to complete but it should be appreciated that adsorbed water is not liquid in the normal sense of the term so that it travels by molecular diffusion, governed by its energy and the size of the gel pores. For this reason, creep occurs more rapidly at higher temperatures, especially in the case of young concretes. It might be supposed that creep should impose severe restrictions on loads applied to concrete. This is not the case, however, since strain due to creep does not become significant until stresses of

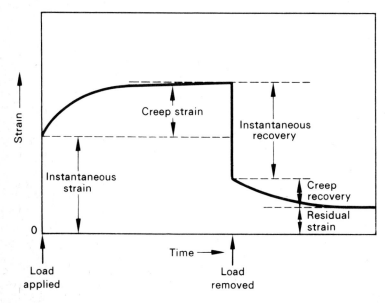

Fig. 3.28 Creep and creep recovery in concrete

about 50 per cent of the ultimate strength are reached. Problems may, however, arise; for example, in mass concrete when internal regions which become warm due to cement hydration at first become compressed, the stresses being relieved by creep. Over a period of time the temperature reduces and the now more mature concrete is able to creep less under the tensile stresses caused by cooling. Hence cracking may occur. (The process is rather similar to that by which glass is toughened.) Creep must be allowed for in prestressed concrete. CP. 110 requires allowances of up to 48 microstrain per N/mm^2 of applied stress depending on concrete type and age.

Thermal properties and fire resistance

It need hardly be mentioned that, owing to the moisture in concrete, it is not possible to quote a coefficient of thermal expansion as would be possible with, for example, steel. When concrete is heated, water diffuses from gel pores into capillary pores and the concrete as a whole tends to lose weight. Hence an initial expansion may be offset by the consequent moisture change which may take some considerable time to complete. A further effect which influences expansion is the decrease of surface tension of water with increase of temperature. This results in a further expansion of concrete due to the reduction of the compressive effect of water in capillary pores. This capillary effect is greatest at humidities of about 50 per cent since at high humidities capillaries are full of water and there are fewer water/air interfaces, while at low humidities they are almost empty. The expansion coefficient of concrete also depends on that of the aggregate used. As far as it is possible to quote an 'average'

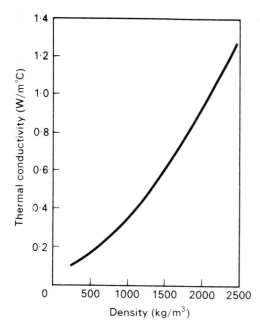

Fig. 3.29 Approximate relationship between the thermal conductivity and density of dry concrete. The exact relationship depends on aggregate type and moisture content.

value, normal concretes have coefficients of thermal movement around $11 \times 10^{-6}/°C$, which fortunately is similar to that of steel, so that relative movement in reinforced concrete is usually insufficient to destroy the steel/concrete bond.

The thermal conductivity of concrete is dependent on its density (Fig. 3.29), though it is also affected by aggregate type. Generally speaking, dense concrete has a thermal conductivity of about 1.0 W/m °C. The fire resistance of concrete depends on its thermal conductivity since concrete with low conductivities will heat up more slowly. Hence lightweight concretes tend to have better fire resistance than dense concretes. Failure normally occurs by spalling due to stress concentrations caused by the heat. Fire resistance is also affected by the coefficient of expansion of the aggregate and it is known that limestone aggregate which has a low coefficient of expansion produces a concrete of better fire resistance than siliceous aggregate concretes. Above about 300°C the bonding in the cement paste begins to break down, the concrete becomes virtually useless by about 800°C. If spalling of the surface of structural concrete exposes reinforcement, then failure takes place more rapidly due to its consequent expansion. Hence cover to reinforcement must be related to the fire resistance required.

Resistance to chemical attack

The effecs of some acids and sugar on concrete have already been mentioned (see 'Organic impurities' and 'Admixtures') but the most common form of chemical attack is due to the presence of sulphates in the soil or ground water. (See 'Cements' for details of the chemical effect.) The resistance of cements to sulphate attack increases in the order: ordinary Portland cement, Portland blast furnace cement, low heat cement, sulphate resisting cement, super sulphated cement and high alumina cement. When in doubt, tests for sulphates should be carried out, especially in clay soils; BS 1377 (1967) gives methods for these. The sulphates from a measured sample of dried soil or ground water are extracted using barium chloride, which forms an insoluble precipitate of barium sulphate. Alternatively, an ion exchange method may be used. Quantities of sulphates are measured as a percentage of the original oven-dry weight for soils or in grammes per litre for ground water.

Increased resistance to sulphates is obtained by use of low water/cement ratio concretes which are relatively impermeable to water. When concreting in a heavily sulphated soil (over 2 per cent for example), high alumina cement with a cement content of about 350 kg/m^3 of concrete and a water/cement ratio not exceeding 0·40 should be used. Less aggressive conditions, for example 0·5 per cent sulphates, would allow the use of sulphate resisting or super sulphated cements with about 300 kg/m^3 of cement and a water/cement ratio not exceeding 0·5. Low heat or Portland blast furnace cement should only be used where sulphate contamination is slight (say, 0·2 per cent or less).

MORTARS

These may be defined as mixtures of sand, cementitious material such as lime or cement and water, used for jointing or surfacing. The plastic properties of mortars are of considerable importance: they must combine good cohesion with high workability and adequate suction to the background. (It should be emphasised that mortars do not bond chemically to the background, they 'key' on to the material by absorption of mortar into surface layers. Hence a porous or open texture provides the best grip.) The strength of mortars is not normally required to be high. In renderings the mortar should be strong enough to resist shrinkage cracking and sufficiently impervious to resist frost damage. When used for jointing, the mortar should be weaker than the units to be joined, so that if relative movement occurs cracking will occur in the mortar rather than in the units themselves. Furthermore, since mortar joints are normally thin, failure in them due to shear is unlikely and walling units may have strengths as much as five times greater than the mortars used in them. On the other hand, brickwork normally has a strength between 25 and 40 per cent that of the strength of the bricks used as determined by the test of BS 3921. (These facts reflect the type of test used on bricks, mortar and brickwork.) One of the most likely modes of failure in brickwork with a large slenderness ratio is by buckling caused by tensile stresses due to eccentricity of load. Lateral loads may contribute to this kind of failure.

Use of lime in mortars

Hydrated lime is obtained by heating calcium carbonate to form calcium oxide and then adding water to produce calcium hydroxide (hydrated lime) according to the equation:

$$CaO + H_2O \rightarrow Ca(OH)_2 + heat$$

If an excess of water is added, lime putty is produced which was formerly popular because it could be stored in tubs on site for considerable periods of time. If, however, the quantity of water added is chemically correct according to the above equation, a powder is produced which may be marketed in bags and lime is now more commonly used in this form. Ordinary (non-hydraulic limes) sets by combination with carbon dioxide in the atmosphere:

$$Ca(OH)_2 + CO_2 \rightarrow CaCO_3 + H_2O$$

Hence such limes set gradually by exposure to the atmosphere, the surface layers hardening first. Limes containing impurities (for example, magnesium carbonate, obtained in dolomitic limestone) are known as hydraulic limes and these limes harden to some extent without the necessity for carbonation by the atmosphere.

The most important use of lime is to achieve a workable yet plastic mortar without use of large cement contents which would make the mortar too strong. Where strong mortars are required, as for engineering bricks, little or no lime is necessary, due to the relatively large quantity of cement. Lime also increases the suction of mortar to brickwork since, on account of its high specific surface, it helps the mortar retain its moisture against the suction of the bricks. Lime mortars may be used without cement, have admirable working properties and will retain plasticity for some time if occasionally retempered. However, they harden slowly, cannot be used for foundations or other situations where not exposed to the atmosphere, and are not highly frost resistant. Hydraulic limes are better than non-hydraulic limes in these respects and are normally used without cement. The cement/sand ratio (by volume) may vary from 1 : 3 for engineering bricks to 1 : 12 for internal partitions. Lime content may vary from 10 per cent by volume for stronger mortars to about 25 per cent by volume for weaker mortars. Pure (hydraulic) lime–sand mixes are normally either 1 : 2 or 1 : 3 by volume. Richer mixes are suitable for more exposed situations or for use in colder weather. Air entraining agents and inert mineral plasticisers have been successfully used instead of lime and are the basic additives in masonry cements.

PRECAST CONCRETE

Precast concrete products in the form of building blocks, paving slabs and similar units have been in existence for some time but recent years have seen a considerable increase in the size and variety of products manufactured. The reasons for these developments are as follows:

1. The increase in modular types of construction and system building has lead to large numbers of identical numbers of units being required, such types of unit being most economically produced using closely controlled factory production techniques.
2. Advances in mechanical plant have enabled a greater degree of automation to be used.
3. Development in pre-stressing and post-tensioning techniques enables large structural units for buildings, roads and bridges to be manufactured in precast form.
4. Precast units lead to faster construction with less environmental disturbance than *in situ* techniques.
5. Some more traditional types of construction, for example brickwork, are now very expensive. Precast concrete units such as tiles and blocks are often larger than fired clay equivalents so that labour cost of installation is reduced.

A very wide range of precast concrete products exists, blocks and tiles being briefly described below for comparison with similar products manufactured from clay.

Precast concrete blocks BS 2028, 1364: 1968.

Blocks, as distinct from bricks, are defined by BS 2028 as being greater in size than 337·5 x 225 x 112·5 mm. Concrete blocks of all types are in common use today, dense blocks often being used as finished walling units; lightweight or aerated blocks being used similarly for internal walls or partitions. BS 2028 classifies blocks into groups A, B and C; group A being dense blocks for general use including below damp proof courses. Group B refers to lightweight blocks which are not suitable for use below damp proof courses unless:

(a) they are made from dense aggregate; or
(b) they have an average strength of at least 7 N/mm^2;
(c) they are protected in some way from damp, for example by tanking; or
(d) the manufacturer considers them suitable.

Group C blocks are intended for use in non-load-bearing walls and partitions.

Strengths of group A range from 3·5 to 35 N/mm^2 and those of group B from 2·8 to 7 N/mm^2. There is no strength requirement for group C blocks but instead a flexural strength requirement for blocks laid on their side and loaded in a vertical direction.

Drying shrinkage limits are also given, ranging from 0·05 per cent for lower strength group A blocks to 0·09 per cent for lower density group C blocks.

Concrete tiles for roofing (BS 473 and 550 Pt. II)

These have largely replaced clay tiles owing to their relative cheapness, ease of fixing and contemporary appearance. BS 473 describes a flexural test for these tiles similar to that for clay roofing tiles. Durability is, however, measured in terms of permeability—that is, the rate of water absorption per unit area under a standard water pressure (200 mm). There are two classes of tile, Class A having a permeability of not more than 1.0 ml/m^2 per minute after 24 hours under test and class B having a value not more than 2.0 ml/m^2 per minute.

Steam curing

This process is commonly applied to precast products in order to reduce time in the mould. Steam curing may be carried out at low (atmospheric) pressure or high pressure:

Low pressure steam curing. Steam at a temperature of 55–80°C is passed through chambers containing the units for a period of about 12 hours. The final strength of units is comparable to that obtained ultimately by normal curing provided the temperature is increased gradually and does not exceed about 80°C. It is also found that a delay of 2–5 hours after moulding before steam curing is beneficial. The 12-hour strength of a steam-cured concrete may be three to four times that obtained by normal curing. The product formed has a similar chemical structure to that of hydrated cement paste. Low-pressure steam curing of concrete cubes is becoming increasingly used for obtaining rapid estimates of the 28-day strength of concrete.

High pressure steam curing (Autoclaving). This is quite different to the method described above, the units being heated in pressure vessels at about eight atmospheres pressure to approximately 180°C. The addition of finely ground silica increases the strength by a reaction similar to that which occurs in the manufacture of sand lime bricks, the lime being provided by the hydrating cement—in particular the tricalcium silicate.

The specific surface of the resulting hardened paste is much lower than that of normally cured cement paste and the hydrate should be regarded as microcrystalline rather than in 'gel' form. As a result, drying shrinkage, moisture and thermal movements are smaller due to reduced quantities of adsorbed water. Hence, the concrete is more durable than normally cured concrete and its resistance to sulphate attack is greater. High-pressure steam curing produces normal 28-day strength in about one day but is not suitable for reinforced concrete since bond strength is reduced.

Steam curing by either process cannot be carried out on high alumina cement, which in any case develops strength rapidly under normal curing. The high cost of cement in the latter is balanced by the cost of steam curing apparatus and power in the former.

Problems

3.1. The table shows the chemical composition of five cements which are ordinary Portland cement, rapid hardening Portland cement, sulphate resisting Portland cement, white Portland cement and low heat Portland cement.

Compound (per cent)	Cement A	Cement B	Cement C	Cement D	Cement E
C_3S	57·5	55·9	33·0	45·3	29·7
C_2S	15·9	23·8	35·0	26·9	41·9
C_3A	8·5	13·0	9·4	2·0	2·1
C_4AF	6·7	1·0	10·0	16·9	18·0

Identify each cement. What cement could be used in place of
(a) sulphate-resisting cement;
(b) rapid-hardening Portland cement?
Why, in the second case, would the use of the substitute be unlikely?

3.2 A chemical analysis of a cement gives the following composition:

	Per cent
SiO_2	23·3
Al_2O_3	5·2
Fe_2O_3	2·6
free CaO	66·3

By use of the Bogue equations, give the likely properties of this cement.

3.3. Describe what is meant by conversion in high alumina cements and how adverse effects caused by it can be avoided. Discuss the use of high alumina cement for precast products.

3.4. Give three important tests which should be carried out on an aggregate in order to assess its suitability for use in high quality concrete.

3.5. For a cubic metre of particular lightweight concrete mix, the masses of fine and coarse aggregate required are 395 kg and 850 kg respectively. The aggregates have absorption coefficients of 4 and 10 per cent and moisture contents of 10 and 5 per cent, fine and coarse, based on wet weight respectively. Calculate corrected batch quantities for the aggregates and the correction to be made in water added at the mixer.

3.6. Use the American Concrete Institute method together with the graph of Fig. 3.9 to calculate batch masses for an air entrained concrete mix with 25–50 mm slump, to have a 28 day strength of 45 N/mm^2 using ordinary Portland cement with a specific gravity of 3·15; 20-mm coarse aggregate with a rodded bulk volume of 1800 kg/m^3, specific gravity 2·7 and fine aggregate with a fineness modulus of 2·4, specific gravity 2·6.

3.7. Explain the meaning of:
(a) 'nominal' mixes;
(b) 'standard' mixes;
(c) 'designed' mixes
and discuss the situations in which they might be used.

3.8. In concrete practice, the addition of extra water to a mix just before placing is quite a common occurrence. Discuss the effect of water content adjustment on
(a) the plastic properties; and
(b) the hardened properties of concrete.

3.9. Define 'maturity' of concrete. Some codes of practice restrict the placing of concrete at a temperature of 5°C or less on a falling thermometer. Give the reasons for this and methods by which concrete could be protected from the possible consequences.

3.10. Describe carefully the procedure for sampling concrete to make concrete cubes and the curing and crushing of cubes. Discuss the possible causes of a very high cube result. Explain how such a result would affect the standard deviation of a set of cube results.

3.11. An ultrasonic pulse takes 33·3 μs to travel through a 100-m cube of density 2400 kg/m^3. Find the dynamic 'E' value for the concrete assuming Poisson's ratio = 0·2. At what frequency would a 500-mm beam made of the same concrete at the same time resonate if clamped at its midpoint? A 100-mm cube made from the same mix failed at a load of 300 kN. If the static 'E' value is 0·8 times the dynamic value, calculate the strain at failure of the cube.

3.12. Define the terms 'characteristic strength' and 'standard deviation'.

A concrete mix was designed to give a characteristic strength of 27 N/mm² at 28 days with an anticipated standard deviation of 4·0 N/mm² and 2 per cent failures being permitted. The first fifty cube results were as follows, in N/mm²:

36·3	41·2	36·1	38·9	39·1	36·7	42·0	43·9	41·6	37·8
39·9	40·8	42·0	40·3	38·1	36·2	44·0	40·5	38·6	43·4
44·3	40·7	37·5	37·5	36·1	48·9	43·6	40·2	38·6	37·8
29·7	36·1	34·5	37·9	31·3	47·5	43·6	41·6	46·1	36·0
34·4	39·7	45·8	43·4	43·7	38·6	32·5	47·5	46·0	41·4

Assuming that a change in cement content of 5 kg/m³ produces a change in mean strength of 0·8 N/mm², suggest how the cement content of the above mix could be altered.

3.13. Give reasons why lightweight aggregate concrete is becoming increasingly widely used. State two ways in which design or production techniques differ from those of dense concretes and indicate typical applications of lightweight concretes.

3.14. Calculate batch masses for 1 m³ of lean mix concrete to conform to the minimum Ministry of Transport requirements for road bases. Assume that the fully compacted concrete has a density of 2300 kg/m³.

3.15. Discuss the connections between
(a) moisture movement and creep; and
(b) drying shrinkage and carbonation shrinkage in concrete.

References

1. F. M. Lea, *The Chemistry of Cements and Concrete,* Arnold, 1970.
2. A. M. Neville, *Properties of Concrete,* Pitman, 1970.
3. T. D. Robson, 'The Characteristics and Applications of Mixtures of Portland and High Alumina Cements', *Chemistry and Industry*, 1952.
4. *Road Note 4—Design of Concrete Mixes,* Road Research Laboratory, H.M.S.O., 1950.
5. *Design and Control of Concrete Mixtures.* Portland Cement Association U.S.A., 1968.
6. J. D. Dewar, 'Relations between various Workability Control Tests for Ready-Mixed Concrete', *Cement and Concrete Association Technical Report TRA 375,* 1964.
7. *Hot Weather Concreting.* Cement and Concrete Association Advisory Note 10, 1966.
8. A. Pink, 'Winter Concreting', *Cement and Concrete Association Technical Advisory Series,* 1967
9. D. C. Spooner, 'Discrepancies in Concrete Cube Testing', *Cement and Concrete Association Paper pp/25,* 1968.
10. 'The Performance of Existing Testing Machines'. *Concrete Society Working Party Report. PCS 62,* 1971.
11. J. Kolek, 'An Appreciation of the Schmidt Rebound Hammer', *Magazine of Concrete Research,* Vol. 10, No. 28, 1958.
12. 'Introduction to Statistical Methods for Quality Control', *Cement and Concrete Association Advisory Note No. 8,* 1965.
13. *Authorization Scheme for Ready Mixed Concrete.* British Ready Mixed Concrete Association, 1972.
14. H. C. Erntroy and B. W. Shacklock, *Design of High Strength Concrete Mixes,* Cement and Concrete Association, 1954.
15. L. S. Blake, 'Lean Mix Concrete Bases', *The Surveyor,* No. 117, 1958.
16. *Specification for Roads and Bridges.* Ministry of Transport, H.M.S.O., 1967.
17. A. Short and W. Kinniburgh, *Lightweight Concrete,* Publishers Concrete Record Ltd.
18. 'Admixtures for Concrete'. *Technical Report TRCSI,* Concrete Society, 1967.
19. *Principles of Modern Building,* Vol. 1, H.M.S.O., 1959.

Relevant British Standards

Cements
BS 12: Part 2: 1971. *Portland cement (ordinary and rapid hardening).*
BS 146: 1958. *Portland blastfurnace cement.*
BS 4027: 1966. *Sulphate resisting Portland cement.*
BS 1370: 1958. *Low heat Portland cement.*
BS 4246: 1968. *Low heat Portland blastfurnace cement.*
BS 915: 1947. *High alumina cement.*

Aggregates
BS 812: 1967. *Methods for sampling and testing of mineral aggregates, sands and fillers.*
BS 882 & 1201: 1965. *Aggregates from natural sources for concrete (including granolithic).*
BS 3681: 1963. *Methods of sampling and testing of lightweight aggregates for concrete.*
BS 3797: 1964. *Lightweight aggregates for concrete.*

Concrete
BS 1881: Parts 1–5. *Methods of testing concrete.*
BS 4408: Parts 1–4. *Recommendations for non-destructive methods of test for concrete.*
BS 3148: 1959. *Tests for water for making concrete.*
BS 2028 & 1364: 1968. *Precast concrete blocks.*
BS 473 & 550: Part 2: 1971. *Concrete roofing tiles and fittings.*
BS 1926: 1962. *Ready mixed concrete.*

BS Code of Practice C.P. 110: *The Structural use of concrete.*

Chapter 4
METALS

Metals display a considerable number of properties not found in any other major group of materials; for example, high tensile and compressive strength as well as the ability to deform plastically without damage; rapid surface oxidation in the atmosphere, good heat and electrical conduction properties. The latter properties are easily explained by reference to the nature of the metallic bond, but other properties require a more detailed examination of metal structure if they are to be understood.

METALLIC CRYSTALS

Crystals have been defined as very large, regular arrays of atoms conforming to a given pattern and the basic repeat unit is known as the unit cell. Virtually all pure elements, when in solid form, pack in a crystalline manner and metals are no exception. Unit cells of metals are also quite simple, since the metallic bond is non-directional in character; it results in close packing of metallic ions such that attraction due to bonding is balanced by ion–ion repulsion. Corresponding to any one metal ion is an equilibrium distance at which neighbouring ions will try to position themselves.

The shape of unit cell produced may be predicted easily by studies of close packing of spheres. The maximum number of spheres that can be made to touch a single sphere of equal size is twelve and this can be obtained in two ways, the sphere in each case being surrounded by a hexagon of spheres with all spheres in the same plane. The other six occur in two groups of three above and below this hexagon, fitting in the spaces between those in the original hexagon. In one case, however, the upper triplet is directly above the lower triplet, and in the other case each upper sphere is above a gap in the lower triplet (see Fig. 4.1). The former is known as a hexagonal close-packed lattice (HCP) and the latter as a face-centred cubic lattice (FCC). In the latter, the corners of the face-centred cube have been shaded in case it is difficult to see the relationship between the hexagonal structure and the cubic unit cell. These unit cells are more commonly represented as in Fig. 4.2. Also included is the body-centred cubic (BCC) unit cell in which the atoms of some metals (for example, iron at room temperature) pack. This structure is less close packed, each atom having eight near neighbours. The reason for this is that iron at room temperature has a degree of covalency in its bonding, with the BCC structure in this case being of lower energy than either of the above forms and therefore more stable, owing to the partial directionality of bonds which results. The FCC and HCP structures are also of

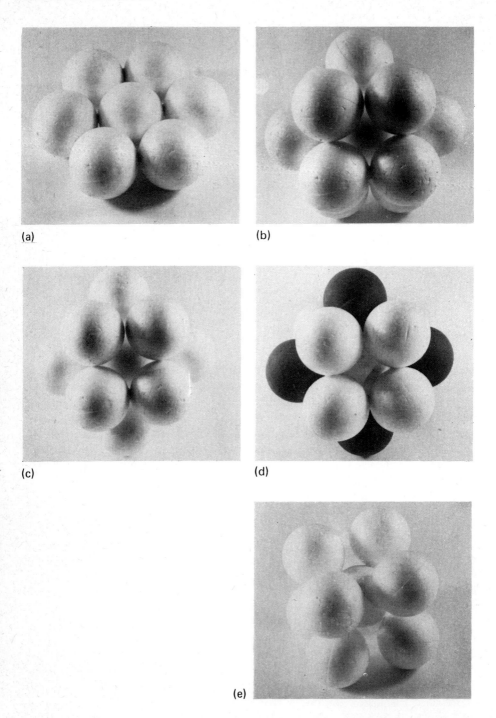

Fig. 4.1 (a) Basic hexagon shape. (b) Upper triplet directly above lower triplet. (c) Upper triplet above gaps in lower triplet. (d) As (c), but coloured to show face-centred cubic structure. (e) The body centred cubic lattice

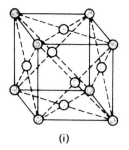 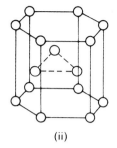 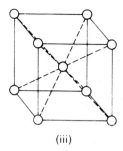

(i)   (ii)   (iii)

Fig. 4.2 Simple crystal lattices. (i) Face-centred cubic. (ii) Hexagonal close packed. (iii) Body-centred cubic

different energy and it is normal for metal atoms to pack in one or other form in given conditions. Table 4.1 shows the classification of some common metals.

The deformation properties of pure metals in particular groups are similar and they depend on the symmetry of atoms within the crystals. If a crystal could be observed

Table 4.1

Crystalline form of some common metals

Crystalline structure		
FCC	HCP	BCC
Aluminium	Zinc	Iron
	Magnesium	(below 910°C)
Nickel		Niobium
Copper		Molybdenum
Lead		Vanadium
		Chromium

under the microscope, planes of atoms would be immediately apparent rather like lines of plants in a mechanically planted array, only in three dimensions. The strength and deformation of metals depends on the population and spacing of these planes, which are described by Miller indices.

Miller indices

This is a system of indices in which parallel planes are described by a series of numbers dependent on the orientation of the plane to the axes of the unit cell. In the cubic unit cell, for example, the axes are orthogonal (x, y and z axes). The Miller indices of any plane are obtained by noting the intercept of that plane on the x, y and z axes respectively, in terms of the unit cell length. In Fig. 4.3, for example, the plane intercepts the axes of a cubic unit cell at $x = \frac{1}{2}a$, $y = 1a$ and $z = \frac{1}{2}a$. The Miller indices are then the *reciprocals* of these numbers, i.e. 212, enclosed in brackets thus: (212). If

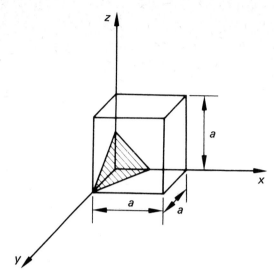

Fig. 4.3 A (212) plane in a cubic crystal

the intercept on any axis is outside the unit cell, giving a fractional component in the Miller index, it is normal to increase all the indices by a common factor to eliminate the fraction. Figure 4.4, for example, shows a (211) plane with this property. Similarly, if indices have a common factor, (for example, (420)) then they would be condensed by this factor (i.e. (210)). In this case, the '0' means that the plane is parallel to the z axis. Planes in hexagonal crystals are described by three axes at 120°

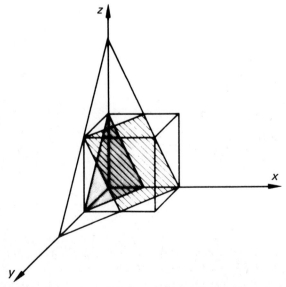

Fig. 4.4 A (211) plane. The larger plane gives intercepts of 1, 2, 2 on the x, y and z axes respectively. This would result in indices $(1\frac{1}{2}\frac{1}{2})$. Removing the fractions, this gives (211) as the Miller indices. The smaller plane is also a (211) plane

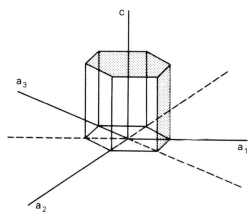

Fig. 4.5 The system of axes for an hexagonal crystal. The vertical plane shaded is a (10$\bar{1}$0) plane. The horizontal plane shaded is a (0001) plane

to one another in the basal plane, and a 'vertical' axis (Fig. 4.5). There are four indices, given the generalised letters h, k, i and l, and since the first three are not independent $h + k$ is always equal to $-i$.

It is also useful to be able to describe directions in crystals since, when deformation occurs, it must be in a certain direction within a plane. Directions are easily obtained if one end of the vector intersects the origin. Then the reciprocals of the co-ordinates of

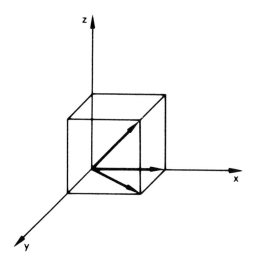

Fig. 4.6 The [100], [110] and [111] directions in a cubic cell

the point where the other end of the vector intersects the unit cell are the indices of that direction. Figure 4.6 shows the [100], [110] and [111] directions in a cubic cell, these indices being enclosed in square brackets. Planes and directions may have negative indices if intercepts occur on the negative side of the origin. Figure 4.7, for example, shows how the [$\bar{1}$11] direction in the unit cell could be identified.

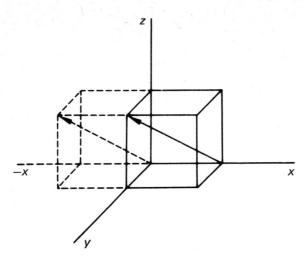

Fig. 4.7 The [$\bar{1}$11] direction in a cubic unit cell. The dotted lines show the construction of the direction, though it is normal to draw it within the unit cell

Families of planes and directions

Owing to the symmetry of cubic unit cells, the x, y and z axes in a cubic crystal would be indistinguishable from one another, since they contain identical atomic distributions. Hence the (100), (010) and (001) planes in a given cubic system are identical and are known as equivalent planes or members of the same 'family'. In this case, the family would be designated $\{100\}$ which would include planes represented by all possible permutations of the digits in the brackets, including negative values. Directions occur also in families and are distinguished thus $\langle\ \rangle$. For example, the $\langle 111\rangle$ family of directions would represent the four possible body diagonals of a cubic unit cell. Families of planes and directions can be similarly identified in hexagonal cells.

Slip planes

It was mentioned in Chapter 1 that since the atoms in a pure metal are identical, it is possible for planes of atoms to slip over one another without any 'damage' whatsoever to the metal. In practice, however, slip only takes place along certain planes and in certain directions in any one crystal type and the number of these (known as slip systems) in any given system will influence the ductility of that system.

In any type of crystal, the planes and directions in which slip takes place are usually those in which the greatest population of atoms is found since these are, as a consequence of their dense population, farther apart from one another and therefore need smaller shear forces to cause them to slide. Close-packed directions appear to be most important and by inspection of Figs. 4.1 and 4.2 they are easily seen to be face diagonals of FCC crystals (for example, [110]), any one of three directions in the basal plane for HCP crystals (for example, [11$\bar{2}$0]) and body diagonals of the BCC structure (for example, [111]). Slip can only take place in these directions and therefore all slip planes must contain these directions. Close-packed planes which satisfy these conditions are {111} for FCC crystals, {0001} for HCP crystals and {110} for BCC crystals respectively. There are four planes in the {111} family and each plane contains three different ⟨110⟩ directions so that FCC crystals have twelve possible modes of slip or slip systems. HCP crystals have only three slip systems—the three directions in the basal plane. BCC crystals have twelve slip systems in {110} planes, though, owing to the reduced packing density of these planes, BCC metals are not as ductile as FCC metals. Hence ductility generally decreases in the order: FCC, BCC, HCP (see Table 4.1). It should be added that in BCC crystals the {121} and {132} planes also contain the body diagonal and are important in slip processes. (See Questions at end of chapter.)

Note, however, that the number of slip systems in a crystal is not the only factor affecting ductility. It is greatly affected, for example, by the presence of impurities in the metal.

Elastic behaviour of metals

The resultant position of metallic ions in a crystal lattice has been explained in terms of the attraction caused by the metallic bond and short range ion–ion repulsion forces. The ion finds the position of lowest potential energy. The potential energy of any ion in the lattice, in terms of its separation from another, may be represented graphically as in Fig. 4.8(a). The sum of the two energy curves is shown and the equilibrium position of the ion is at the lowest point. Note that very large potential energies arise when ions are very close and that only when the separation is infinite is the resultant energy zero, indicating that there is no bonding tendency. For a bond to be stable, the resultant potential must be negative, implying that work must be done to pull the ions apart. The thermal expansion and melting of the metals is explained by the graph since, if the ions have thermal energy, total energy will correspond to some position above the lowest point of the curve. The curve is asymmetric and this means that the equilibrium position will move to the right corresponding to expansion of the solid; melting will occur when the thermal energy is equal to the original negative value of the potential energy.

The effect of increasing the separation artificially by force may be seen also. By plotting the gradient of the curve of Fig. 4.8(a) against r (Fig. 4.8(b)), the minimum force needed to separate the ions (i.e. cause the metal to 'yield') is obtained, since $F = \partial V / \partial r$. The 'E' value of the metal is the gradient of the force-distance curve. These curves, in fact, apply to the elastic behaviour of any type of crystal, metallic or otherwise.

The force required to cause the ions in a given plane to slide over one another can be estimated for a certain crystal type using these arguments and it is found that the results obtained are far greater than the forces required experimentally to cause metals to yield. Furthermore, many real metals become stronger (work harden) after yielding. These properties are the result of certain defects in real metals.

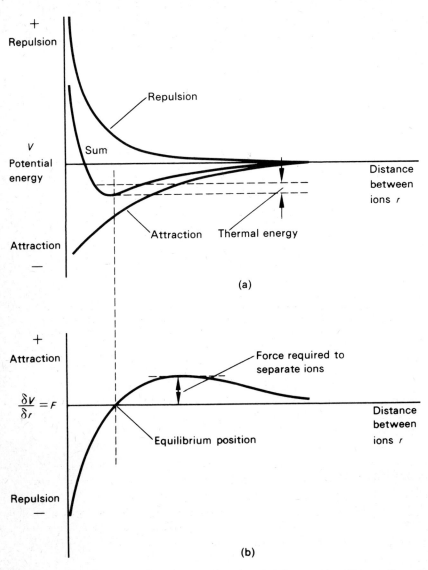

Fig. 4.8 (a) The potential energy of two ions as a function of their separation. The negative energy curve represents the metallic bonding tendency. The positive curve represents short range repulsion. (b) The force–distance curve obtained by differentiating curve (a)

DEFECTS IN CRYSTALS

These may be classified as point defects, line defects and surface defects. All types of defect are common in ordinary metal components such as rolled steel beams and play an important part in their manufacture and working properties.

Point imperfections

There are three possible types of point imperfection. They are illustrated in Fig. 4.9.

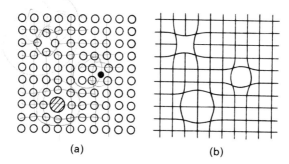

(a)   (b)

Fig. 4.9 Point imperfections. (a) Representation of a vacancy, a large substitutional impurity and an interstitial impurity. (b) The lattice lines which indicate the stresses resulting from the imperfections in (a). Where lattice lines are close together, there are compression zones. Where they are farther apart, there are tensile zones

1. *Vacancy.* A lattice site is unoccupied. This defect arises if the speed at which the crystal is grown is too high for perfect packing to take place. Slower cooled metals contain fewer vacancies.

2. *Substitutional impurities.* These may occur if a foreign material is present in the metal. Provided the atoms are of similar size (for example, zinc and copper, whose atomic diameters are in the ratio 1 : 1·04), the impurity ions may fit into lattice sites of the host element. If the ionic diameters are quite different, then the impurity material cannot 'dissolve' in the parent metal in this way. This type of process is the basis of many alloys which are formed when the atoms of metals become intimately mixed.

3. *Interstitial impurities.* If foreign atoms which are much smaller than the host ions are present they may occupy space between lattice sites, causing slight distortion of the lattice. Carbon in iron, forming steel, is an example of this type of impurity. There will be a limit to the amount of such 'impurities' which can be 'dissolved' in the metal; in the case of iron at room temperature, this limit is less than 0·01 per cent by weight of carbon since its presence causes considerable distortion of the BCC iron lattice.

Line imperfections (dislocations)

Although these are already present in large numbers in unstressed metals, their nature may be understood by considering the effect of stresses on a metal block consisting of a large, perfect crystal (Fig. 4.10).

If the block is fixed at the base (Fig. 4.10(a)), the application of force in the position and direction shown would cause a distortion of the lattice such that, in the most heavily stressed areas of the crystal, upper atoms will tend to occupy positions almost over atoms adjacent to those they were previously above. On increasing the stress, the crystal will finally slip along a slip plane by one atom spacing, producing a *screw dislocation* as in Fig. 4.10(b). Screw dislocations are represented by the symbol ↻ or ↺, since they may have a clockwise or anticlockwise sense. Note that, apart from the distortion of the lattice, it is perfect all round the dislocation which extends as a line through the crystal; hence the term 'line imperfection'. On increasing the stress, a further plane of atoms slips and the dislocation moves at *right angles to the stress direction* until finally the entire upper half of the crystal has moved one atom spacing to the left (Fig. 4.10(d)).

If the stress is applied centrally to the block, then the distortion would be as in Fig. 4.10(e). The dislocation would, in this case, be an extra plane of atoms in the upper part of the crystal in a plane at right angles to the stress direction, known as an *edge dislocation,* and represented thus: ⊥ (Fig. 4.10(f)). On increasing the stress, the dislocation will move *parallel to the stress direction* until the entire upper half of the crystal has slipped one atom spacing.

Note that the slipped crystal finishes up with a perfect lattice as a result of each kind of dislocation movement. This process may continue further by repeated dislocation formation and movement, causing eventual failure of the crystal, unless the dislocations are obstructed in some way.

Burger's vector. This is obtained by counting equal numbers of lattice spacings around the dislocation. For example, if, for the edge dislocation in Fig. 4.10(f), five spacings are travelled, downwards, to the right, upwards and then to the left, a gap is found to remain and this is the Burger's vector of the dislocation. This is equal to the distance which the crystal will slip as a result of the dislocation movement and, since a larger distance will require more energy, dislocations tend to operate in planes which are close packed, these planes having smaller values of Burger's vector.

The effect of dislocations. The importance of dislocations is due to the fact that they allow the slip process to take place in small steps, in lines of atoms, instead of whole planes, so that the deformation occurs at a stress much lower than that which would be required to cause the upper part of the block to slip bodily by simultaneous disruption of all bonds in the slip plane. Dislocations act as a 'low gear', producing the same net effect as slip of complete planes but at much lower stresses. Although the example of stressing a crystal, given above, was used to explain the origin of dislocations, these defects are in fact present in large numbers in unstressed materials due to imperfect crystal formation during cooling. They may also occur in closed loops in the metal, the dislocations in places then being partially edge and partially screw dislocations. When

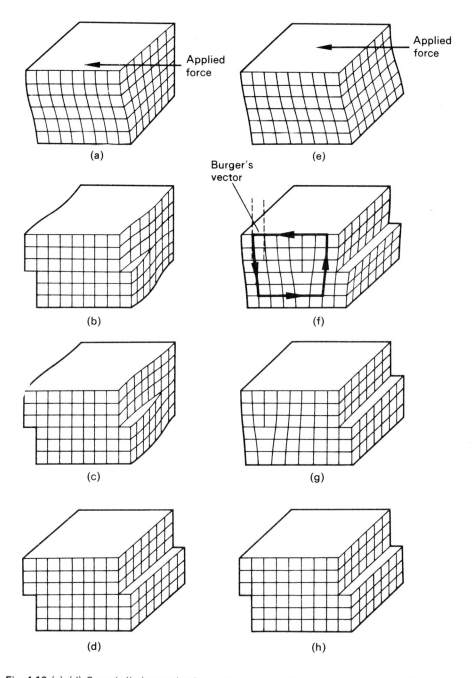

Fig. 4.10 (a)–(d) Crystal slip by production and movement of a screw dislocation. (e)–(h) Crystal slip by production and movement of an edge dislocation

materials are stressed, plastic flow takes place by movement and multiplication of dislocations already present, rather than by creation of dislocations as above.

Surface imperfections

These arise due to the fact that, on cooling from liquid, metal crystals begin to form on a multitude of nuclei simultaneously, rather than by gradual growth of single crystals. The crystals grow to a point where they meet and then, since orientations of different crystals will be different, there will be narrow bands of semi-ordered structure known as grain boundaries (Fig. 4.11). The size of crystal formed depends on

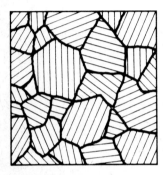

Fig. 4.11 Grain boundaries in metals. The straight lines represent atomic planes

the cooling rate of the metal; if cooling is slow, as in annealed metals, crystals tend to be large as they form fewer nuclei and have more time to form. Rapid cooling reduces crystal size and very rapid cooling (for example, quenching) may completely prevent crystal formation.

Deformation of metals

A large number of metal components are made by mechanical deformation of metal in the cold state. The following general effects occur when load is applied:

On first stressing the metal beyond its elastic limit, crystal planes will begin to slip by movement of dislocations already present. If the metal crystals are large and the metal is pure (for example, wrought iron or lead) considerable distortion will be possible without weakening although the material will gradually harden as dislocations arrive at grain boundaries where they must stop. (Adjacent crystals, having different orientations, cannot normally allow continued movement.) Hence dislocations will tend to pile up behind one another if they are of the same type (Fig. 4.12(a)). This process is known as work hardening. It is a disadvantage in many manufacturing processes, since it is accompanied by decreased ductility, resulting in increased power consumption in shaping processes, greater wear on machinery and increased likelihood of damage to the component being made. Heating of the component at an intermediate stage in the shaping process (annealing) allows crystals to redistribute themselves so that softening occurs and, provided cooling is slow, the original properties of the metal will be restored. Some metals, notably lead, recrystallise at

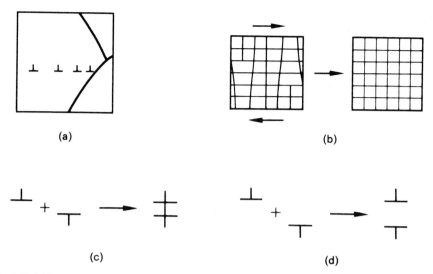

Fig. 4.12 (a) Pile up of edge dislocations caused by a grain boundary. (b) Annihilation of dislocations by plastic flow. (c) Simple representation of the situation in (b). (d) Combination of dislocations to form a vacancy

room temperature and therefore do do not work harden (see Table 4.2). To some degree, dislocations may, on movement, cancel one another; for example, if an extra plane of atoms in upper layers of the metal travelling one way encounters a similar plane in lower layers, travelling in the opposite direction, the two dislocations will cancel (Fig. 4.12(b), (c)). If the upper plane were one spacing above the lower plane, a vacancy would be formed (Fig. 4.12(d)). If crystals are small, the metal will be correspondingly harder and less deformable. This is because dislocations are not able to move as far as previously since they are nearer grain boundaries. Stressing such metals beyond a point will cause bond failure at grain boundaries where bonding is weak, leading to cracking and eventual failure.

If metals contain 'impurities' these will in general tend to make it harder since they are apt to interact with dislocations, blocking their paths. For example, an interstitial

Table 4.2

Approximate recrystallisation temperature of some common metals

Metal	Recrystallisation temp. (°C)
Iron	450
Copper	200
Aluminium	150
Zinc	Below room temp.
Lead	Below room temp.

impurity at the end of an extra plane of atoms will cause the dislocation to 'lock' at this point (Fig. 4.13(a)). If the foreign metal is present to a degree above its solubility, it may form separate compounds at grain boundaries. It is for this reason that carbon is included in steel; it has a strengthening and hardening effect on iron. Another means of strengthening metals is by substitutional impurities; for example, two substitutional impurities, atoms slightly larger than the host atoms, just below a dislocation plane, would cause the dislocation to stop unless a higher stress were applied (Fig. 4.13(b)).

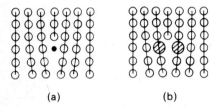

(a)   (b)

Fig. 4.13 Relief of the tensile stress at the end of an edge dislocation by (a) an interstitial impurity atom and (b) two substitutional impurity atoms

Where dislocations are locked at each end of the line, it is possible, on continued increase of stress, for the centre part of it to move further, bowing out and eventually completely enclosing the original obstructions, giving rise to a new dislocation (Fig. 4.14). This is known as a Frank Read source. There are several other ways also in which dislocations can overcome obstructions.

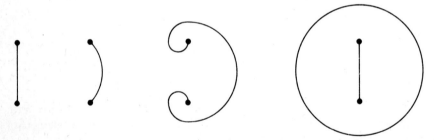

Fig. 4.14 Stages in the distortion by stress of a locked dislocation to form a new dislocation

ALLOYS

An alloy consists of a metal mixed intimately with one or more metals (or in some cases, non-metals) of a different type. The other metal may be dispersed in the first, possibly in the form of a 'solid solution', though metals do not have to be soluble in one another to form alloys. For one metal to 'dissolve' in another, the atoms of the former must be accepted into the lattice of the other and this may be possible in two ways—interstitially or substitutionally. In each case, the solubility of the foreign material will depend on its size; in the former, atoms should be small, while in the latter, they should be within about 15 per cent of the size of those of the host material. Certain valency requirements must also be satisfied. Substitutional alloys are the most common; there is a very large range of these and many metals used in the construction industry today are alloyed in this way to some degree. If atomic diameters are very similar, then solubility may be complete so that, on cooling, any proportions of two metals in liquid form, a single crystalline material is formed. This is not to say that the two metals are evenly mixed in all crystals in the solid. A property of all alloys, whether or not solubility is complete, is that different crystals have different proportions of the constituent metals, unless after formation the structure has been able to diffuse to a uniform composition.

The basic principle of alloy formation can be considered by reference to temperature-composition diagrams. Consider two metals A and B which are completely soluble in one another, having melting points as shown in Fig. 4.15. On cooling a mixture, for example of composition 60 : 40, A : B (indicated by the vertical line), solid will first

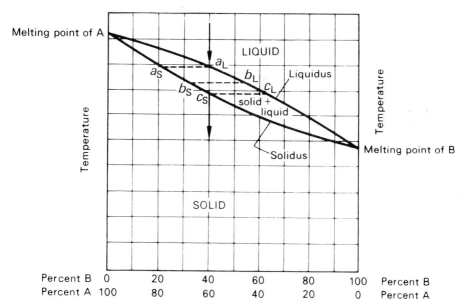

Fig. 4.15 Equilibrium diagram for two metals A and B which are completely soluble in one another

begin to form at the temperature represented by points a and it will be of composition corresponding to point a_S. As the temperature falls to a value corresponding to points b, solid with $b_S\%$ of A exists so that the remaining liquid will be richer in metal B and will, in fact, be of composition corresponding to point b_L. (The lower and upper lines are on this account known as the solidus and liquidus lines respectively. At any given composition, the alloy cannot be all solid above the solidus line and it cannot be all liquid below the liquidus line at that composition.) Eventually, on reaching points c, the average composition of the solid will be denoted by c_S and, since this is that of the original liquid, the metal must now be completely solid. Between temperatures corresponding to a and c, solid and liquid exist together in equilibrium—hence alloys show a plastic stage on cooling. This property in itself has been most useful, with application for instance in wiping joints using lead pipes. The resultant solid is known as a single phase solid, since all crystals are of one type though with varying composition, the core of each crystal being rich in metal A and the outer parts rich in metal B. In fact, if thermal energy were sufficient, diffusion of each metal would take place from richer to leaner areas, ultimately causing even distribution.

Alloys in which the two metals are completely soluble do exist; for example, copper and nickel, but their mechanical properties are very similar to those of the pure metals and there may not always be much advantage in using them in alloy form.

Most commonly used alloys consist of metals which are only partially soluble in one another; for example, zinc and copper-producing brass. When copper contains up to 36 per cent zinc, an FCC crystalline form known as 'alpha' brass results, as in pure copper. Between 36 and 46 per cent zinc, a second type of crystal appears, known as 'beta' brass which is of BCC structure. Finally, above 46 per cent zinc, a complex phase known as 'gamma' brass is produced.

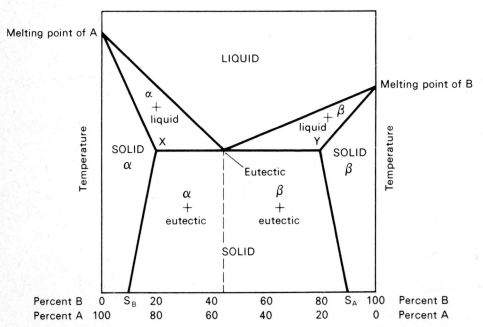

Fig. 4.16 Equilibrium diagram for two metals A and B which are partially soluble in one another

The simplest general form of temperature composition diagrams for metals which are partially soluble in one another is shown in Fig. 4.16. The material (phase) produced when B dissolves in A is known as alpha phase and when A dissolves in B as beta phase. Note that these solubilities, denoted by the sloping lines at the left and right of the figure at the base, increase with temperature, as do all solubilities. The liquidus line this time reaches a minimum value at a point known as the eutectic point, signifying that the melting point of two phase metal alloys is, for most proportions of its constituent metals, lower than the melting points of each of the pure metals. The products which result on cooling a mixture of these metals are as follows (see Fig. 4.16):

1. Percentage of B below the percentage solubility s_B at room temperature. The alloy will begin to solidify at the temperature where the vertical composition line intersects the liquidus and finish solidifying where this line intersects the solidus. The properties of the resultant product will be similar to those of pure metal A.

   A similar argument applies to percentages of A below the solubility limit s_A dissolved in B.

2. Percentage of B below the high temperature solubility level X but above the room temperature level. The alloy will solidify as in (1) except that, when the temperature at which the α phase becomes saturated occurs, pure metal B containing some of A (i.e. β phase) must begin to separate. If cooling is slow, the β phase will form in grain boundaries, but if cooling is rapid, the metal will be trapped, producing quite different properties in the alloy.

3. If the percentage of metal B is higher than that in (2) but below the eutectic composition, the liquid will commence to solidify, producing α phase material at the point given by the intersection of the composition line with the liquidus, as before. Solidification will continue until the temperature has fallen to the solidus line, the remaining liquid at this temperature having eutectic composition. However, because, owing to the limited solubility of each metal in the other, formation of a single phase of this composition is not possible, the solid which solidifies must contain proportions of α (B in A) and β (A in B) phases at their respective solubility limits X and Y. Hence the resulting alloy contains some α crystals and some of the $\alpha + \beta$ mixture. As the $\alpha + \beta$ mixture cools, argument (2) applies owing to the decreasing solubilities. A similar argument applies if the composition of the liquid is between the eutectic value and that corresponding to point Y.

The nature of the $\alpha + \beta$ mixture (eutectic) is such that the alloys containing it are usually brittle. Alloys containing some eutectic therefore are normally cast rather than cold worked. Cast iron is a typical example.

MECHANICAL PROPERTIES OF METALS

These may be described under the headings of tensile strength; creep; impact strength; fatigue; hardness.

Tensile strength

The elastic nature of metal deformation has already been described and this is obviously of prime importance, since nearly all metal components are designed to undergo elastic movement only. But to estimate factors of safety, it is essential to know at what point a metal would be incapable of taking its allotted stress with acceptable strains, and since plastic movement during manufacture is responsible for considerable modification of metal properties, a knowledge of both the elastic and plastic parts of stress–strain curves is of advantage. Although most components in service may be under compressive or shear stresses as well as tensile stresses, tensile tests are the standard way of assessing strength and this is perhaps appropriate since, for example, steel for reinforcement is principally under tension, as is the lower flange in a simply supported beam.

Tensile tests are carried out by loading uniformly to destruction either bars or wires (as in the case of reinforcement or pre-stressing wire) or carefully cut strips of the metal component.

The exact nature and significance of stress–strain curves produced by tensile testing depends on the nature and formation process of the alloy and the differences are best understood by consideration of the form of the curve produced by some types of simplified structure.

For example, if a single, perfect crystal of a pure metal were stressed, the stress–strain curve may appear as in Fig. 4.17. The stress would increase elastically to a point dependent on the relative orientation of preferred slip planes and tensile stress, at which dislocations would form, moving almost unhindered through the perfect crystal to cause failure without any significant further stress increase. Note, however,

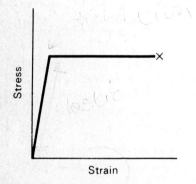

Fig. 4.17 Stress–strain diagram for a single, perfect metal crystal. The yield point would depend on the crystal orientation

that the 'yield' point would be heavily dependent on the relative orientations of the tensile stress and slip planes. Different orientations would produce totally different yield points.

If the metal were polycrystalline and perfect, plastic flow would begin this time at a certain fixed tensile stress which would be proportional to the shear stress required to cause crystal slip but modified by a factor which arises due to the random orientations of the crystals. Since dislocations cannot now proceed unhindered between different grains, which in general have different orientation continued deformation of the metal will require increased stress, the stress–strain curve consequently appearing as in Fig. 4.18.

The point at which plastic flow begins (the yield point) will depend in practice on the grain size since dislocations will be present, even in the unstressed metal. The dislocations in smaller grains travel smaller distances before meeting the next grain so that greater shear forces will be necessary to cause plastic movement. It is well known that more rapid cooling of metals, which decreases grain size, increases their yield point.

The effect of alloying metals depends on whether the alloy is based on substitutional or interstitial 'impurities'.

In the case of substitutional alloys, the crystal lattice is distorted due to the presence of atoms of slightly different size. This makes it less easy for dislocations to move since they tend to linger at points where their presence reduces the lattice strains. As a result, the yield point increases and on the same account, work hardening is greater and the metal improves considerably in strength.

A feature of interstitial alloys—for example, steel—is that the dislocations present, which are points of stress in the lattice, tend to gather congregations ('atmospheres') of interstitial impurities around them. These may be, for example, carbon or nitrogen. On stressing the material, these atmospheres restrain the movement of dislocations, causing an artificially high yield point. As a consequence, when the yield point is reached and the dislocations move clear of the impurities, they become more mobile and the stress in the metal suddenly drops. An alternative possible cause could be the creation of new dislocations just before yielding which then multiply rapidly, moving

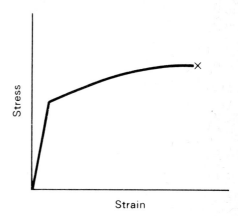

Fig. 4.18 Stress–strain diagram for a poly-crystalline sample of metal

more slowly as they multiply, assuming the strain rate to be constant. This multiplication of dislocations on yielding allows straining to continue at a reduced stress. The form of a stress–strain curve is therefore as in Fig. 4.19.

The reduction in stress is known as a yield point drop (point A) and cannot occur in substitutional alloys because the larger substitutional impurities have much lower mobility than interstitial impurities. On removal of load at point X, the dotted line is followed as the stress reduces, being retraced on reloading so that the material is now effectively stronger than originally in the sense that its yield point is now higher. Note also there will be no yield point drop on retesting. On the other hand, if the metal is left for some days, the interstitial atoms will diffuse back to dislocation sites so that, on loading, a yield point drop again occurs. This process is known as strain ageing and the metal becomes effectively stronger by the action of dislocation pinning. The yield point drop may be restored quite quickly by heating the metal to about 200°C or higher.

(In the case of alloys which show no yield point drop, the stress value which is normally used for calculation of factors of safety is based on the stress at which 0·2 per cent plastic strain occurs and is known as the 0·2 per cent proof stress (Fig. 4.20). Where a yield point drop occurs, design codes are normally based on the lower yield

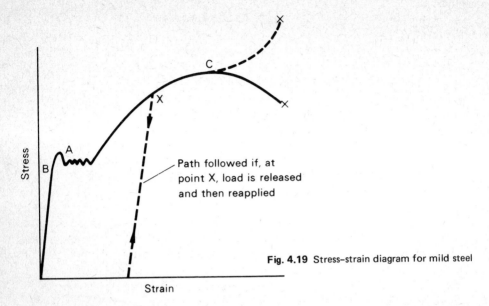

Fig. 4.19 Stress–strain diagram for mild steel

Strain

Path followed if, at point X, load is released and then reapplied

stress, since the upper point is difficult to measure and varies from specimen to specimen).

Figure 4.19 is, in fact, typical of the form of the stress–strain curve for mild steel. In addition to the above features, the following points are worthy of note:

1. There is normally a slight deviation from Hooke's law (i.e. stress proportional to strain) before the elastic limit is reached–point B.

2. As strains increase, the metal will become thinner so that the true stress in the metal is actually higher than that obtained by calculations based on the original cross sectional area.

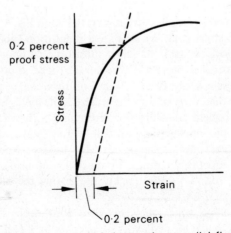

Fig. 4.20 Stress–strain diagram for a metal which does not have a well-defined yield point. Instead of yield stress, a stress corresponding to 0·2 per cent plastic strain and known as the 0·2 per cent proof stress is used

3. From point C onwards, deformation continues at a single point on the bar only, since, due to a stress concentration at this point, perhaps caused by a slight dent in the bar, plastic movement is sufficient to cause a local reduction in cross sectional area known as 'necking'. The apparent stress–strain curve appears to have a negative gradient from this point but, in fact, the true stress in the necked region is still increasing (dotted line).

4. Failure occurs when the bonds at grain boundaries in the heavily stressed central area of the bar fail. Cracks propagate in this way on planes of maximum shear (45° to the tensile axis), reversing so that they stay within the most heavily stressed central part of the necked area. Eventually, the shear stress on the reducing intact area becomes sufficient to cause overall shear, again at 45° to the tensile axis, causing a 'cup and cone' fracture.

Ductile and brittle modes of fracture. Some substances, notably impure metals such as cast irons and ionic or covalent compounds, have great resistance to crystal slip so that grain boundary strength, or in some cases crystal strength, is exceeded before any slip can take place. Such materials fraction in a brittle manner; they display no plastic movement. Other materials, such as some plastics, can be deformed to the extent that their cross sectional area reduces almost to zero before failure, rather like a viscous liquid. This would result in a perfectly ductile fracture. The mild steel fracture described above, on this basis, would be partially ductile since plastic deformation continued to a point and then the crystal structure itself failed, giving a brittle end point to the stress–strain curve. Ductility of metals is usually measured by the elongation at failure of a given gauge length, during the tensile test.

Creep

This is defined as time-dependent strains which occur when steady stresses are maintained. The phenomenon has been described in concrete, but although the same effect occurs in metals the cause is quite different.

Creep in metals can be satisfactorily explained by reference to the dislocations they contain. All dislocations have a certain amount of thermal energy and this will fluctuate according to statistical laws from place to place in the metal and with time. If occasions arise when a dislocation, previously locked by other dislocations or defects, has sufficient thermal energy then it will, when the metal is under stress, tend to climb over the obstacle and thereby allow some plastic movement in the metal. A typical strain–time diagram for a metal undergoing creep is shown in Fig. 4.21. During the first stage, known as primary creep, strain increases rapidly from the initial instantaneous value, the rate falling off as dislocations become trapped. During the secondary stage, diffusion of atoms leads to a gradual increase of strain as dislocations interact and annihilate one another. The process is known as 'recovery'. Finally, in the third stage, necking occurs with eventual failure. It is clear that increasing stress and increasing temperature will both contribute to creep strain so that the scale of the time axis will depend on the stress, temperature and metal used; it may vary between minutes and years. It would seem likely also that some creep could occur even at low temperatures, since even then there would be some statistical probability of dislocation movement. Although creep does occur at low temperatures, significant strains do not normally occur at temperatures below about 40 per cent of the melting point temperature of the metal in K. Lead, for example, has a melting point of 327°C = 600 K. Room temperature (20°C) equals 293 K and this is 49 per cent of 600 K, so that lead would be expected to creep at normal temperatures. This fact is well known and adequate restraint of lead components which are stressed due to their weight is essential in order to avoid distortion with time. The melting point of iron is, on the other hand, 1539°C so that creep would not be expected in ferrous metals at normal temperatures. A related phenomenon does, however, occur in cold-worked ferrous metals on stressing. The distortion of the crystals on cold working leads to stresses in

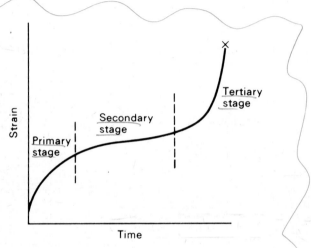

Fig. 4.21 Stages in the fracture of a metal, due to creep

steels which tend to reduce by dislocation movement when a component is stressed in service. This is known as 'relaxation' and allowances must be made, for example, for the loss of pre-stress that occurs in pre-stressed concrete, particularly when the working stress is near the characteristic strength of the material. Relaxation is not, however, like creep in that it does not lead to ultimate failure of the component and it can be removed by initially stressing the wire beyond its in-service stress. If a metal is at a temperature at which creep is likely, its performance will be improved with increase of grain size (and therefore reduction in the number of grain boundaries), since grain boundaries at such temperatures tend to be receptive to dislocations, thus permitting plastic flow. Work hardening increases creep resistance provided recrystallisation does not occur (as it would in lead at room temperature).

Impact strength

Impact testing measures the toughness of metals; that is, their ability to absorb energy quickly. There are many possible causes of shock loading in buildings—even the slamming of a door may produce considerable impact stresses. When a structure is subject, for example, to the use of heavy loading equipment, failure may occur due to the shock of impacts on it. Some idea of impact strength can be gathered from the area under the stress–strain graph obtained from a tensile test since this is related to the energy absorbed during the test. Brittle metals exhibit very little strain before failure so that the area is small, while annealed pure metals may undergo very large strains before failure. However, the object of impact testing is to determine performance under rapid or shock loading and stress–strain curves tend to change in form under such conditions so that their use is limited.

The energy absorbed by impact of a metal in practice is measured by an impact of standard energy on a small notched specimen of the metal (Fig. 4.22). The impact is

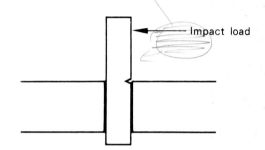

Impact load

Fig. 4.22 One form of impact-testing apparatus

produced by a pendulum and the energy absorbed by the specimen is proportional to the difference in heights of the pendulum when at rest before and after impact. The energy absorbed is affected by the following factors:

1. *The geometry of the notch at which failure occurs.* A smaller radius at the root of the notch produces a larger stress at this point so that cracks, which originate here, form more quickly. The impact strength of metals in service depends similarly on surface defects and stress concentrations in them.

2. *The temperature.* The impact strength of metals depends on the degree to which plastic flow can take place in the small interval of time between initial impact and fracture. If the yield point of the metal is increased, as occurs on cooling, thermal energy of dislocations is reduced and therefore plastic flow will be more difficult. As a result, the energy absorbed during impact will decrease. In the case of some metals, notably of BCC structures such as ferrous metals, the impact strength may drop very rapidly with temperature (Fig. 4.23). This may be attributed to the fact that, on cooling, a temperature is reached at which the yield point exceeds the fracture strength, so that virtually no plastic movement occurs. This transition is known as the ductile–brittle transition and for low carbon steels it takes place between 0 and $-50°C$, dependent on the type of impact (see (4)). The ductile–brittle transition is more gradual for higher carbon steels, but note that impact strength of medium/high carbon steels is quite sensitive to temperature changes at normal temperatures. The effect of lowering temperature on HCP metals such as titanium and zinc is similar to BCC metals but, in the case of FCC metals such as aluminium, copper and lead, there is no such transition and ductile behaviour is exhibited even at very low temperatures.

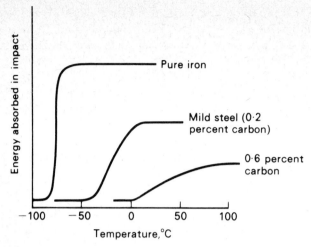

Fig. 4.23 The nature of the ductile–brittle transition for steels of different carbon contents

3. *Grain size.* Although finer-grained metals tend to have higher yield points, given slip planes in any one crystal are shorter and therefore contain fewer dislocations. As a result, the stress on any plane due to impact will be reduced with consequently decreased possibility of cracking and failure. Therefore, by 'grain refining', as occurs in normalising or by addition of some alloying metals (such as niobium or manganese in steel), impact strength may be increased.

4. *The straining rate caused by the impact.* The more suddenly the impact occurs, the less time will be available for absorption of energy by yielding. It is known that in fact yield stresses tend to be higher when loading is more rapid because dislocations take a finite time to move, causing yield. Hence a very severe impact may cause metals that are normally ductile to behave in a brittle manner.

Fatigue

This is defined as a reduction in strength caused by continued variations in loading. The phenomenon came to light as a result of aircraft crashes caused by fatigue in wing structures due to continued vibration and load reversal. It is quite possible for fatigue to occur in bridges where, due to traffic movement, stresses are continually fluctuating.

Fatigue damage normally starts at a fault in the metal, such as a weld fault. When, the stress fluctuates, plastic movement, which would be possible in the case of static stresses, cannot take place, since there is insufficient time. This may be regarded as equivalent to the increase of yield stress of metals which occurs on rapid loading. Therefore, a crack eventually occurs at the stressed point, leading to further stress concentration and propagation of the crack, until finally brittle failure occurs.

Fatigue performance of metals may be investigated by rotation of a bar supported at both ends and loaded at its centre point about its own axis. As the bar turns, the load causes rotation of the bending moment. Alternatively, in the case of larger components, for example steel beams, a fluctuating load may be applied to the mid-point of a simply supported span. The number of stress reversals N to cause fracture at a given stress S is measured and results are plotted in the form of an S–N curve (Fig. 4.24).

Curves are of two types. Metals in which strain ageing occurs show a certain stress below which fatigue does not occur. This is because, for example, in the case of steel, the carbon 'atmospheres' prevent dislocation movement from occurring. The stress is, in the case of mild steel, about 0·4 times the ultimate tensile strength (known as the endurance ratio). In metals which do not exhibit strain ageing (for example, aluminium) failure may occur at very low stresses on continued stress reversal.

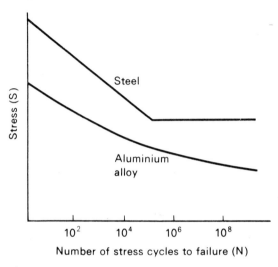

Fig. 4.24 S–N curves for steel and an aluminium alloy

Fatigue strengths increase with tensile strength or decrease of temperature and decrease in the presence of impurities, surface defects and corrosive environments. Tensile stresses result in lower fatigue strengths than compressive stresses so that, if a compressive stress can be imparted to the surface, as for example by carburising or nitriding, fatigue strength will be increased. Refining grain structure also increases fatigue resistance.

Hardness

The hardness, as such, of metals for constructional purposes is not normally an important criterion. Hardness testing, however, has been used for quality control purposes during the manufacture of, for example, rolled steel joists, since local deformation of metal is involved and it is possible for a given metal to correlate hardness and tensile strength. 'Brinell' hardness is measured by pressing a hardened steel ball into the surface of the metal under a load appropriate to the softness of the metal. In the case of steel, the load is normally about 30 kN with a 10-mm diameter ball. The diameter of the dent is measured microscopically and the Brinell hardness is then equal to

$$\frac{\text{load}}{\text{surface area of the indention}}$$

In some metals, hardness may be limited to a maximum value since it is indicative of a brittle structure. For example, BS 4622 for grey cast iron pipes includes the use of the hardness test for this purpose.

METALLIC CORROSION

This may be described under the headings oxidation; electrolytic and acidic corrosion.

Oxidation

Although the metallic bond has shown itself to be such that metals often have considerable strength and toughness in a mechanical sense, almost all metals are intrinsically unstable in an oxygen-containing atmosphere at normal temperatures. This is due to the fact that it is not possible for a crystal lattice to be perfect at the surface of the metal grains. Therefore, the metal atoms at the surface tend to be highly reactive and, in the case of most metals, combine very quickly with oxygen to form a more stable arrangement. Oxygen molecules in the atmosphere split into atoms, each of which contains six electrons in its outer shell, therefore requiring two electrons to make a stable octet. These electrons are supplied by atoms at the surface of the metal so that ionic bonding occurs and a metallic oxide is formed (Fig. 4.25). The precise

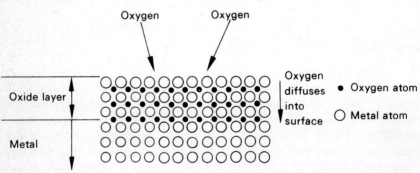

Fig. 4.25 The combination of oxygen with the surface film of a metal to form an oxide layer. In this case, the oxide lattice is coherent with the metallic lattice and the oxide coating is therefore tenacious and impermeable

behaviour of a particular metal with its oxide coating depends on a number of factors as follows:

1. *The relative stabilities of the metal and its oxide.* This varies from metal to metal—gold is, in fact, more stable than its oxide in normal conditions, although a surface layer of oxygen atoms does exist to satisfy the bonding requirements of surface atoms. Other metals such as silver and copper have relatively small heats of

formation with respect to their oxides; that is, the energy release when the oxides are formed is small so that the oxides are not extremely stable and the metals are corrosion resistant in clean atmospheres. Increasing oxygen pressure always increases stability of oxides in the same way that an increase of humidity in the atmosphere increases the tendency for water to exist in liquid form.

2. *The physical properties of the oxide layer.* In order for the oxidation process to continue, oxygen must have access to metallic ions below the surface of the existing oxide layer. The rate at which this can happen depends on the permeability of the oxide coating to metallic ions and/or oxygen ions. In the case of some metals, notably those whose atoms have only one or two electrons in their outer shell, the metallic ion is smaller than that of the metal from which it was formed. Thus, shrinkage of the metal on oxidation occurs, resulting in stresses in the oxide film and possibly cracking. The film will therefore be porous and will allow further oxygen to penetrate it so that oxidation continues. Such behaviour is shown by, for example, magnesium, whose oxidation rate with respect to time is linear, that is, the film thickness is proportional to time.

In other metals, ionic sizes may be comparable to or larger than pure metal atoms so that the oxide film is impervious and possibly in compression. Iron and copper are examples of this and since, in this case, ions must diffuse through the oxide coating, oxidation rates will decrease as the film thickness increases, though oxidation will never cease completely. This may be expressed in the form:

$$\frac{dx}{dt} = \frac{k}{x} \quad \text{where } x = \text{film thickness}, t = \text{time and } k = \text{a constant}$$

$$x^2 = kt + C \quad (C = 0 \text{ if } x = 0 \text{ when } t = 0)$$

or $\quad x = \sqrt{kt}$

The equation represents a parabolic relationship between film thickness and time.

In some cases, the oxide itself may be very tightly bound to the metal or it may be so stable that it will not permit diffusion of ions or electrons through it to allow further oxidation. In this case, the growth rate of the film will decrease exponentially and, after a time, oxidation will cease. Zinc chromium, lead and aluminium exhibit this behaviour, each having wide use in building as a result. Aluminium goods are often artificially oxidised (anodised) after manufacture to give a uniform protective coating. The above arguments apply to dry non-polluted oxygen-containing atmospheres. Pollutants or dampness may give rise to other reactions, accelerating corrosion.

3. *Temperature.* As with any chemical reaction, oxidation proceeds by 'chance encounters' of oxygen and metallic ions, and since temperature increases thermal energy and diffusion rates of ions, it will inevitably increase oxidation rates. Hence, for example, metals obeying the exponential law at room temperature may obey the parabolic law at higher temperatures. Steel ingots, before rolling, may form considerable thicknesses of 'mill scale' in quite short times and most metals in the earth's crust exist in the form of oxides ('ores') which is indicative of high temperatures at some stage in their history.

4. *The effect of alloying elements.* Alloying elements are often added to metals in order to produce a protective film on their surface. Restrictions are, however, placed on alloying elements since they may also alter the mechanical properties of the parent metal. For example, aluminium, when alloyed with iron, forms an effective oxide coating but affects its forming properties. Hence, use in percentages required for protection is confined to treatments applied to the finished article. Perhaps the most important alloying elements for iron are chromium and nickel. Chromium forms a protective oxide layer while nickel has the effect of preserving the austenitic state (see 'stainless steel'). Alloying elements added for other reasons may, by oxidation, affect the properties of the parent metal. Carbon in steel, for example, oxidises more quickly than iron and is lost as a gas so that the surfaces of carbon steel components tend to soften on ageing.

Electrolytic and acidic corrosion

These are caused in the first instance by the tendency for metals to dissolve (ionise) in aqueous solutions. If the surface of a metal becomes moist, metallic ions enter the water, leaving behind a negative charge on the remaining solid metal:

$$M \rightleftharpoons M^{(n+)} + n(e^-) \quad \text{n equals the valency}$$

$$\text{metal} \qquad \text{metal ion} \qquad \text{electron(s)–(remain on metal)}$$

The arrow shown indicates that the reaction may proceed in either direction. This reaction, theoretically, may take place to some degree in any solid material in an attempt to balance the concentration of ions in the solid and adjacent liquid, but, in the case of metals, it is particularly important due to the effect of the negative potential which builds up on the remaining metal with respect to the solution. Metallic ions continue to form until the electrons which are left behind have set up a sufficient negative voltage to oppose further release of positive ions. Even then, the equilibrium should be regarded as dynamic rather than static, that is, ionisation still occurs but is balanced by the opposite process—deposition or 'plating out' of metal.

The actual value of the negative voltage which arises depends on the type of metal, the temperature and other factors. In practice, there is the problem of measurement of this potential since the other 'reference' electrode which must be used for measuring the difference in voltage between the metal and the solution will itself produce an electrode potential, so that a relative reading only is obtained. The problem is overcome by use of a standard 'hydrogen' electrode. Table 4.3 gives the standard electrode potentials of some common metals in solutions of their ions, with respect to the hydrogen reference electrode. Metals which are more reactive than the hydrogen electrode produce negative voltages, while those that are less reactive produce positive voltages. The former are known as anodic metals and the latter as cathodic or noble metals. Electrode potentials are also affected by the state of the surface of the metal. Imperfections in the surface, such as grain boundaries or points of intersection of dislocation lines with the surface, will result in weaker bonding of atoms, easier dissolution and higher effective electrode potentials at these points.

So far, although the basic mechanism of ionisation and electrode potentials has been explained, the causes of continued corrosion which occurs when ionisation

Table 4.3

Standard electrode potentials of pure metals.
Note that the most reactive metals are the
alkali and alkaline earth metals which hold
their electrons most loosely

Metal	Electrode potential (Volts)
Magnesium	−2·4
Aluminium	−1·7
Zinc	−0·76
Chromium	−0·65
Iron (ferrous)	−0·44
Nickel	−0·23
Tin	−0·14
Lead	−0·12
Hydrogen (reference)	0·00
Copper (cupric)	+0·34
Silver	+0·80
Gold	+1·4

proceeds with little or no hindrance over long periods of time is not yet apparent; in the above examples, corrosion stops when the electrode potential is reached. Corrosion can only continue if the actual potential of the metal for some reason changes so that more metal must dissolve to restore its original value; that is, the electrons which are the cause of the potential, must somehow 'drain away' from the metal. This electron-consuming reaction may occur in two ways:

In the presence of acids: acidic corrosion. Acids contain free hydrogen ions which, on reaction with electrons, produce hydrogen gas:

$$2H^+ \quad + \quad 2e^- \quad \rightarrow \quad H_2\uparrow$$
$$\text{in solution} \quad \text{from metal} \quad \text{gas}$$

The supply of electrons required for this reaction is obtainable from metals which are above hydrogen in the table of electrode potentials. Hence, these metals dissolve in many acids. The more concentrated the acid is, the more rapidly will a metal corrode since such acids contain greater concentrations of hydrogen ions. Metals below hydrogen in the table do not corrode in normal acids because hydrogen itself, which may be regarded as a 'metal', tends to ionise to a greater degree than these metals; therefore, hydrogen rather than the metal will remain in ion form.

If the metal is joined to a different metal which gives rise to a lower negative potential: electrolytic corrosion. Consider, for example, strips of copper and zinc immersed in the same solution and joined by an electrical conductor (Fig. 4.26). The zinc would

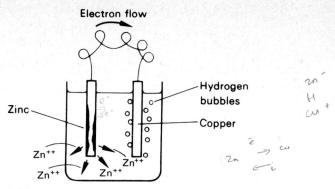

Fig. 4.26 Electrolytic corrosion resulting from zinc and copper rods immersed in an aqueous solution while in electrical contact

normally reach a voltage of -0.76 V on the hydrogen scale and the copper $+0.34$ V. Therefore, on joining them, there must be a potential difference of 1.1 V between the zinc and copper. Electrons will flow through the wire from the zinc to the copper (corresponding to a flow of conventional current in the opposite direction) and the zinc will continue to dissolve in an attempt to replace them, since the process will cause a reduction in its negative electric potential. The copper, on the other hand, will donate electrons to positive ions in solution in an attempt to maintain its former voltage of $+0.34$ V. If the solution contains hydrogen ions, then they will collect electrons from the copper, forming hydrogen gas:

$$2H^+ \quad + \quad 2e^- \quad \rightarrow \quad H_2\uparrow$$

in solution   from copper   gas

The zinc ions which dissolve will form a zinc salt by combination with negative ions in solution. If, for example, the solution contained sulphate ions then zinc sulphate would form.

The corroding metal (in this case, the zinc) is known as the anode and the protected metal (in this case, the copper) as the cathode. Electron flow is always from the anode to the cathode. Note that the above arrangement is the principle of the Daniell cell in which the electromotive force of 1.1 V is used for the supply of small quantities of electric power. As with the Daniell cell, however, the electrolytic action does not proceed unhindered until the zinc is destroyed. Many other corrosion reactions are similarly slowed down due to the resistance to ion movement in the solution. This may be caused, for example, by formation of insoluble films on the anode. Aluminium for this reason normally behaves *cathodically* to zinc and chromium is corrosion resistant in the same way. Alternatively, hydrogen gas bubbles evolved at the cathode tend to form a 'third electrode' and also resist the flow of further positive ions to the cathode. This is known as polarisation.

Alternative causes of electrolytic corrosion

There are a number of instances where commonly used combinations of different metals in building or constructional engineering result in electrolytic corrosion;

examples are given in Table 4.4. Just as important, however, and less obvious, are instances in which electrolytic corrosion cells may form within a single metal in the presence of moisture. Table 4.5 gives a number of possible causes. The effect of grains and electrolyte concentration in causing corrosion will be readily appreciated, since

Table 4.4

Some common situations in which electrolytic corrosion occurs

Situation	Metal which corrodes	Remedy
Galvanised water cistern or cylinder with copper pipes; traces of copper deposited due to water flow	Galvanised film corrodes electrolytically at point of contact with the copper particles. Film is destroyed, then steel corrodes similarly	Use a sacrificial anode in cistern. Otherwise use a plastic cistern or copper cylinder
Brass plumbing fittings in certain types of water	Zinc-dezincification	Use low zinc content brass or gunmetal fittings
Copper ballcock soldered to brass arm	Corrosion of solder occurs in the damp atmosphere resulting in fracture of joint	Use plastic ball on ballcock
Copper flashing secured by steel nails	Steel corrodes rapidly	Use copper tacks for securing copper sheeting
Iron or steel railings set in stone plinth using lead	Steel corrodes near the base	Ensure that steel is effectively protected by paint
Steel radiators with copper pipes and cast iron boiler	Steel radiators corrode	Corrosion can be reduced by means of inhibitors

these both cause changes of electrode potential but the effects of oxygen and stresses require some amplification, since both occur commonly and steps must be taken to prevent consequent deterioration of metals as a result.

The role of oxygen in electrolytic corrosion. Oxygen plays a part in many corrosion processes but the case of steel is particularly important and therefore, by way of example, the effects of oxygen on steel will be discussed. If steel is immersed in fairly pure water, there is only a very slight chemical reaction, producing ferric oxide. Rusting of steel is chiefly electrolytic, the anodes and the cathodes being different parts of the same piece of steel. The anodes may be stressed regions; for example, the head of a nail, or grain boundaries. Although the electrode potential of steel varies

Table 4.5

Situations in which electrolytic corrosion of a single metal may occur

Cause	Anode	Examples	Remedy
Grain structure of metals	Grain boundary	Any steel component subject to dampness	Keep steel dry
Variations in concentration of electrolyte	Low concentration areas	All types of soil	Cathodic protection
Differential aeration of a metal surface	Oxygen-remote area	Improperly protected under-ground steel pipes	Cathodic protection
Dirt or scale	Dirty area (oxygen remote)	Exposure of some types of stainless steel to atmospheric dirt	Use more resistant quality or keep the surface clean
Stressed areas	Most heavily stressed region	Steel rivets	Protect from dampness

slightly from place to place, on this basis, corrosion of the metal in pure water is very slow. Ions form at anodes:

$$Fe \rightarrow Fe^{++} + 2e$$
$$\text{metal} \quad \text{ferrous ion} \quad \text{electrons remain}$$
$$\text{in solution} \quad \text{on metal}$$

In the water:

$$H_2O \rightarrow H^+ + OH^-$$

At the cathode:

$$2H^+ + 2e^- \rightarrow H_2\uparrow$$
$$\text{from the} \quad \text{electrons} \quad \text{gas}$$
$$\text{water} \quad \text{from cathodes}$$

and in the water:

$$Fe^{++} + 2(OH)^- \rightarrow Fe(OH)_2\downarrow$$
$$\text{ferrous hydroxide}$$
$$\text{precipitate (green)}$$

The reaction is so slow that a steel nail immersed in boiled or distilled water may not show any visible corrosion product for some time.

Steel corrodes quite rapidly in ordinary water, however, and this is due to the presence of oxygen which reacts with electrons from cathodes to form the hydroxyl ions required by the above equation, to cause rusting:

$$2H_2O + O_2 + 4e^- \rightarrow 4(OH)^-$$
$$\text{from cathode}$$
$$\text{hydroxyl ions}$$

Then:

$$Fe^{++} + 2(OH)^- \rightarrow Fe(OH)_2$$
$$\text{ferrous-hydroxide}$$

Iron exhibits two valencies—of two and three—and 'rust' is in fact *ferric* hydroxide, $Fe(OH)_3$, obtained when ferrous hydroxide is further oxidised by air, although the product will be black—anhydrous magnetite, Fe_3O_4—if the air supply is limited, as in many closed heating circuits. The corrosion product forms in solution rather than at anodes or cathodes and the exact position depends on the diffusion rates of the positive and negative ions. In the case of steel, Fe^{++} ions are smaller and therefore more mobile than $(OH)^-$ ions, so that they meet near the cathode. Hence, unlike atmospheric corrosion, the corrosion product is incapable of protecting the metal, since it does not form on the corroding part—the anode.

A further common feature of corroded steel is pitting. This occurs because ferric oxide (mill scale) itself behaves cathodically with respect to iron which may be exposed by a scratch in the oxide coating so that the steel continues to corrode, causing cavities, while rust builds up on cathodes until it covers the entire surface (Fig. 4.27). Another factor contributing to pitting is the fact that the anode, being

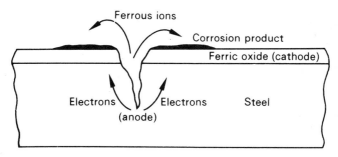

Fig. 4.27 Pitting of steel originating from a crack in the oxide coating

normally much smaller in area than the cathodic area, corrodes at a faster rate (even so, the total loss of weight caused by pitting will be less than that caused by uniform corrosion of the surface under similar conditions since the small anodic area acts as a 'bottle neck' in the corrosion process).

Steel corrosion may also occur by 'differential aeration'; that is, when different parts of the same piece of metal are exposed in different degrees to oxygen. Oxygenated areas tend to form cathodes due to the production of hydroxyl ions as explained above. Steel posts, for example, tend to corrode just below ground level, the corrosion cell consisting of an anode just below the ground where the oxygen level is relatively low and a cathode just above the ground where the oxygen level is higher. Underground steel pipes are sometimes seriously corroded by the action of bacteria in anaerobic (that is, oxygen-free) soils such as clays which contain sulphates and organic matter. The bacteria cause the sulphates to react with and remove the hydrogen which would normally prevent corrosion by causing polarisation at cathodes.

The effect of pH values. Yet another factor affecting corrosion of metals is the pH value of the moisture with which they are in contact. Just as a reaction involving electrons such as $Fe \rightarrow Fe^{++} + 2e$ depends on the e.m.f. of the metal with respect to solution, so a reaction such as $Fe^{++} + 2(OH)^- \rightarrow Fe(OH)_2$ will be pH dependent since it affects the balance of hydroxyl ions in solution. The equation $2H_2O + O_2 + 4e^- \rightarrow 4(OH)^-$ will be affected both by the electrode potential of the metal and the pH of the solution. Diagrams relating the relative stability of different states of a metal to their electric potential and the pH of the solution are known as Pourbaix diagrams. A simplified form of that for iron is shown in Fig. 4.28.

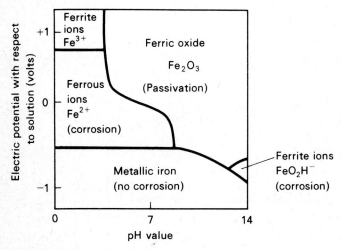

Fig. 4.28 Pourbaix diagram for iron/water

The boundary line between Fe and Fe^{++} is horizontal since, as explained above, electrons only are involved in the change; pH has no effect. Note however, that at higher pH values—that is, alkaline environments—ferric oxide, Fe_2O_3, is, within a range of voltages, more stable than the metal and forms a protective coating on it. This process is known as passivation and it prevents electrolytic corrosion occurring.

The passivating effect of alkaline environments in steel is, of course, responsible for the protection of steel in reinforced concrete and is the basis of some types of corrosion inhibitor for boiler systems. The effects of alkaline and acidic environments on steel are also well illustrated by the fact that a bricklayer's trowel, left uncleaned, will not corrode for some time, whereas a plasterer's float, if left in this way, will corrode rapidly due to the acidic solution resulting from gypsum plasters. Corrosion of steel, similarly, is greatly accelerated if saline solutions are present as in sea water or in concrete containing chlorides.

Although Pourbaix diagrams are extremely useful in showing how metals react to varying conditions, they should not be taken as a final indication of their corrosion properties, since factors already mentioned such as polarisation, the nature of the corrosion product, impurities in the metal and water and movement of the latter also play a part.

Stress corrosion cracking

Some alloys, when under a tensile stress and in corrosive conditions simultaneously, have exhibited cracking, leading to sudden failure without warning. This may occur in certain environments well below the yield point of the metal and may have disastrous consequences where considerable loads or pressures are sustained.

Stress corrosion may be caused either because a tensile stress at a point assists dissolution of metal, effectively altering its electrode potential, or simply due to corrosion of parts of a metal which would otherwise prevent spreading of a crack.

Stress corrosion may be regarded, in some cases, as an extension of pitting, as occurs in steel. As a pit becomes deeper, the stress at the root becomes higher causing increased corrosion at this point, so that a crack propagates through the metal. This type of cracking has led to explosions of riveted boilers. Seepage of treated boiler water past rivets and subsequent evaporation leads to concentration of alkali around them (the alkali is used in water treatments for passivation of the metal). As the Pourbaix diagram indicates (Fig. 4.28), large concentrations of alkali which produce high pH values may lead to local corrosion of the steel rivets, causing pitting and eventual failure as above. Riveted connections are particularly vulnerable to this type of attack, since some are inevitably stressed more than others, but stress corrosion may also occur in welded connections which are more common today.

Some alloys tend to exhibit stress corrosion due to electrochemical differences between the grain boundaries and the grains themselves, particularly if grain boundaries contain a different phase, as in the case of annealed steels. In certain stainless steels in particular, chromium carbide forms at grain boundaries when it is heated, as in welding, so that, in certain environments, electrolytic corrosion will occur with chromium carbide as cathodes and neighbouring chromium depleted areas as cathodes. This leads to cracking and eventual fracture under stress.

PROTECTION OF METALS AGAINST CORROSION

Wherever possible, the choice of metal for a given situation should be such that electrolytic corrosion does not arise, since effective protection methods involve, firstly, the initial cost of treatment, and in many cases the subsequent cost of maintenance. In damp atmospheres, metals which form impervious corrosion films are most suitable and the use of different metals in contact in these situations should be, if possible, avoided. Particular care is necessary in polluted atmospheres or corrosive environments which will accelerate corrosion. A number of metals are very prone to certain types of chemical in solution; these are described under the headings of individual metals. The task of protection of metals in corrosive situations may be tackled from several standpoints: a metal may be protected by coating with an impervious coating, by reversal of the corrosion reaction making it into a cathode (cathodic protection), passivation or by means of inhibitors.

Protection by impervious coating

This is a very common method of protection of metals since it is cheap and in many cases the only feasible method; for example, protection of structural steels, though some types of paint possess an inhibitive property in addition to their waterproofing qualities. The provision of a waterproof coating on metals depends on a number of factors relating to the paint and its application. The most important are outlined below:

1. Crevices as formed by joints where metal components touch tend to trap moisture by capillarity. Evaporation is in any case slower due to reduced air circulation and the latter itself will tend to create anodes in crevices, as explained above. Furthermore, the corrosion product will tend to trap moisture, and in the case of riveted connections cause stresses due to the volume increase which accompanies corrosion. These stresses will increase the corrosion rate and accelerate failure. Particular attention should therefore be paid to restricted spaces and they should not be painted when damp. Protection may be achieved by insertion of a protective paste; for example, red lead for steel.
2. The film must be unbroken for effective protection unless it is an inhibitive film. For example, although structural steel is often protected by a prefabrication primer, this will be damaged during fabrication and should be made good afterwards. Otherwise, corrosion will occur by differential aeration at discontinuities in the protective coating.
3. The surface of the metal must be suitably prepared. For example, mill scale should be removed from steel before priming, since it has a different coefficient of thermal movement to steel and will tend to flake off in time. In factory processes, scale is normally removed by acids, as in pickling or phosphating. These methods are, however, not suitable for site application, shot or grit blasting is more effective. Wire brushing achieves little if substantial thicknesses of rust are present.
4. No paint is perfectly waterproof; the protection afforded depends, therefore, on the thickness of the film. Sharp edges often protrude through a single coat of paint due to its surface tension effect, so that, if such edges cannot be rounded off before painting, extra coats of paint should be applied at these points. Thixotropic versions of paints have the advantage that greater thickness can be obtained. Polyvinyl chloride (PVC) coatings, factory applied, for the same reason, give excellent protection provided they are not punctured, and are now commonly used for protecting a wide variety of components.

Cathodic protection

If the electric potential of a metal in aqueous solution can be maintained at its standard electrode potential, then corrosion will not take place since, as explained, the metal only ionises in order to try to establish this potential. If the electric potential is held by some means at a value more negative than the electrode potential, then the metal will behave cathodically and, although hydrogen may be generated from solution by the excess electrons in the metal, corrosion cannot occur. This is known as cathodic protection. It would be misleading to suggest that the exact value of the standard electrode potential of the metal must be maintained for full protection. If, for example, in the case of steel pipes in hard waters, a protective 'scale' of a magnesium or calcium salt forms, protection will be achieved at a voltage which would, in normal conditions, cause the steel to behave anodically. On the other hand, if the concentration of ions in solution is reduced, as for example when there is flowing water, there will be a constant diffusion of ions away from the metal and corrosion will occur even though it is held at its normal electrode potential. The corrosion rate is, in all cases, proportional to the difference between the *actual* potential of the metal and its *effective* electrode potential, under the given conditions.

In order to protect a metal from corrosion, electric current must be supplied to it such that the draining away of electrons from it is counterbalanced. Conventional current will therefore be *away* from the metal to be protected. This current may be provided by means of a second cell, either in the form of another more anodic metal known as a sacrificial anode, or by a direct current source connected into the corrosion cell.

Sacrificial anodes

The use of these in protection of steel is very widespread. To be effective, metals used must be higher in the electrochemical series than iron. It might be considered that protection would automatically be achieved with any such metal but this is not the case, since initially the corroding metal will be some margin below its standard electrode potential and the sacrificial anode must be of sufficiently negative potential to increase the negative potential of the corroding metal by this margin. The impressed e.m.f. required depends on the resistance of the solution; if it is low, then a metal near to iron in the table will be satisfactory; for example, aluminium or zinc. High resistance solutions will require a higher metal in the series such as magnesium, if the steel is to be fully protected. The situation is exemplified in Fig. 4.29.

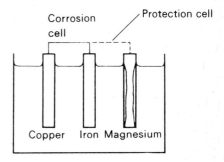

Corrosion cell / Protection cell

Copper   Iron   Magnesium

Fig. 4.29 Cathodic protection using a sacrificial anode. The protection cell must be sufficiently active to restore iron to its standard electrode potential in spite of the influence of the copper

The metal which was formerly corroding is now behaving as a cathode with respect to the sacrificial anode which must therefore be near to the protected metal. A good example is galvanised steel in which a zinc coating behaves as a sacrificial anode. The period of protection of the zinc coating depends primarily on its thickness. Hot-dip galvanising produces a thickness of about 100 μm of zinc, alloyed into surface layers of steel which may give full protection for 10 years or more if uniform thickness is achieved. Sheradising (heating in powdered zinc and zinc oxide to about 300°C) produces a thickness of about 10 μm which will give full protection for possibly a few years. Electroplating of zinc may produce only very thin coats which are not recommended for use without painting.

Impressed current method

Protection of underground steel pipes has, in the past, been successfully achieved by this method. By connection of the negative terminal of a direct current source to the steel, the positive terminal being connected to a further electrode in the soil, electrons are supplied to the iron, maintaining it at a sufficiently negative voltage to avoid corrosion (Fig. 4.30). As with sacrificial anodes, this supply of electrons at any one part of the pipe depends on a completed cell being formed at that point, with the d.c. source. Hence, due to soil resistance, electrodes must be positioned at intervals along the pipe, the actual interval depending on the resistance of the soil. The current consumed will also depend on the soil resistance, being higher in more corrosive conditions. The other electrode will be at a positive potential and will therefore corrode unless made out of a noble metal. Steel electrodes, for example, will require

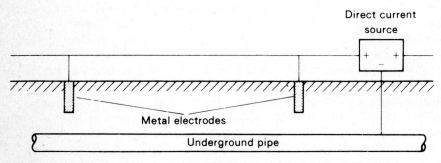

Fig. 4.30 Protection of an underground steel pipe by the impressed current method

replacement whereas more expensive platinum or carbon electrodes would be corrosion resistant. Impressed currents used for protection of underground steel pipes may adversely affect neighbouring buried metals. Also, direct currents in populated areas may interfere with the pipes themselves; such currents were at one time produced by electric railway power supplies. Alternating currents are now more common but even these may adversely affect some buried metals such as aluminium, whose oxide has a rectifying action. Neither the above impressed current nor the sacrificial anode method is intended to obviate the need for painting of underground pipes. Complete protection by these methods alone would be very costly; they are merely intended to supplement the protection given by traditional waterproof coatings such as bitumen coatings which may not be 100 per cent effective due to, for example, incomplete coverage or damage during laying of the pipe.

Passivation and use of inhibitors

Passivation is based on Pourbaix diagrams. If the pH value of a certain environment and the potential of the metal are such that it is covered by a stable, impervious corrosion film, then corrosion will cease. For example, steel in an alkaline environment is passivated, though aggressive ions, such as chlorine ions, will destroy the protective film, allowing corrosion to continue. Hence, steel in reinforced or pre-stressed concrete is protected, though the use of calcium chloride in such concretes is not recommended.

Inhibition (anodic-cathodic). Inhibitors are added to corrosive media to resist corrosion of metals immersed in them. They may retard either the anodic or cathodic reactions of a system. For example, if steel anodes can be coated with a layer of ferric oxide, Fe_2O_3, corrosion will not be possible. This requires an oxidising agent; for example, sodium chromate. This chemical will work in a de-aerated solution but other inhibitors such as sodium carbonate or sodium silicate require an external supply of oxygen. Hence, these inhibitors would not be effective in, for example, boiler circuits where oxygen contents are low. The above might seem contradictory to earlier statements about the accelerating effect of oxygen on corrosion. The accelerating effect is still theoretically present but, in this case, the oxygen in combined form with the metal produces a situation in which corrosion cannot occur in spite of the fact that the oxygen in solution behaves as a depolariser. The Pourbaix diagram for iron shows that oxide coatings are not stable at low pH values so that other methods must, in these cases, be used.

An example of inhibition by the interference of salts with cathodic products occurs in hard natural water. Calcium carbonate and magnesium hydroxide which form a scale on the metal prevent the penetration of oxygen to act as a depolariser. Unfortunately, such scales tend to accumulate, increasing the frictional resistance of pipes and adversely affecting their heat-conduction properties. Other inhibitors such as polyphosphates retard cathodic and anodic reactions, though, as in the case of all inhibitors, the presence of aggressive ions such as nitrates, sulphates and chlorides, tends to reduce their efficiency. Soft waters, which often contain carbon dioxide dissolved to form carbonic acid, may be improved by addition of alkalis such as sodium carbonate (washing soda), which will precipitate calcium carbonate from solution. Excess use of alkalis is, however, not recommended; it can lead to localised corrosion cells.

FERROUS METALS

The element iron, in abundance, is second only to aluminium, it is relatively easily extracted from its ore and can be modified by alloying to form a vast number of products with widely different properties. These facts account for the dominant role played by this metal in many aspects of construction.

Production of iron

Iron, like many metals, occurs in the form of an ore, generally iron oxide, together with earthy material such as silica and alumina. The first stage in the production of iron involves the blast furnace in which the iron oxide is reduced to iron by carbon monoxide produced from ignition of coal and limestone, combustible gases providing the necessary heat. The impurities and calcium oxide from the limestone collect as a slag on top of the liquid iron, which is run off. The iron itself is run into moulds forming 'pigs' which contain between 2 and 4 per cent carbon and quantities of silicon, sulphur, phosphorous and manganese.

PRODUCTS BASED ON IRON

The impurities listed above have a marked effect on the properties of iron and by modification of pig iron to differing degrees, materials having apparently quite different properties are produced. Classification of products is normally based on the carbon content and in order of increasing percentages, the following are obtained:

Wrought iron—very low carbon content..
Steel—low carbon, medium carbon and high carbon.
Cast iron—high carbon content.

The properties of each of these groups may be modified by alloying with other metals.

Wrought iron (BS 51).

This is the purest form of iron, containing about 0·02 per cent carbon which is almost completely dissolved interstitially in the iron lattice. The metal is tough and ductile with a yield point of about 210 N/mm^2 and a tensile strength of about 350 N/mm^2. It is produced from pig iron by melting in a reverberatory furnace in which impurities are oxidised into slag. As the iron becomes purer, its melting point rises and it therefore becomes 'pasty'. Balls of iron are withdrawn and the slag, which is more fluid than the iron, is forced out by steam hammering. The iron is then rolled into bars or the process repeated to obtain greater purity.

Wrought iron was formerly used for structural members subject to tensile stresses (compression members being made from cast iron). Steel has, of course, replaced these materials in such situations, though wrought iron is still used for ornamental ironwork, chains and hooks since it has admirable working properties and great toughness and corrosion resistance. More general use of the metal has, however, given way to that of steel, since the latter is much cheaper to produce.

Steel

This is an alloy of iron and carbon containing between 0·10 and 1·7 per cent carbon. The solubility of carbon in iron is very low—about 0·007 per cent at room temperature, since the carbon atom is larger than any of the interstitial spaces in the BCC iron crystal lattice and too small to act as a substitutional impurity. Therefore, only small quantities of carbon actually dissolve in the iron and the percentages of carbon in steel given above result in quite different properties. It is clear that some of the carbon in steel must be in a different form than alpha iron or ferrite, as the iron containing dissolved carbon is known. This other material contains 6·67 per cent carbon and is known as cementite. Cementite has a different crystal structure to that of iron or ferrite, having properties more like a ceramic than a metal, since the high percentage of carbon atoms in the lattice (6·67 per cent by weight, 25 per cent numerically) increases strength and prevents plastic deformation.

In order to understand the parts played by ferrite and cementite in steels of varying composition, it is necessary to investigate the way in which steel ingots cool during manufacture. The structure of hot steel is different to that at normal temperatures since, on heating to a temperature above 910°C, iron changes from BCC to an FCC structure known as gamma iron. The interstitial spaces in the lattice thereby increase so that up to 1·7 per cent carbon by weight, corresponding to nine atoms per hundred of iron, can dissolve. The resulting material is known as austenite. Thus, the carbon in steels at high temperature is fully dissolved and, as would be expected, the resultant material is soft, ductile and suitable for rolling and forging. It is important to note that even austenite is solid; iron, on further heating, undergoes yet another change in crystal structure before it finally melts at 1539°C.

When austenitic steel cools slowly so that alpha iron is produced, the resulting material must contain suitably balanced proportions of ferrite and cementite and the mechanism of changes is rather similar to that by which a two-phase alloy solidifies from the liquid mixture. The temperature-composition diagram for iron–carbon alloys up to 1·5 per cent carbon and approximately 1000° C is shown in Fig. 4.31. The rules as given for two-phase alloys apply:

1. If the carbon content is to the left of line (i), pure ferrite is formed.
2. If the carbon content corresponds to the area between lines (i) and (ii), ferrite forms but since the solubility of carbon decreases at reducing temperatures, cementite crystals must begin to form, occupying space between grain boundaries.

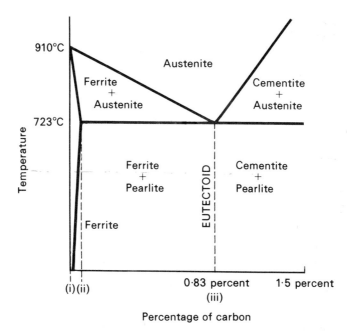

Fig. 4.31 Part of the equilibrium diagram for iron–carbon compounds

3. If the carbon content is between lines (ii) and (iii), ferrite grains will begin to form and the carbon rejected will diffuse into remaining austenite grains until they contain a percentage corresponding to line (iii). At this point, which occurs at a temperature of 723°C and 0·83 per cent carbon, an intimately mixed combination of ferrite and cementite will form, this combination being known as pearlite since, under the microscope, polished and etched specimens of steel have a pearly appearance. The point is known as the *eutectoid* (as distinct from the *eutectic* which would be used for a liquid–solid equilibrium diagram). The above steels are known as hypoeutectoid steels; that is, they contain less than 0·83 per cent carbon. If a eutectoid steel—one containing 0·83 per cent carbon—is cooled, then pearlite is the only material formed and the transition does not begin until the temperature decreases to 723°C.

4. If the percentage of carbon is above line (iii) (hypereutectoid) then, on cooling, cementite is first produced appearing at grain boundaries, the remaining austenite becoming less rich in carbon until the eutectoid is reached, pearlite then forming as before.

The above transformations will only take place as stated if cooling is very slow, allowing diffusion of carbon from within the austenite crystals to form ferrite and cementite products.

The properties of ferrite are similar to those of pure iron, such as wrought iron, while cementite is intensely hard and brittle. Pearlite, a mixture of these two in the proportions 88 per cent ferrite and 12 per cent cementite, is, as would be expected, intermediate in properties. The material is much harder than ferrite but less hard than cementite; stronger than ferrite but weaker than cementite.

The effect of carbon content on the appearance of sections of steel when polished and etched under a microscope is as shown in Fig. 4.32.

Steels may be divided in this respect into:

Low carbon steels containing up to 0·15 per cent carbon.
Mild steels containing 0·15–0·25 per cent carbon.
Medium carbon steels containing 0·2–0·5 per cent carbon.
High carbon steels containing 0·5–1·4 per cent carbon.

Note that eutectoid steels which contain pearlite only rank as high carbon steels. Low carbon steels are soft and ductile and are suitable for cold drawn wire and thin sheeting. Mild steels are strong but ductile and suitable for rolling, hence they are commonly used as structural steels. Medium carbon steels are suitable for forging, that is, modification of shape by pressure or impact. They are used for many engineering purposes. High carbon steels are very hard and strong but, on this account, brittle. They are used for casting, for manufacture of machine tools and for high strength wire.

Although the carbon content has an important bearing on the properties of the final steel product, it is by no means the only significant factor. The following will also be accountable to some degree for the performance of the finished product.

(a) *The size and shape of the metal grains.* The basic grain structure of a steel depends on the history of the product while in the austenitic state. Within the austenitic range of temperatures, thermal energy is high and the crystals tend to grow continuously so that products kept in the austenitic state tend to have a coarse grain structure. Generally speaking, a fine grain structure is preferable since it results in increased yield strength, toughness and ease of heat treatment, though creep resistance is reduced. There are, of course, practical limitations to the size of grain which can be obtained. Ingots allowed to cool in air will tend to have a finer grain structure in external layers than internal layers which cool more slowly. Hot rolling breaks down

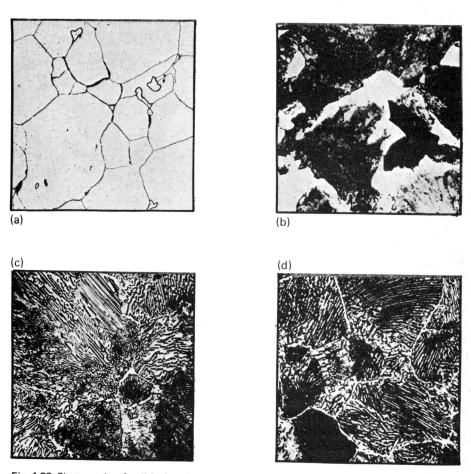

(a) (b) (c) (d)

Fig. 4.32 Photographs of polished, etched sections of steel having different carbon contents. (a) Carbon content almost zero. Grain boundaries are clearly visible. (b) 0·5 per cent carbon. Ferrite grains are light and pearlite grains dark. (c) 0·83 per cent carbon, eutectoid steel. In this case, the ferrite/cementite layers are clearly visible. (d) Hyper-eutectoid steel. Cementite appears as light-coloured layers around the pearlite grain boundaries

the grains and results in a more even size distribution, recrystallisation taking place immediately after. Cold rolling distorts or breaks down the grains and leaves the structure in a stressed, though harder and stronger state, since cold rolling is carried out at a temperature which is too low to allow recrystallisation to occur. Larger steel components, for example steel joists, would require too much energy to be produced by cold rolling, hence they are hot rolled. Smaller products, for example wire, can be cold worked or 'drawn', however, and this process results in smaller grain size and higher strength.

(b) *The effects of heat treatment.* The term, as used here, is used to denote treatment by heat that may produce a change of phase, crystal redistribution or passage of a constituent into or out of solid solution. The phase diagram given above only applies to steels cooled so slowly that carbon is able to diffuse from austenite grains to form equilibrium products. When the cooling rate is faster than this, diffusion to equilibrium states cannot complete and a frozen condition of non-equilibrium is obtained. In order of decreasing rapidity, the main processes are. quenching (cooling by immersion in water, oil or iced brine), normalising (controlled cooling in still air) and annealing, in which, by slow cooling, steel is brought more or less to equilibrium conditions.

Quenching completely prevents diffusion of carbon atoms so that they are held in an unstable condition in a body-centred tetragonal lattice. As would be expected, the resultant material, known as martensite, is very hard and brittle since no plastic deformation is possible (Fig. 4.33(a)). For this reason, it is normal to temper quenched steels to increase to some degree their ductility and toughness. Tempering involves heating to a temperature which is sufficient to allow some diffusion of carbon to form small cementite crystals. Temperatures of about 200–400°C are normally used; higher temperatures cause greater loss of tensile strength and hardness, as increased quantities of carbon are rejected and ferrite begins to form. This structure is known as a sorbitic structure.

Normalising allows some diffusion of carbon atoms to form cementite but large ferrite crystals do not have time to form and the resulting structure consists of large numbers of small crystals of ferrite and pearlite (Fig. 4.33(b)). Normalised steels have properties intermediate between quenched steels and annealed steels.

Annealing normally involves heating of the steel to form austenite. This allows carbon to dissolve so that, on cooling slowly, equilibrium products are formed. The process is often carried out after welding when the initial cooling may have been rapid, leading to brittleness in the joint. Annealing initially refines grain structure since new crystals of austenite grow, but annealing times should be sufficient only to allow carbon to dissolve in the austenite since, if they are greater than this, crystals tend to grow larger, causing reduced strength and increased ductility in the resulting steel (Fig. 4.33(c)). If the annealing temperature is too high, a similar effect occurs. Steel sections are heated to a point below the austenite transition temperature at stages during rolling to allow redistribution of crystals distorted by rolling. Higher temperatures in this case are not necessary since the carbon distribution in the steel in the section is undisturbed during rolling. This process is known as sub-critical annealing.

(c) *The effect of alloying elements.* Steels may be classified as 'plain carbon steels' or 'alloy steels' according to the quantities of alloying elements they contain, though even plain carbon steels often contain small quantities of other elements which have significant effects on their properties. The most common elements found in plain carbon steels are:

1. Sulphur and phosphorous. These both increase the brittleness of steels so that very small percentages only are allowable (for example, 0·05 per cent).

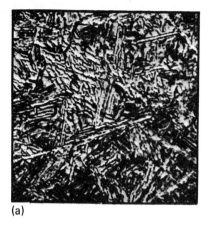

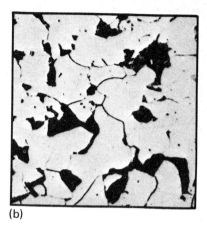

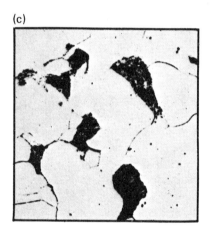

Fig. 4.33 The effect of heat treatment on a 0·13 per cent carbon steel. (a) Martensite, obtained by quenching. (b) Fine grain structure, obtained by normalising. (c) Coarse grained structure, obtained by annealing

2. Manganese. This may be used for deoxidation purposes, in which case it would be removed as a slag, but mild steels still benefit from its presence since it 'dissolves' in ferrite and refines the grain structure, increasing strength and hardness. High yield steels normally contain more manganese than mild steel, which usually contains about 0·5 per cent.
3. Silicon. This has a similar effect to that of manganese only to a lesser degree.
4. Niobium. This element forms a carbide within the ferrite lattice refining the grain structure and increasing the yield strength of steels. It also tends to increase the temperature of the 'ductile-brittle' transition but the problem may be overcome by normalising if high impact strength is required.

(d) *The degree of deoxidation of the steel.* Iron oxide forms on the surface of molten steel very quickly due to its high temperature and combines with carbon in the steel forming carbon monoxide gas. The gas dissolves in the steel but tends to form bubbles on cooling as its solubility decreases. To avoid porosity in the ingots therefore, the evolution of gas must be controlled. The addition of manganese, silicon or aluminium prevents gas formation. A steel in which no gas forms is known as a 'killed' steel. Shrinkage in these ingots produces, however, a waste area at the top so that killed steels are more expensive than the forms described below.

Semi-killed steels contain a proportion of gas which compensates for shrinkage and enables more efficient use of ingots. They are also known as balanced steels.

Rimming steels (non-deoxidised) contain large quantities of gas in the form of blow holes. Although this might seem unsatisfactory, rimming steels have the advantage that the surface layers are usually very pure since the gases sweep away impurities from the ingot surface, hence these steels are suitable for drawing and pressing. Working of the metal closes and welds the blow holes provided they are deep seated, so that they do not adversely affect mechanical properties.

STEEL FOR STRUCTURAL USES

Steel for structural uses may be divided into hot or cold rolled steel sections for structural steelwork on the one hand and bars or wire for reinforced and pre-stressed concrete on the other. Each material is covered by relevant British Standards which form the bases of codes of practice.

Weldable structural steels (BS 4360: Part II)

Since welding has largely replaced riveting in both shop and site fabrication of steelwork, the above British Standard forms the basis of hot rolled structural steel sections. The standard describes four grades of steel which are equally suitable for welded, riveted or bolted connections. The grades are designated 40, 43, 50 and 55, corresponding to minimum tensile strengths of 400, 430, 500 and 550 N/mm^2 respectively, as measured in accordance with BS 18: *Methods of tensile testing of metals.* Each grade of steel contains sub-divisions corresponding to steels of different yield stress and impact requirements. Steels should be in the 'semi-killed' deoxidation condition unless used in thin sections to minimise risk of blow holes. Table 4.6 shows selected properties for steel sections up to 16 mm thick and over 63 mm thick. Note the following:

1. Carbon contents generally decrease from sub-division A to E, corresponding to increased impact resistance of the latter. In each case, impact strength is indicated by the energy absorbed by standard notched specimens at a given temperature. Steels with higher impact strength will absorb more energy at a given temperature (or equal energy at a lower temperature). Sub-division 'E' steels, particularly high grade types, are likely to be normalised.

Table 4.6

Some properties of weldable structural steels; BS 4360: Part II

Grade	Max. Carbon content (Ladle analysis)	Typical minimum yield stresses (N/mm^2)		Minimum elongation on gauge length of 200 mm	Charpy V-notch impact test		
		Up to 16 mm thick	Over 63 mm thick		Temp. (°C)	Energy (J)	Maximum Thickness (mm)
40 A	0·22	–	–	22	–	–	–
40 B	0·20	240	210	22	Room temp.	27	50
40 C	0·18	240	210	22	0	27	50
40 D	0·18	240	210	22	–15	27	50
40 E	0·16	255	225	22	{ –20	27	50
					–30	27	50
43 A1	0·25	–	–	20	–	–	–
43 A	0·25	255	225	20	–	–	–
43 B	0·22	255	225	20	Room temp.	27	50
43 C	0·18	255	225	20	0	27	50
43 D	0·18	255	225	20	–15	27	50
43 E	0·16	270	240	20	{ –20	34	50
					–30	27	50
50 A	0·23	–	–	18	–	–	–
50 B	0·20	355	325	18	–	–	–
50 C	0·20	355	325	18	0	27	40
50 D	0·18	355	By agreement	18	–10	27	40
55 C	0·22	450	–	17	0	27	19
55 E	0·22	450	–	17	{ –20	47	63
					–30	41	
					–40	27	

2. Thicker sections tend to cool more slowly, resulting in coarser grain structure and reduced yield strengths.

3. Yield strengths increase as tensile strengths (represented by grade designation) increase. Grade 43 A, for example, is the normally used 'mild steel' for general structural purposes while grades 50 B and C correspond to 'high yield steel' without and with impact strength requirements respectively. Note that high yield steel does not necessarily contain more carbon than mild steel. The manganese content of high yield steel is, however, normally higher than that of mild steel, typical figures being 0·8 and 0·5 per cent respectively. (BS 4360 requires a maximum of 1·5 per cent for most steels to ensure weldability.) Alternatively, higher strengths

may be obtained by additions of the metal niobium or normalising, both of which refine the grain structure of the steel.

4. Ductility of steels decreases as their strengths increase. This factor is measured by the elongation of steel samples during tensile testing, ductile samples showing greater elongation.

BS 4360 gives similar requirements for plates, round and square bars and hollow sections, together with diagrams showing the positions from which samples should be cut for tensile and impact tests and bending tests. The standard also specifies a maximum 'equivalent carbon content' which is important for welding and takes into account the presence of alloying elements such as manganese, chromium and copper.

Requirements relating to quality: width, length, flatness and weight tolerances are given.

Hot rolled sections (BS 4: Parts I and II)

These may be in the form of universal beams, columns and bearing piles, joists, T bars, channels, angles and bulb flats, or alternatively, hollow sections. They are normally manufactured from weldable structural steels as described above. BS 4 gives dimensions and tolerances of hot rolled sections and hollow sections. For example, mass per unit length tolerances are −4 per cent on minimum mass/unit length for hollow sections and $\pm 2\frac{1}{2}$ per cent on specified mass/unit length for universal beams, columns and bearing piles. Tolerances under the specified depth of joists and channels are of considerable importance since extreme fibre stresses and deflections increase greatly for a small decrease in overall depth of sections. Table 4.7 shows required tolerances. Hot rolled sections have a very wide application in all aspects of structural engineering and building for load-bearing purposes.

Table 4.7
Dimensional tolerances for hot rolled joints and channels (BS 4)

Nominal depth		Maximum permissible variation from specified depth	
Over (mm)	Up to and including (mm)	Over (mm)	Under (mm)
—	305	3·2	0·8
305	381	4·0	1·6
381	432	4·8	1·6

Cold rolled steel sections (BS 2994)

These are produced by cold rolling from steel strip. The material specifications are described in BS 1449; Parts IIIA, IIIB and IV, which cover hot rolled, cold rolled and stainless/heat resisting strip respectively. In Part IIIA, for example, mechanical and chemical composition requirements are specified, and on this basis steels are given 'HS' classifications. Mild steels, designated HS1 to HS4, contain increasing quantities of carbon and manganese up to maxima of 0·13 and 0·6 per cent respectively and are used for cold forming and drawing, HS1 being the most ductile and in the 'killed' condition. HS12, 17, 22, 23 steels are higher strength though less ductile; HS20, 30, 40 are medium carbon/manganese steels more suitable for hot forming, as are HS50–100 high carbon steels. BS 2994 gives sizes in common production together with dimensions and tolerances. This method of production is used for sections of low or medium load bearing capacity such as channels, angles and lintels.

Use of structural steel (BS 449)

The stability of any metal component in a given situation depends on the magnitude of the load, the types of stresses it induces and also on the properties of the component. The properties of steel have been outlined by the British Standards mentioned above and BS 449 shows how, by consideration of loading types and arrangements, members of suitable dimensions can be selected.

BS 449 gives certain requirements relating to impact strength of welded elements manufactured from BS 4360 steels during erection or in the completed structure, since brittle failure may occur at joints if impact strength is low. The impact energy requirements of BS 4360 apply to certain thicknesses only (see Table 4.6) and since impact strengths of thicker sections which have a coarser grain structure are less, BS 449 specifies a separate impact strength for such welded sections, when in tension, of at least 27 Joules by the Charpy V-notch test at $0°C$. The standard also requires that steel to be used in cold climates should have an impact strength of not less than 27 Joules at the lowest ambient temperature likely to be encountered. This may require one of the C, D, or E types of steel from BS 4360. Again, if a member is of critical importance, subject to high restraint or shock loading, a steel with high impact resistance should be specified.

In the section on design and details of construction, BS 449 specifies that the thickness of steel used for external constructions exposed to weather should not be less than 8 mm, or 6 mm for unexposed steel (with the exception of webs or packings). Sealed tubes or sections may be of 4 mm minimum thickness in exposed situations or 3 mm in unexposed situations, since corrosion in these cases can only occur from the external face. The above figures need not be adhered to if special measures are taken to protect steel from corrosion. Design methods for members in bending, compression and tension are given.

The allowable tensile or compressive stress due to bending depends on the grade of steel and the thickness and possibly the type of section. Table 4.8 shows typical maximum allowable stresses. These may be compared with the minimum yield point stresses from BS 4360 given in Table 4.5. The compressive stresses allowed in Table 4.8 are reduced in cases of long, slender beams to ensure satisfactory performance. In some cases, other criteria may be involved in selection of suitable sections, for example, deflection.

All BS 4 sections are available in grades 43 and 50 steels though the majority of

Table 4.8
*Maximum permissible stresses for steel members in bending
(BS 449). There are, of course, requirements for bearing and
shear stresses in sections; the above tensile and compressive
stresses are given for comparison (a) with yield stresses in
steel and (b) with other metals or materials*

Form	Grade	Thickness	Maximum allowable tensile or compressive stress (N/mm^2)
Rolled I	43	All	165
beams	50	Up to and incl. 65 mm	230
		Over 65 mm	Ys/1·52
	55	Up to and incl. 40 mm	280
		Over 40 mm	260
Plate girders	43	Up to and incl. 40 mm	165
		Over 40 mm	150
	50	Up to and incl. 65 mm	215
		Over 65 mm	Ys/1·63
	55	Up to and incl. 40 mm	265
		Over 40 mm	245

Value of Ys to be agreed with manufacturer and not greater than
350 N/mm².

rolled steel sections are grade 43–'mild steel'–since it is more economical for manufacturer and supplier alike to concentrate on larger quantities of a particular grade of steel. In some cases, however, high yield–grade 50–steel may be more economical, generally where higher stresses are encountered, where a required section falls in a 'gap' in standard sizes of grade 43 steel and particularly for fabrication of plate girders which may be used for large spans as in bridges. (There is, in fact, a separate British Standard for the structural use of steel in bridges: BS 153.) More recently, higher grades of steel have become available; for example, a grade 77 weldable steel which has low carbon content (0·08–0·17 per cent) but significant quantities of manganese, molybdenum, silicon and titanium. Quenching and tempering fully killed steel results in a fine grained material of minimum yield point 700 N/mm². This material has been used for hollow sections of thickness up to 10 mm and outside measurements up to 150 mm (round or square). Its use is, on account of its high cost, restricted to crane jibs and similar situations where a high strength/weight ratio is essential.

The use of cold rolled steel sections in building is covered by Addendum No.1 to BS 449. The metal thickness is, of course, lower than in hot rolled sections so that, although light in weight and economical, additional factors such as local weakness or torsional stiffness, must be considered in design. Hence, although cold rolling tends to increase yield strengths, particularly at corners, permissible stresses are in general slightly lower than in hot rolled section.

STEEL FOR REINFORCEMENT OF CONCRETE

Reinforcement is used for the following reasons:

1. To take the tensile load of concrete beams or slabs.
2. To withstand shear stresses in beams which are greatest near the supports. These give rise to complementary tensile stresses in these regions which require the use of additional reinforcement. These may be in the form of stirrups or bent-up bars at the end of simply supported beams.
3. To carry a proportion of the compressive stress and to withstand tensile stresses which may arise due to eccentric loading, as in columns.
4. Reinforcement may be used near the surface of mass concrete structures to reduce cracking by drying or carbonation shrinkage.
5. In some cases secondary reinforcement is used to prevent spalling of concrete surfaces due to fire.

The bond between concrete and steel

When reinforced concrete is loaded such that the reinforcement is under a tensile stress, some strain in the concrete must occur before the steel provides the necessary restraint and therefore cracking in tensile regions may occur. If there were no stress transfer between the steel and concrete, the steel would clearly be of no use at all in restraining it, and if a steel reinforcing bar were fixed only at its ends a single large crack would almost certainly appear at the point of maximum tensile stress. For example, the mid-point of a simply supported beam under a uniformly distributed load would crack if the beam were reinforced in this way. If the steel is bonded to the concrete, stress transfer would occur at all points along the length of tension members, and if cracks occur they would be in the form of a large number of very small cracks. Such cracks are more acceptable since they are less likely to allow penetration of air and moisture which would corrode steel. The precise nature of the bond between steel and concrete is not fully understood but its strength depends on the following factors:

(a) The area of contact between the steel and the concrete. This may be increased by use of larger numbers of smaller-diameter bars which would have a higher surface area for a given sectional area. In the case of higher stresses in the steel, bars having hooked ends may be used, though they may result in larger cracks than the equivalent in straight bars of similar total surface area, since there would be lower stress transfer per unit length of bar over the central section.

(b) The strength of the concrete. Bond strength increases with the crushing strength of the concrete, though the relationship is not linear.

(c) The condition of the steel surface. It is known that a thin layer of adherent rust increases the bond, possibly due to the increased roughness of surface obtained. Loose or flaky rust and mill scale do not have this effect and should be removed before steel is used. Twisted bars also result in a greater bond strength and are commonly used for high yield or cold rolled reinforcement to effect transfer of the higher working stresses used. Ribbed bars produce a still greater bond strength to concrete, though secondary reinforcement may be necessary to prevent bursting of concrete reinforced in this way.

It is unfortunate that high-strength bars for reinforcement do not have a significantly greater modulus of elasticity than mild steel bars so that strains will be greater at the larger stresses which are permissible. In these cases, therefore, twisted or deformed bars are normally used to provide the increase in bond strength necessary. Table 4.9 shows selected properties of the most commonly used reinforcing steels.

Table 4.9

Properties of steels for reinforcing concrete. Characteristic strength of hot rolled bars is based on yield strength with 5 per cent failures. In the case of cold worked bars or drawn wire, it is based on 0·2 per cent proof stress with 5 per cent failures. The value of S_0, used to determine gauge length for elongation measurements, is equal to the original cross sectional area of the test piece

Designation	Size	Charact. strength N/mm^2	Carbon (per cent)	Per cent minimum elongation at failure on $5·65\sqrt{S_0}$
Hot rolled mild steel (BS 4449)	All	250	0·25 max	22
Hot rolled high yield steel (BS 4449)	All	410	0·25 max	14
Cold worked high yield steel (BS 4461)	⩽ 16 mm > 16 mm	460 425	0·25 max	12 14
Hard drawn steel wire (BS 4482)	⩽ 12 mm	485	0·25 max	—

In addition to the above requirements, the British Standards specify chemical impurities, ultimate tensile strength, elongation at failure and bending test requirements. The hard drawn steel wire is commonly used for fabric reinforcement and precast products, such as pipes. There is as yet no classification in British Standards for the local bond strengths obtained from plain, twisted or ribbed bars, though C.P. 110

allows them to be used in the approximate ratios, 1 : 1·25 : 1·5. Design may be based on a local bond stress in tension of between 1·7 and 2·7 N/m^2 for plain bars, depending on the concrete strength. C.P. 110 specifies separate values for anchorage bond strengths.

STEELS FOR PRE-STRESSING CONCRETE

These are designed primarily for strength, so that they tend to contain higher percentages of carbon than steels for reinforcement and are not as malleable or ductile. Note that the drawn wires have the greatest tensile strength. The drawing process relies on the fact that, on reduction of the diameter of a wire on drawing through a die, the increase in tensile strength due to work hardening more than offsets the increase of stress resulting from the decrease of cross sectional area of wire. Table 4.10 shows some properties of typical pre-stressing bars and wires.

Table 4.10

Properties of steels for prestressing concrete. Characteristic strengths are based on breaking load with 5 per cent failures, though minimum proof stress values are also specified. By using strand, the greater tensile strength and increased ductility of wire are utilised to withstand high loads (compare 18 mm BS 4757 strand to 20 mm BS 4486 high tensile alloy steel bar)

Material	Examples of sizes available (mm)	Specified character-istic load (kN)	Equivalent stress N/mm²	Minimum elongation on 5·65 $\sqrt{S_0}$	Relaxation (per cent) at 70 per cent of character-istic stress for 1000 hours Normal	Low	Carbon content (per cent)
Cold worked high-tensile alloy steel bars (BS 4486)	20 40	325 1250	1030 995	6 per cent	–	–	–
Steel wire (BS 2691)	4 7	– –	1720 1470	–	5	2	0·6–0·9
Seven wire strand (BS 3617)	6·4 15·2	44·5 227·0	1820⎫ 1637⎭	3·5 per cent gauge length ≮ 600 mm	7	2·5	0·6–0·9
Nineteen wire strand (BS 4757)							
As spun	18	370	1762⎫	3·5 per cent	9	–	
Treated	25·4	659	1558⎬	gauge length	7	2·5	0·6–0·9
Treated	31·8	979	1483⎭	≮ 600 mm	7	2·5	

Standards also deal with quality and impurities of pre-stressing steels and wire to BS 2691 is required to satisfy a reverse bend test instead of the elongation requirement of other standards. Relaxation in bars or wires tends to be a problem at stresses over 50 per cent of the characteristic strength, so that design codes must allow for this particularly if untreated (normal relaxation) steel is used. In any case, it is not normal to load pre-stressing wires to stresses above 80% of their characteristic strength.

Site heating, welding and cutting of steels

> $450°C$

Reference to Table 4.2 shows that, if heated to temperatures above about 450°C, steels are likely to change in properties, by recrystallisation, annealing or even chemically, in order of increasing temperature. Welding of mild steel does not pose problems since the metal welds easily and is not likely to be severely affected by the process. There is, however, much skill involved in the welding process and brittleness and cracking will result if the weld is of poor quality. At high temperatures, grain boundaries tend to accommodate stresses due to shrinkage and therefore a fine grained weld structure is preferable. This is obtained by avoiding overheating, which would also damage surrounding parent metal. Welding of high yield steel presents greater problems and preheating of the heat-affected zone may be necessary to avoid metallurgical changes during the welding process. Cold worked steels will recrystallise on welding so that yield strength will be reduced. In all cases, particular care is needed when members are in tension. Pre-stressing steels are not normally welded—this should not be necessary, and in any case their high carbon/alloy content makes welding difficult.

If heat is required to assist in bending reinforcement, this should be in the form of steam only.

Cutting is best carried out by a high speed abrasive wheel which avoids heating of the steel, though an oxyacetylene flame will produce a cutting rather than a melting action if an excess of oxygen is used. The ends of bars or wire are not normally under stress, but in post-tensioned prestressing systems it is particularly important that a tendon at its anchorage is not overheated.

Fire resistance of steel

$550°C$

It is unfortunate that the electronic properties of metals which give rise to their formability also result in high thermal conductivity and decrease of strength at only moderate temperatures. The high conductivity of metals results in rapid transfer of heat to metal structures in case of fire unless in some way protected, so that collapse of steel structures may occur very rapidly in serious fires. On heating to a temperature of about 550°C steel weakens to the point where, based on normal factors of safety, yield is likely to occur. However, even before this has occurred, considerable distortion of the structure by expansion of the softening material may take place. For example, a 10-m beam heated to 400°C will expand by approximately 50 mm. It is clear, therefore, that steel structures must be protected as far as possible from fire and this is usually achieved by cladding, either in concrete or, better, lightweight insulating materials such as asbestos, vermiculite, lightweight concrete and lightweight plasters. Cold drawn steels for reinforcing or pre-stressing concrete will be seriously affected at relatively low temperatures, for example, 300°C, though a considerable degree of protection is afforded by the concrete itself.

ALLOY STEELS

These contain substantial proportions of alloying elements. They may be included for the following reasons:

(a) To increase strength and hardness. For a given cooling rate, the BCC elements tungsten, molybdenum and vanadium enhance these properties.

(b) To increase hardenability. It is very difficult to harden effectively large steel sections by quenching, since, although martensite will be produced on surface layers, the bulk of the metal will tend to form pearlite. In any case, quenching is drastic and results in a distorted, brittle structure. By incorporating alloying elements in steels, they can be made to produce martensite without quenching, so that the material will harden uniformly throughout its section. Elements having this effect are manganese, molybdenum and chromium.

(c) To increase corrosion resistance. Aluminium, copper and chromium have this effect. Structural steels and sheet containing 0·2 per cent copper are available; these form a protective brown oxide layer on exposure. These could have application in buildings, allowing the steel frame to be situated externally, perhaps as an architectural feature and with less danger of damage by fire. Most important, at present, however, are stainless steels which are based on the effect of chromium (see below).

(d) To preserve the austenitic state. Metals such as manganese and nickel which are FCC tend to preserve the austenitic structure of steel down to temperatures as low as room temperature. For example, a 13 per cent manganese steel is used on the teeth of mechanical shovels to resist the severe abrasion encountered. Impact or abrasion changes the surface layers of the austenite structure into martensite which resists wear and damage.

(e) To produce special properties. Steels containing 36 per cent nickel, for example, have a very low thermal movement (approximately $2 \times 10^{-6}/°C$ at normal temperatures compared to $11·6 \times 10^{-6}/°C$ for ordinary steel). They are known as 'invar' steels and are used in surveyors' tapes and similar applications.

A very large number of alloy steels can be produced by the addition of alloying elements as above, though these are mainly used in mechanical engineering applications. In addition, surface hardening may be used; for example, flame hardening in which, by heating of the surface of a metal component and then quenching immediately, martensitic surface layers are produced on a tough, resilient core. A similar effect may be obtained by nitriding or carburising which involve heating components in nitrogen- or carbon-rich atmospheres which combine with surface layers, giving a hardening effect.

Stainless steels

Owing to their corrosion resistance, these are the most widely used alloy steels in the construction industry. Resistance to corrosion is achieved by incorporation of chromium in steel. On immersion in water or dilute acids which contain oxygen, an impervious chromium oxide film is formed and any faults in the coating are quickly repaired. Chromium in quantities up to 27 per cent of the steel may be used, 18 per cent being a common figure. Best results are obtained with a single-phase metal, since two phases (for example, ferrite and pearlite in ordinary steel) will tend to corrode electrolytically with one another. The addition of nickel preserves the austenitic state, and for this reason up to 10 per cent nickel is included in the austenitic steels. The most common types of stainless steel are 18–8 (percentages of chromium and nickel respectively) and 18–10–3 (the last figure indicating 3 per cent molybdenum) steels. The second type is more expensive but has greater corrosion resistance and is more suitable for external use, for example in cladding or internally where cleaning is not practicable. Caution is necessary when welding austenitic stainless steels, since, at the high temperatures involved, chromium carbide forms at grain boundaries which may cause corrosion of chromium-depleted regions nearby. This problem may be avoided if very low carbon contents are used or if the steel is stabilised with niobium or titanium which themselves combine with the carbon present.

Ferritic stainless steels also exist and though they are cheaper than austenitic stainless steel due to their low nickel content, they have relatively poor corrosion resistance especially if welded. Hence they are used internally; for example in balustrades, lift fittings and similar applications.

A harder steel is obtained by quenching from about 1000°C, producing martensitic stainless steel. However, although used for cutlery, corrosion resistance and formability are not as good as austenitic steels.

Since stainless steels depend for their protection on a chromium oxide coating, resistance to corrosion will be reduced in oxygen-remote situations, or where there is differential aeration, as, for example, in underground pipes. The effect will be exaggerated in the presence of chlorides or sulphates. The 18–10–3 grade is most resistant to such conditions.

Use of stainless steel. Stainless steel is manufactured mainly in the form of steel plate, sheet and strip (BS 1449; Part IV) or light gauge tubing (BS 4127). The material is now used for a wide variety of pressed fittings, internally and externally; for example, cladding of window sections, toilet and kitchen furniture, flue pipes and roof coverings. Stainless steel tubing for domestic purposes is comparable in price with copper and prices fluctuate less than those of the latter. Although work hardening makes bending rather more difficult, stainless steel tubes have much greater bursting pressures than copper, such that when compression fittings are used, freezing of the tube will tend to cause sliding at the joints rather than bursting of the tubes. This obviates the need for pipe replacement, though it may result in the emission of a full bore of water on complete failure of a joint. When soldering tubing, the use of chloride-based fluxes is not recommended, since they cause corrosion of the tubing, especially if jointing is completed some time before the system is brought into use or flushed out. Special fluxes such as those based on phosphoric acid should be used.

CAST IRON

Carbon dissolves to the extent of 1·7 per cent in austenite and cast iron may be conveniently defined as a carbon/iron alloy containing carbon in excess of this percentage. It will be recalled that the compound cementite contains 6·67 per cent carbon, so that cast irons containing up to this percentage of carbon might be expected to exist in the form of gamma iron plus cementite above 723°C and pearlite plus cementite below 723°C. This may be the case, but carbon in the form of graphite may also occur in the metal due to decomposition of cementite. This will result in much reduced strength owing to the flakey nature of graphite. There are several forms of cast iron depending on the condition of the carbon in the metal but they are all eminently castable (hence the name) and, as a result of their high carbon content, have a melting point as low as 1130°C—much lower than that of steel. In fact, the solid/liquid portion of the iron–carbon equilibrium diagram is of eutectic form, 1130°C being the eutectic temperature obtained with 4·3 per cent carbon. The following are the chief forms of cast iron:

Grey cast iron (BS 1452)

This is graphitic and therefore not as strong as other forms, having a tensile strength of about 200 N/mm^2. The presence of flakes of graphite also gives rise to stress concentrations and brittleness. However, in the thicknesses cast, corrosion is not normally a problem and grey cast iron has been extensively used for boiler castings, radiators, pipes, baths and gutters. Its use for external rainwater systems is diminishing as a result of developments in plastics, but it remains the only material for the purpose which has been proved to have first-class durability over the course of many years. BS 1452 describes various grades of grey cast iron in the form of pipes and fittings, cast either in sand moulds or centrifugally cast. The latter process produces a stronger, harder product.

Spheroidal cast iron (BS 2789)

In this type of iron, the flake graphite in the molten iron is made to crystallise into spheres by addition of silicon and magnesium. Hence, the stress concentrations are removed and a more ductile material is produced. By annealing after casting, the cementite can be made to decompose resulting in a ferritic structure with even greater ductility. BS 4772 describes ductile iron pipes containing carbon in the spheroidal state which are likely to have wide use in underground applications. Casting methods are as for grey pipes but tensile strengths are much improved, being not less than 420 N/mm^2.

White cast iron

This contains carbon in the form of cementite and may be produced by rapid cooling of a casting or by the effect of sulphur which tends to stabilise cementite. White cast iron is intensely hard and brittle, but where greater toughness is required, castings can be rendered malleable by heat treatment which causes decomposition of cementite and formation of a ferritic structure.

NON-FERROUS METALS

Aluminium

It is seldom appreciated that aluminium, in the form of Al_2O_3, is the most common metallic element in the earth's crust, being present, for example, in most types of rock and clay. It is unfortunate that extraction of aluminium is expensive and is not normally economical in the case of rocks and clays. Bauxite, $Al_2O_3.2H_2O$, is the chief mineral used for extraction of aluminium. Extraction of the metal is not possible by means of reducing agents such as carbon used for steel; an electrolytic method is used after conversion of the bauxite to aluminium hydroxide. Hence, aluminium is expensive due to the cost of extraction rather than to any lack of abundance.

The widespread use of a reactive metal such as aluminium stems directly from the fact that a coherent, impervious oxide film forms on the surface of the metal immediately on exposure to air. The oxide coating conducts positive aluminium ions but not electrons (hence, its action as a rectifier), so that, once a certain thickness is reached, the resistance of the corrosion film will prevent further corrosion. If increased protection to corrosion is required, anodising may be carried out. This involves immersion of aluminium in chromic, oxalic or sulphuric acid solutions and inducing corrosion electrolytically using a direct current source of about 50 V with the aluminium as the anode and a steel cathode. The oxide film forms as in normal corrosion but in a more uniform and greater thickness due to the increased voltage. The films obtained using some acids are initially porous so that dyes can be used producing a coloured finish and the surface then sealed. Film thickness may vary between 35 μm, suitable for aggressive environments, and 1 μm, which must be painted. Aluminium oxide films are very vulnerable in the presence of certain ions, notably OH^- ions, as occur in caustic environments. For example, anodised aluminium is corroded by fresh or damp cement paste with production of hydrogen, hence it should not be used in contact with damp concrete, indeed, the same reaction is used for generation of hydrogen during production of 'aerated' concretes. BS 1615 (1961) describes a number of tests relating to physical and chemical properties of anodic coatings on aluminium. In general, aluminium should not be allowed to come into contact with damp brickwork, plaster, timber or soil. The unprotected metal also corrodes in the presence of chloride ions, as occur in sea water. Coatings of bitumen will be effective in such circumstances. Paints containing copper, mercury, lead or graphite may be harmful and should be avoided; resin-based primers containing chromates and iron oxide may be used. Magnesium oxychloride, as used in flooring should not contact aluminium as it will also cause corrosion.

Pure aluminium, though not of high strength, is very suitable for weatherings and foils. A common use is, for example, as a lining for plasterboard, since it has low emissivity and very high vapour resistivity. A further useful property of aluminium is its high electrical conductivity. This property, combined with its light weight makes it preferable to copper for transmission wires in spite of the higher electrical conductivity of the latter. Most aluminium, however, is manufactured in alloy form.

Aluminium alloys (BS 1470; 1969). There is a very wide range of alloys which may have enhanced strength or corrosion resistance. Alloys containing magnesium are, like the pure metal, corrosion resistant and, since magnesium is of similar atomic size to aluminium (they are adjacent in the periodic table), it will dissolve to a limit of about 5 per cent in aluminium at room temperature. The single phase alloy so formed therefore has considerable ductility which, combined with its corrosion resistance, makes it suitable for pressed components of moderate strength; for example, corrugated roofing or where superior corrosion resistance is essential. However, since pure magnesium alloys are single phase, they do not benefit from heat treatment. Incorporation of silica, magnesium and manganese produces alloys which can be

Table 4.11

Properties and uses of some aluminium products

| Alloy | Essential alloying elements (per cent maximum) | | | | $0 \cdot 2$ per cent proof stress | Application |
	Mn	Si	Mg	Cu	N/mm^2	
NSIB–H4	—	—	—	—	—	Flashings, weatherings, can be hand formed
	(Al content 99·5 per cent min.)					
NS3–H4	1·25	—	—	—	—	Roofing, general applications. good durability
HE9–TF	—	0·375	0·625	—	130	Extrusions for window frames
HE30–TF	0·5	1·0	0·625	—	240	Structural sections

welded and extruded and yet have 0·2 per cent proof strengths of up to 300 N/mm^2 on heat treatment (cf. grade 43 A steel, maximum permissible stress— 165 N/mm^2). The extrudability of such alloys makes them ideal for relatively complex extruded sections such as complete window frames.

The presence of silicon or copper in aluminium increases its strength by the process of precipitation or age-hardening. At high temperatures, these elements dissolve to the extent of several per cent in aluminium. However, on cooling, the solubility decreases so that metal crystals tend to precipitate at grain boundaries. If aluminium is cooled quickly, there will be insufficient time for precipitation and a super-saturated (solid) solution of silicon or copper in aluminium is obtained. The 'impurities' will then diffuse within the aluminium lattice to form clusters which oppose dislocation movement, strengthening and hardening the metal. Diffusion may be accelerated by heating to say 200°C but overheating will result in a separate metallic phase at grain boundaries where its benefit will be lost. These treatments are known as solution and precipitation treatments respectively. Alloys containing copper should be protected if used externally. Protection may be in the form of sprayed pure aluminium, or, for aluminium alloy sheets, pure aluminium cladding.

A large range of alloys exists, being described in BS 1470–1475 and a complete explanation of the letter code is not possible here but Table 4.11 shows the codes, chief properties and applications of some alloy products used in building. The prefix 'N' refers to metals which do not benefit from heat treatment, though strength and ductility still depend on temper, '0' being annealed and 'H1' to 'H8' indicating the degree of strain hardening. The prefix 'H' denotes a heat treatable alloy. 'S' stands for sheet and 'E' for extrusions. The number in each code relates to the alloy composition. The letters 'TF' imply that the alloy has been solution heat treated and precipitation treated. Aluminium is also available in cast form, denoted 'LM', being used in components such as door handles and ornamental work.

Structural use of aluminium. The chief advantage of aluminium lies in its low density compared to that of steel; densities are in the approximate ratio 3 : 1, steel : aluminium. Some of this advantage is, of course, lost owing to the reduced stiffness of the latter but even so, an aluminium structure is not likely to be more than half the weight of its equivalent in steel. A further advantage is that, in mild, non-polluted atmospheres, aluminium may be left unpainted. The embrittlement which occurs in steels on cooling is also absent in aluminium owing to the FCC structure, although, at temperatures above 150°C, loss of strength is rapid and aluminium alloys melt at about 600°C. Temperature movement of aluminium is almost double that of steel, though its modulus of elasticity is only about one-third, so that, although allowances for expansion are necessary, temperature stresses in a restrained member will be only about two-thirds of those in a similarly restrained steel member. The low elastic modulus of aluminium is a disadvantage with respect to lateral stability in compression members; this should be carefully checked during design.

Aluminium alloy sections for structural use are normally extruded rather than rolled, and since this process is more versatile than rolling a large number of sections is available, so that, provided care is taken to select the best section for a given purpose, there is some compensation for the extra cost of aluminium compared to steel, which is only available in standard sections. Design codes are therefore inevitably different to those of steel and this is perhaps one of the reasons why the structural use of aluminium is not more widespread.

Welding of aluminium has, in the past, presented problems partly due to the oxide film which must, of course, be removed before joining components. This may be achieved by electric arc welding in an inert gas such as argon which excludes oxygen. Porosity in welds also reduces strength and 'joint efficiency' factors are used when designing welded connections. Alloys, if welded in the 'TF' condition, will revert to the 'TB' condition (that is, solution-treated only) though the original properties can be restored by heat treatment. Tempered metals, for example NS 1B–H4, will revert to the annealed '0' condition in welded zones.

Lead

The excellent durability and ease of working lead are responsible for the former widespread use of the metal in weatherings, flashings and pipes. Its use in these situations is now declining since the material, as formerly used, is expensive and the lower ductility of other metals is no disadvantage for components which are formed by machine. Lead occurs naturally in the form of galena (lead sulphide) which is imported from the U.S.A., Australia or Canada. The metal is extracted by conversion of lead sulphide to lead oxide which is then reduced, by carbon, to the metal.

Lead is the densest common metal, having a specific gravity of 11·34. It also has a low melting point, equal to $327°C$ and high thermal movement—$29·5 \times 10^{-6}/°C$. The strength of the metal is low, ultimate strengths ranging from about 20 N/mm^2 for impure leads to 11 N/mm^2 for very pure lead.

On exposure to the atmosphere, lead forms a protective coating of lead carbonate which is innocuous and does not stain adjacent brickwork or stonework. Although lead is by no means the most reactive of metals used in building, it may undergo electrolytic corrosion with metals such as copper if, in damp conditions, the metals touch. However, corrosion will only be serious where relatively large areas are in contact and lead coverings may be secured by copper nails due to the small area of the latter and protection afforded by the corrosion product. (Galvanised or steel nails are not suitable for use with lead, since they may corrode rapidly as a result of the relatively reactive nature of zinc or steel and the small anodic area provided by the nails.) Lead is also attacked by some types of organic acid—notably acetic acid, which forms the basis of vinegar—and is not highly suitable for domestic waste systems in soft water areas. Moisture which has been in contact with peat, oak or teak and, to some extent, pitch pine, may also have a corrosive effect. Lead components are best protected by bitumen-impregnated tape in such situations.

Uses of lead

Lead pipes (BS 602 and 1085). As would be expected with a metal fairly near its melting point, lead creeps above a certain stress. BS 602 and 1085 (1965) recommend minimum pipe thicknesses for water service and distributing pipes. BS 602 describes pure lead pipes while BS 1085 relates to silver copper lead which contains 0·003–0·005 per cent of silver and copper. Such material has greater tensile strength and creep resistance so that it can be used with slightly reduced wall thicknesses for a given water pressure. Waste pipes and gas pipes which are not subject to hydrostatic pressure are normally thinner than water service pipes. The working properties of lead pipes depend on the grain size distribution, the grains being visible if a section of a pipe is polished and etched. The above British Standards give qualitative requirements for the size and uniformity of grain structure in lead pipes, to obtain a suitable balance between creep resistance (improved by coarse grain structure) and tensile strength to resist pressure 'surges' (improved by fine grain structure).

Extruded lead pipes and meter connections for gas supplies are still widely used due to their corrosion resistance and ductility, though their use for water service pipes is decreasing due to cost, competition from plastics and possibility of contamination of water. Pure or soft waters tend to dissolve lead, since they contain carbon dioxide which combines with the metal to form a soluble form of lead carbonate. In hard water containing calcium carbonate, a lead carbonate film forms on pipes preventing dissolution of the metal. Local authorities normally restrict the lead content of mains water to 0·1 parts per million and soft water may require treatment to keep lead contamination to this limit.

Owing to their flexibility, water-filled lead pipes will withstand freezing several times, though, on the same account, the infill around underground lead pipes may, over a period of time, cause leaks due to abrasion. Lumps of brick or concrete should not be used in infill materials.

Lead sheet and strip (BS 1178). Lead sheeting for roofing purposes has, to some extent, been replaced by other materials but, even so, there are many modern examples of lead roofing, cladding and fascias which combine great durability with aesthetically pleasing effect, particularly in 'prestige' building. When used in such large areas, joints must be provided to allow for thermal expansion. The maximum dimension in any direction should not exceed 3 m, sheet normally being used in strips about 1 m wide. BS 1178 gives code numbers from 3 to 8 corresponding to thickness between 1·25 and 3·55 mm, together with a colour code; thicker sheets should be used where dressing is required or if mechanical damage, for example, due to foot traffic, is likely. The admirable working properties of lead sheet are, in part, due to the fact that, at room temperature, lead is above its recrystallisation temperature, hence it does not work harden.

Lead strip is still widely used for damp proof courses since it has unsurpassed damp proofing qualities. It should be protected from contamination by cement mortar by coating both sides with a bituminous paint. Lead-cored bituminous felts overcome this problem.

Lead solders (BS 219). These normally consist of a proportion of tin and lead, possibly with a small percentage of antimony. Tin–lead alloys produce the type of phase diagram shown in Fig. 4.16, the melting points being:

327°C—pure lead
232°C—pure tin
183°C—eutectic composition consisting of 37 per cent lead and 63 per cent tin

When a low melting point is required, as for spigot-type joints on lead pipes, the eutectic composition may be used, though this solder is expensive due to its high tin content. Solders for general uses are about 60 : 40, lead : tin, combining relative cheapness with a reasonably low melting point. Solders for wiping joints in lead pipes are about 70 : 30, lead : tin, in order to give a long plastic stage.

COPPER

The element occurs naturally in the form of ores containing copper, iron and sulphur. Since the metal is almost indestructible, a good deal is also recovered as scrap and reprocessed. Some impurities are removed by flotation and then by oxidation in a converter. The metal is then refined either by furnace or electrolytically according to use, the latter producing the purest metal.

Copper is the noblest of metals commonly used in building—it behaves as a cathode to the others with the exception of stainless steel, hence it will be protected by almost any metal it touches, at the expense of the other metal. It forms an attractive green patina of the basic sulphate on exposure to a damp atmosphere, though, unless attention is given to detailing, washings from it may stain adjacent materials. Copper is resistant to most common acids and to sea water (but see below under 'copper tube').

The tensile strength of copper depends on its purity, being about 200 N/mm^2 for the pure metal. Its main applications result either from its ductility or its very high electrical and thermal conductivities, the latter being 385 W/m°C, the highest of any building material. Pure copper has a melting point of 1083°C so that creep is not a problem at normal temperatures.

Uses

Copper tube (BS 2871). Copper is the most commonly used material for central heating and domestic water tubing owing to its lightness and admirable working properties. In the hard drawn form, it can be used with wall thicknesses as low as 0·5 mm and is therefore cheap, though tube in this form will break if bending is attempted; fittings must be used where bends are required. This type of tube is covered by BS 2871 Part I, Table Z. The same standard also specifies Table X tube which is slightly thicker and not work hardened to the same degree, so that bends can be obtained. Table Y tube is available in half hard or annealed forms which have thicker walls, and may be used for forming tighter bends than Table X tube, or for underground service pipes. Copper tubing for water supplies has generally very high corrosion resistance though it has been known to undergo corrosion in some acidic waters such as those obtained from peaty catchment areas, or containing carbonic acid. Such water should be treated with sufficient lime to neutralise acidity without causing pipe scaling. Dirt or impurities in pipes may cause electrolytic corrosion so that cleanliness during installation is essential, especially in soft water areas. It is advisable to protect copper tubes chased into gypsum plasters with a coating of bitumen, particularly if damp conditions are prevalent.

Copper tube is also used in waste and soil systems, pipes over 50 mm diameter normally being bronze welded or silver soldered. Copper fittings may be used with copper tubing, capillary end-feed or solder ring type fittings producing cheap, unobtrusive joints. They are also used with stainless steel tube in the absence, at the present, of any similar product made in stainless steel.

Copper sheeting (BS 2870). This is used for a variety of purposes in building: in damp proof courses, for weatherings and flashings and as a roofing or cladding material. A number of forms are available, having been work hardened to various degrees. Annealed copper is essential for roofing, since manipulation is necessary, but where sheet is to some degree self-supporting, a half-hardened temper should be used. Copper sheeting should be fixed with copper nails since other metals would be prone to rapid electrolytic corrosion. Welding is most easily carried out on deoxidised copper which contains a small percentage of phosphorous; the small amount of cuprous oxide which occurs in non-deoxidised ('tough pitch') sheet tends to react with hydrogen in the flux or gas, causing unsoundness due to steam formation. The presence of arsenic in copper increases its strength at 200°C and above and also improves corrosion resistance. Copper may be alloyed so that it benefits from solution treatment and precipitation hardening where higher-strength sheet is required.

Copper alloys

Brasses. Zinc has an atomic radius similar to that of copper and dissolves to form a single FCC phase alloy in contents up to 36 per cent. The brasses obtained are known as alpha brasses; they are ductile and have high tensile strength, particularly if the zinc content approaches the solubility limit or if work hardened. Since, during the process of work hardening, most distortion takes place at grain boundaries, these may corrode electrolytically with the grain body, leading to 'season cracking' unless stresses are relieved by annealing. Alpha brasses are used for pressing (such as in door furniture), stamping or drawing.

Alpha–beta brasses contain 36–46 per cent zinc, the beta phase (BCC) increasing as percentages approach the upper figure. They are less ductile than alpha brasses but are suitable for high temperature extrusion, rolling or casting. They are used in window sections, often having a bronze colour due to incorporation of a small percentage of manganese. Alpha–beta brasses are used for plumbing fittings, screws and general brass mongery.

Beta brasses contain more than 46 per cent zinc, though brasses containing more than 50 per cent zinc are not used. These brasses have melting points lower than 900°C compared to 1083°C for pure copper and are used for brazing.

Copper and copper alloy tube fittings (BS 864: Part II). These are classified as capillary fittings, non-manipulative fittings (type A), which use compression rings, and manipulative fittings (type B) in which the tube at or near the end is formed into a flange which is compressed on to the fitting. Copper capillary fittings are described under uses of copper, though capillary fittings are also obtainable in brass. Joints are perhaps more conveniently made using compression fittings, though they are rather more obtrusive. 'Pull out' of type A fittings is more likely than in type B fittings and for this reason their use is not permitted underground. If, on the other hand, type B fittings are to be used with stainless steel tube, the latter should be cut with a fine tooth-ed saw rather than a tube cutter, to avoid work hardening of the ends and possible splitting as a result.

Dezincification of brass. Brass is an alloy of zinc which is at the reactive end of the electrochemical series and copper which is at the noble end. It is not surprising, therefore that under certain conditions the zinc may corrode electrolytically with the copper. This will result possibly in blockage of hot water fittings by the corrosion product; leakage or even breakage. The brasses worst affected by dezincification are those with relatively high zinc content, for example, duplex (alpha–beta) brasses, containing about 40 per cent zinc, which are suitable for hot stamping of plumbing fittings (BS 218). In theory, any brass containing 15 per cent or more of zinc may corrode in this way but attack in alpha brasses may be prevented by incorporation of small quantities of arsenic. BS 885–*Brass tubes for general purposes*–describes such brasses.

The severity of dezincification depends on the properties of the water, attack being most likely when the pH value is over 8 (that is, alkaline) or when chlorides are present. The presence of temporary hardness in the latter case tends to reduce attack. The reaction rate increases with temperature so that hot water fittings are most commonly affected. Where such conditions are encountered, an alternative material such as copper, gunmetal (a bronze containing about 2 per cent zinc) or a protected alpha brass, should be used. Note, however, that, since oxygen is involved in the corrosion process, brass fittings in recirculatory systems such as central heating circuits, are largely immune from dezincification.

Bronze

This is an alloy of copper and tin. Most bronzes have a tin content slightly over its solubility limit of about 6 per cent so that they are generally harder and stronger than brasses. They have great durability so that they are used for sculpture and ornamental work and in place of brass where corrosion resistance is essential.

Zinc

The element occurs in the form of zinc sulphide (zinc blende), extraction being carried out by concentration of the ore using a flotation process, conversion to zinc oxide and then reduction, using carbon, to the metal.

The metal has a low melting point (419°C) and high thermal movement–up to $40 \times 10^{-6}/°C$ in sheet form, the actual value depending on the direction of rolling, since the HCP crystal structure is non-isotropic.

The tensile strength of pure zinc is low but it may be increased by hot working or alloying, though the ductility of zinc is, owing to its HCP structure, less than that of copper, lead and aluminium. Cold weather or severe working may make it necessary to warm the metal. It is, however, self-annealing since, at room temperature, it is above its recrystallisation temperature.

Many uses of zinc are based on the fact that it forms a coherent protective coating of zinc oxide or zinc carbonate on exposure to the atmosphere, though polluted or marine atmospheres increase the corrosion rate. Nevertheless, zinc is claimed to have good durability in most environments and rolled zinc sheeting has been used for roofing, weatherings and rainwater goods. The metal forms an impervious corrosion product when in contact with cement but will be corroded by the acids which occur in timbers such as western red cedar or oak. Creep will occur above certain stresses, though resistance can be improved by alloying with metals such as titanium and copper.

The most important use of zinc results from its position in the electrochemical series (Table 4.3). A coating of the metal will protect any metal below it in the series, even if scratched, though durability of the product naturally depends on the thickness of zinc and the aggressiveness of the environment. However, zinc or zinc coatings should not be allowed to contact copper or other more noble metals which would greatly accelerate corrosion. As well as in the processes described under 'electrolytic corrosion', zinc is often used in metallic or in zinc chromate form in anti-corrosive paints, though such paints, being porous, should be regarded as primers.

The low melting point of zinc is advantageous in the above applications but particularly so for die casting in which, when alloyed with aluminium and magnesium, a wide variety of hardware components and fittings is produced.

Problems

4.1. Examine Table 4.1 and give three properties of metals which appear to be characteristic of their crystalline groups.

4.2. Draw a (321) plane and then increase its size by tripling intercepts on the cubic axes. Why is this plane important in the deformation of iron? What are the other important planes and what features do they have in common?

4.3. Draw on orthogonal axes two close packed planes in a face-centred cubic lattice, indicating their Miller indices. Indicate also a close packed direction in each plane.

4.4. Find by drawing how many non-parallel planes there are in the {110} family. In which crystal lattice are these close packed planes?

4.5. Discuss with examples the roles played by point, line and surface imperfections on the deformation properties of metals.

4.6. Explain what is meant by a metal grain; discuss the effects of grain size on the properties of metals and describe procedures by which it may be controlled.

4.7. Explain briefly the conditions in which corrosion of steel is likely to occur. Describe three alternative methods of protection, giving situations in which each is used.

4.8. Calculate the factors of safety based on minimum yield point stresses for grades 43 C, 50 C and 55 C of steels in the form of I beams (Table 4.6) less than 16 mm thick, taking the maximum permissible stresses as given in Table 4.8.

4.9. Compare the requirements for reinforcing and prestressing steels with respect to:
   (a)   strength,
   (b)   geometric properties of bars and wires,
   (c)   ductility,
   (d)   weldability;
   and explain how these are governed by the composition and manufacturing processes.

4.10. Write an account on stainless steels, giving properties and uses of the various grades.

4.11. Contrast the properties of aluminium alloys and steel under the headings:
   (a)   general mechanical properties,
   (b)   protection, durability,
   (c)   high temperatures,
   (d)   low temperatures.

4.12. Compare the properties of lead and copper and contrast their uses in:
   (a)   roofing;
   (b)   water service pipes.

References

1. A. H. Cotrell, *Introduction to Metallurgy,* Arnold, 1968.
2. J. B. Moss. *Properties of Engineering Materials,* Butterworths, 1972.
3. F. W. Bailey, *Fundamentals of Engineering Metallurgy,* Cassell, 1961.
4. U. R. Evans, *The Corrosion and Oxidation of Metals,* Arnold, 1961.
5. J. C. Scully, *Fundamentals of Corrosion,* Pergamon, 1966.
6. L. P. Bowen, *Structural Design in Aluminium,* Hutchinson, 1966.

7. *Design Engineering Handbook: Metals,* Product Journals Ltd, 1968.
8. H. J. Sharp (Ed.). *Engineering Materials,* Heywood, 1966.
Additional information may be obtained from Metal Development Associations. See also general references.

Relevant British Standards

BS 4; Part I: 1962. *Hot rolled steel sections.*
BS 18: *Methods of tensile testing of metals.*
BS 219: 1959. *Soft solders.*
BS 449: Part II: 1969. *Use of Structural Steel in building.*
BS 864: Part II: 1971. *Capillary and compression fittings of copper and copper alloy.*
BS 885: 1963. *Brass tubes for general purposes.*
BS 602 & 1085: 1970. *Lead and alloy pipes for other than chemical purposes.*
BS 1178: 1969. *Milled lead sheet and strip for building purposes.*
BS 1449: *Steel plate and strip.*
BS 1452: 1961. *Grey iron castings.*
BS 1470-1475: 1969. *Wrought aluminium and aluminium alloy products.*
BS 1615: 1961. *Anodic oxidation coatings on aluminium.*
BS 2789: 1961. *Iron castings with spheroidal or nodular graphite.*
BS 2870: 1968. *Rolled copper and copper alloys; sheet strip and foil.*
BS 2871: Part I: 1971. *Copper tubes for water, gas and sanitation.*
BS 2961: *Steel wire for prestressed concrete.*
BS 2994: 1958. *Cold rolled steel sections.*
BS 3617: *Seven strand wire for prestressed concrete.*
BS 4127: 1967. *Light gauge stainless steel tubes.*
BS 4360: Part II: 1969. *Weldable structural steels.*
BS 4449: 1969. *Hot rolled steel bars for the reinforcement of concrete.*
BS 4461: 1969. *Cold worked steel bars for the reinforcement of concrete.*
BS 4462: 1970. *Grey iron pipes and fittings.*
BS 4482: 1969. *Hard drawn mild steel wire for the reinforcement of concrete.*
BS 4483: 1969. *Steel fabric for the reinforcement of concrete.*
BS 4486: 1959. *Cold worked high tensile alloy steel bars for prestressed concrete.*
BS 4757: 1971. *Nineteen wire steel strand for prestressed concrete.*
BS 4772: 1971. *Ductile iron pipes and fittings.*

Chapter 5
ORGANIC MATERIALS

CARBON IN STRUCTURE

The term 'organic' traditionally refers to materials which are or are derived from living tissues; for example, timber, leather and cotton or wool. More recently, the term has come to be used for a wider range of materials which, in common with the above, have properties dependent to a large degree on the presence of carbon in their structure. Plastics, paints, adhesives, mastics and bitumens fall into this larger group.

The 'backbone' of each of these materials is the carbon atom which has two s and two p electrons in its outer shell. These electrons become 'hybridised' (see Chapter 1), giving a valency of four so that carbon is very largely covalent in character—it seeks to gain a stable octet of electrons by sharing with those of other atoms. Elements which often combine with carbon in this way are hydrogen, chlorine and fluorine (valency 1), oxygen (valency 2), nitrogen (valency 3).

Typical products are the *paraffins:*

$$
\begin{array}{cc}
\begin{array}{c}
\text{H} \\
| \\
\text{H—C—H} \\
| \\
\text{H}
\end{array}
&
\begin{array}{c}
\text{H H} \\
| \ | \\
\text{H—C—C—H} \quad \text{etc.} \\
| \ | \\
\text{H H}
\end{array}
\end{array}
$$

methane CH_4 ethane C_2H_6

In ethane, each carbon atom shares one of its electrons with the other carbon.

In a large number of organic materials, carbon atoms share *two* of their electrons with one another, producing a double bond (Fig. 5.1). In this case, there is always the possibility that if extra elements such as oxygen or hydrogen were available, they would share their electrons with such carbon atoms producing a more stable arrangement, since double bonds are not normally as stable as single bonds. For this reason, compounds containing double bonds are said to be *unsaturated*. It will be apparent that the number of compounds that can be formed from the elements listed is enormous—in fact it is unlimited and this accounts for the very wide range of properties and uses that derive from organic materials.

Most constructional applications of organic materials require a solid or semi-solid rather than a liquid form and therefore chemical bonding must be extended in nature. The above compounds are usually liquid at room temperature, which is indicative of the absence of long-range bonding. The mechanism by which the bonding in an organic material is extended is known as polymerisation. 'Monomer' units such as ethylene or styrene are joined together to form a 'polymer' and the resulting structure will be more likely to be solid than the original structure. Unsaturated compounds are ideally suited to polymerisation since they contain double bonds which, if 'opened', could be used to link two molecules together. Repetition of the process produces polymers which may contain many thousands of monomer units. The more units linked, the greater will be the strength and the lower the plasticity of the product. In artificially produced materials, therefore, the process of polymerisation must be controlled to

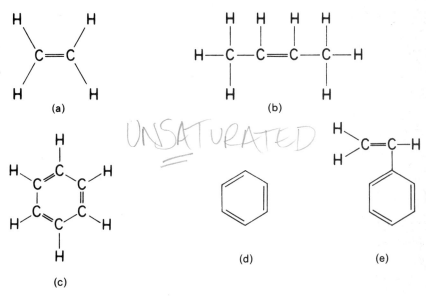

Fig. 5.1 Some examples of unsaturated organic compounds. (a) ethylene, (b) butadiene, (c) benzene (this ring is quite stable even though unsaturated), (d) abbreviated representation of benzene, (e) styrene

obtain the desired balance between strength and flexibility. Mastics, for example, must be flexible while plastics for moulding must be quite rigid. Paints should be in the form of fairly viscous liquids, must harden on exposure to air and still retain sufficient plasticity to withstand movement of the substrate. Having established the differences as well as the similarities between organic materials, it is now necessary to describe them under separate headings.

PLASTIC MATERIALS

The term 'plastic' generally refers to a material which is essentially solid but which can be deformed by applied forces. In this context therefore the term must refer to the formation process rather than to the finished material since most plastics rely on some degree of rigidity for their use and, indeed, many 'plastics' do not return to the truly plastic state even on heating. Plastics are manufactured from monomers obtained from organic substances such as oil or coal. Polymerisation of monomers may be achieved in two ways—by addition or condensation reactions. In the former process, the double

~~double~~ bonded monomer opens and forms a link. The formation of polyethylene (polythene) is the simplest example:

$$\underset{H}{\overset{H}{>}}C=C\underset{H}{\overset{H}{<}} \longrightarrow \left(\begin{array}{c} H\ H \\ -C-C- \\ H\ H \end{array}\right)_n$$

This reaction requires energy at least to start if off and this is provided by the aid of an 'initiator'. Free radical compounds are examples of initiators; they decompose into reactive atoms which cause the initial breakdown of the double bond:

$$I_2 \longrightarrow I- + I-$$

stable initiator molecule   unstable atoms

$$I- + \underset{H}{\overset{H}{>}}C=C\underset{H}{\overset{H}{<}} \longrightarrow I-\underset{H}{\overset{H}{C}}-\underset{H}{\overset{H}{C}}-$$

The product is unstable, since there is an unsatisfied carbon atom. If there is a neighbouring ethylene molecule present, This will therefore link on to the chain, making it larger:

$$I-\underset{H\ H}{\overset{H\ H}{C-C}}- + \underset{H}{\overset{H}{>}}C=C\underset{H}{\overset{H}{<}} \longrightarrow I-\underset{H\ H\ H}{\overset{H\ H\ H}{C-C-C}}-$$

The process will continue very rapidly without further need for the initiator until the free ethylene groups are used up. Termination of the chain may then occur by linking of two chains, by combination of the initiator molecule with the free end of the chain or by other similar reactions in which valency requirements become satisfied. The final polyethylene molecule may have a molecular weight of 50,000 or more depending on the type and amount of initiator and the physical conditions.

Alternatively, addition polymerisation may involve two (or more) basic monomer groups. Products are known as 'co-polymers'. An example is the butadiene styrene polymer shown in Fig. 5.2.

Condensation polymerisation

This is different to addition polymerisation in that a small molecule is produced as a by-product of the polymerisation process, whereas in the addition process there is no rejection of atoms. The molecule is often (though not necessarily) water. A very commonly used reaction is that between urea and formaldehyde (Fig. 5.3). The formaldehyde groups link together the urea groups with rejection of water. Note that

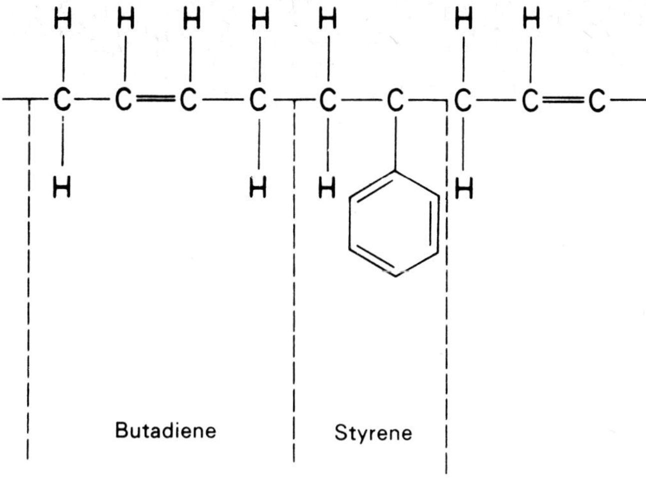

Fig. 5.2 Co-polymer formed from butadiene and styrene. Links are provided when the ethylene-type double bonds of styrene open

in this case there are several 'sites' where the formaldehyde could be added so that the resulting polymer is more likely to be a network than a chain.

Thermoplastic and thermosetting plastics

The two processes described above result in polymers of quite different properties. Addition polymerisation produces a large molecule often in the form of a chain but with few rigid links between adjacent chains. Such polymers will solidify only due to the action of van der Waals forces, and since these forces are relatively weak, will soften readily on heating, producing a viscous liquid or rubbery material. They are therefore known as thermoplastic materials. Urea-formaldehyde which was an example of a polymer produced by condensation polymerisation, is, on the other hand, in the form of a three-dimensional molecular network; in fact, almost all molecules in the structure will be joined by primary bonds resulting in one very large molecule and a rigid

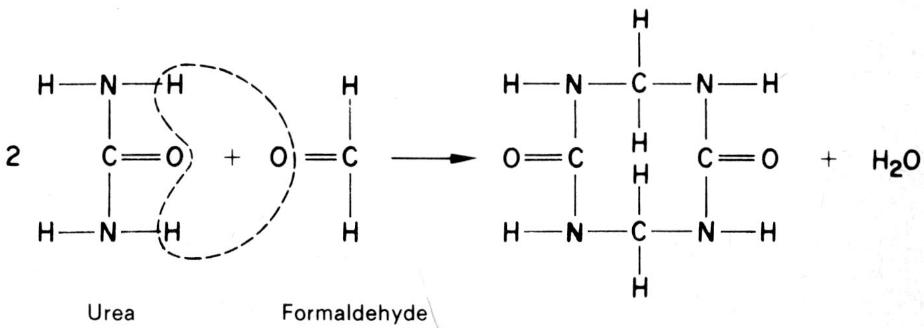

Fig. 5.3 Condensation reaction between urea and formaldehyde. The water molecule is ringed

structure which would not soften on heating. Such polymers are described as thermosetting; if an excess of heat is applied, the bond structure would eventually break down and the plastic would decompose.

Both thermoplastic and thermosetting plastics are valuable, since their properties are conducive to use for different types of product in different situations. Thermoplastics, for example, may be rolled or extruded simply by heating the materials and are used where some flexibility is essential. Their stiffness (modulus of elasticity) is generally low owing to the prevalence of van der Waals bonds which distort readily under stress. Thermosetting plastics are ideal for moulding into components which require rigidity, strength and some resistance to heat.

It would be misleading to suggest that all plastics can be clearly divided into thermoplastic and thermosetting groups. For example, the rigidity (and hence softening point temperature) of some thermoplastics can be increased by cross-linking of molecules. The effect may be produced synthetically, as in vulcanising of rubber using sulphur which increases strength and rigidity to the desired degree. Many thermoplastics harden gradually by cross-linking over a long period of time and may eventually become unfit for their purpose. Thermoplastics may also contain side branches in their chains which, although not necessarily cross-linked to other chains, will affect the packing together of adjacent chains.

A polyethylene chain, for example, should theoretically contain only two methyl groups, one at each end. In practice, it is found that there may be 20 or more groups per 1000 carbon atoms and this must be indicative of some branching (Fig. 5.4).

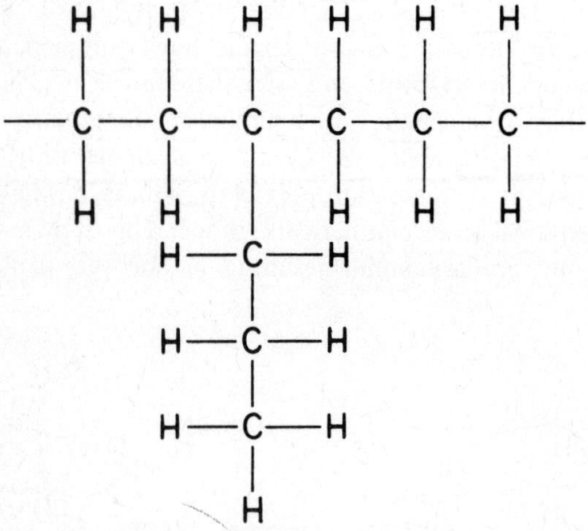

Fig. 5.4 Branching of a polyethylene chain. Each branch ends in a methyl group, CH_3

Branching reduces the closeness of packing of chains, resulting in decreased crystallinity and therefore lower density. Tensile strength and softening temperature are also reduced.

CRYSTALLINITY OF POLYMERS; GLASS TRANSITION TEMPERATURE

Molecular chains may to some extent crystallise as they form, packing together to produce a degree of long-range order in planes at right angles to the chain direction. The amount of crystallisation which can take place depends on the physical conditions but also on the molecular form of the polymer, which is rarely perfect. Long regular chains are most likely to form crystalline solids (Fig. 5.5). Examples are polyethylene

Fig. 5.5 Varying degrees of crystallinity in a branched chain polymer such as polyethylene

and PTFE. However, the majority of plastics are amorphous—that is, the polymer chains are tangled together with little or no order between them. Such types of polymer exhibit marked changes in property on cooling below a certain temperature known as the *glass-transition temperature* (t_g), being rubbery solids when above t_g and brittle glassy solids below their t_g value. When above t_g, they are usually of little structural use, though they can be moulded in this state and are suitable for mastics. Below t_g, plastics are rigid, though plasticisers, which are in fact stable, non-volatile solvents, can be used in some cases to increase ductility effectively lowering t_g. Cross-linking of molecules increases their t_g value until, in highly cross-linked structures such as phenolic resins, t_g is higher than their disintegration temperature. Figure 5.6 shows typical stiffness temperature curves for a crystalline polymer and an amorphous polymer. Note that the effect of the glass transition on crystalline polymers is much less marked than that on amorphous polymers.

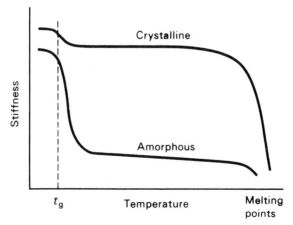

Fig. 5.6 Schematic form of stiffness–temperature graph for crystalline and amorphous polymers

Amorphous materials are often transparent, and plastics are no exception—most plastics are amorphous and can therefore be obtained in transparent forms, though fillers would obviously destroy this property.

THERMOPLASTIC MATERIALS

Polyethylene (polythene) $(C_2H_4)_n$

This has the simplest chemical structure of any polymer (see p. 180) and is also one of the cheapest and most widely used plastics. The plastic is manufactured in two basic forms; by a high-pressure process which produces a low-density polyethylene (specific gravity 0·92) of softening temperature 86°C, and a low-pressure process which results in a higher-density polymer (specific gravity 0·96) of softening temperature 120–130°C. The chief use of polyethylene is in sheeting for damp-proof membranes, vapour barriers and temporary shelters, though, on account of its crystallinity, optical properties are not as good as those of, for example, clear pvc sheeting. Further uses include tubes, down pipes and cisterns, though allowance must be made for thermal movement, the coefficient of linear expansion of low-density polythene is approximately $160 \times 10^{-6}/°C$, one of the highest values of any solid material and approximately thirteen times that of steel. The plastic is prone to degradation and embrittlement by sunlight due to cross-linking but performance can be improved by incorporation of black pigments such as carbon black in the plastic which absorbs rays and prevents damage. Underground, polythene is not so affected and has excellent resistance to salts and bacteria, though thicknesses of sheet used in damp-proof membranes should be such as to avoid damage by abrasion. Polythenes, particularly the low-density type, have a high permeability to gases so that they are not considered suitable for gas pipes. Low-density polythene is suitable for cold water pipes but is less rigid than high-density polythene and begins to soften at temperatures above about 75°C so that it cannot be used for hot water. The impact resistance of polythene at ordinary or low temperatures is excellent, as is chemical resistance—polythene is not attacked by concentrated acids or alkalis. Polythene surfaces have a rather greasy touch and do not form a good base for paints unless roughened. The material is also unaffected by most organic solvents, though this means that it cannot be solvent welded. Joining can be carried out by fusion welding but not by epoxy resins unless the surface is first treated. Electrical insulation properties of polyethylene are excellent and it is used for insulation of coaxial cables such as television aerial leads.

Polypropylene

This has the formula $(CH_2–CH.CH_3)_n$. It has properties similar to those of polythene except that its rigidity and softening temperature are higher. It is used for rigid units such as manhole mouldings and waste systems and may be a possibility for hot water pipes and cylinders. If drawn, it produces a fibre of fairly high strength and flexibility, used in some types of fibre reinforcement and for general purpose string. Although partially crystalline, a transition occurs at approximately 0°C so that brittleness is a problem below this temperature. Polythene and polypropylene are the only common plastics which are less dense than water.

Polyvinyl chloride (PVC) $(CH_3Cl)_n$

PVC is the cheapest and most widely used plastic in the building industry. It is different from polyethylene in that one in four hydrogen atoms is replaced by a chlorine atom:

$$
\begin{array}{cc}
H & H \\
| & | \\
-C- & C- \\
| & | \\
H & Cl
\end{array}
$$

this leads to greater rigidity than polythene though PVC may be plasticised, being used then for flooring, sheet products and flexible coatings. Unplasticised PVC is the most commonly used plastic for rainwater goods, being easily extruded and moulded to the desired shapes and fittings. Cutting and assembly is also easy and rapid. However, it is important that adequate support be given, since the plastic is prone to distortion. Thermal movement is high; for example, a 10-m length of gutter between $0°C$ and $30°C$ will move approximately 15 mm. Sliding expansion joints must therefore be provided. These may be in the form of rubber gaskets or 'O' ring joints. When rigid joints are acceptable, they are easily and cheaply obtained by solvent welding. The two units are joined by a collar and the joint is made by solution and resolidification of surface layers in contact. PVC waste systems are commonly employed, though if the effluent is at a high temperature (as may occur, for example, with automatic washing machines), pipes may soften and distort, especially where a full bore of water is discharged, since the glass-transition temperature (or softening point) is only $80°C$. A post-chlorinated form of PVC has been developed having a softening point of $120°C$ and this may find application in such situations; otherwise, the use of other materials in these situations is preferable. The impact strength of PVC is adversely affected by reduction in temperature such that brittle failure may occur under impact in cold weather. The properties of PVC can in fact be varied widely by use of plasticisers, fillers, stabilisers and other materials, and tests are often necessary to ascertain suitability for a given purpose. PVC is available in a transparent form for roof-lights or corrugated roofing, though light transmission properties and resistance to impact invariably deteriorate with time.

Polyvinyl fluoride (PVF)

This material, characteristic of fluorine-containing polymers, has much better weathering resistance than PVC, hence it forms a very suitable plastic coating for metals. Early problems arising due to the low frictional coefficient and consequent poor bonding properties have now been overcome.

Polytetrafluoroethylene (PTFE) $(C_2F_4)_n$

The fluorine atom is larger than the hydrogen atom so that the chain must twist in order to accommodate them. The resulting polymer has high crystallinity and is therefore very stable, having a high melting point relative to other plastics (300°C). The smooth molecular profile also results in a very low coefficient of frictional resistance, less than that of wet ice upon wet ice, and this forms the basis of most applications of PTFE. The plastic is used, for example, to line pipes which carry solid materials; for bridge bearings and for coating cooking utensils. It is also available in tape form for sealing threaded joints in water or gas pipes. The material is expensive on a volume basis so that its chief applications are as a coating material.

Styrene-based polymers

Styrene consists of a simple combination of ethylene and benzene in which the double bond structure of the former is retained (Fig. 5.1 (e)). This is responsible for its willingness to polymerise. The chief polymers based on styrene are polystyrene and acrylonitrile butadiene styrene which are both thermoplastic.

Polystyrene. Polystyrene has the same structure as polyethylene except that every fourth hydrogen atom is replaced by a benzene ring. It may be produced simply by heating the monomer without need for initiators. Polystyrene is quite cheap, has good formability and reasonable chemical resistance. Softening temperature depends on grade, varying from 75 to 100°C. Polystyrene is an amorphous plastic and at room temperature is below its glass-transition temperature so that it is hard and brittle. The rigidity of the plastic forms the basis of many uses; for example, in containers, for packaging and as lining material in refrigerators.

A large amount of the polymer is produced in the form of expanded polystyrene which has one of the lowest thermal conductivities obtainable—approximately 0·033 W/m°C. The polymer in the form of small beads is heated such that great expansion occurs. The beads are then softened by steam and pressurised so that they stick together. Expanded polystyrene is widely used as an insulating material for general household purposes, in rolls for application to wall surfaces, in floor and roof insulation, as a preformed cavity infill and for ceiling tiles. The plastic burns readily, however, and may therefore constitute a fire hazard. This can be reduced if ceiling tiles are continuously fixed to the ceiling instead of using 'dabs' of adhesive which would allow the softening material to hang down in the case of fire. Fire-resistant grades or treatments are also available. Expanded polystyrene in sufficient thickness may have vapour-resistive qualities but it is not as effective as foil or polythene vapour barriers. Further important applications of the foam include use as a preformed insulant for cavity walls and as a void former in structural concrete.

Acrylonitrile butadiene styrene (ABS). A large range of variants may be produced under the name 'ABS' but their main applications are based on high impact strength at normal and low temperatures and good surface appearance. They are more expensive than common plastics but have nevertheless found application in window fasteners, rainwater goods and moulded articles such as telephones. They have a higher softening temperature than PVC and are therefore more suitable for domestic waste systems.

Acrylic plastics. These are based on acrylic acid, $CH_2=CH.COOH$ (note the ethylene group). The commonest acrylic polymer is polymethyl methacrylate

$$(-CH_2 - \overset{\overset{\displaystyle CH_3}{|}}{\underset{\underset{\displaystyle COOCH_3}{|}}{C}} -)_n$$

commonly known as Perspex. The monomer polymerises readily by application of heat so that acrylic sheet is formed simply by pouring into a mould a partly polymerised syrup and then warming. The polymer is amorphous and below its glass transition temperature at room temperature so that it is a hard, rigid, transparent material. Very good surface finishes can be obtained with good weathering properties. The plastic is used for diffusion of light as in illuminated ceilings and signs. Baths are now made out of the polymer, being cheaper and easier to install, though of inferior durability and stability to the traditional material, cast iron. Scratches may be polished out but the plastic is susceptible to burns and to some organic solvents. Some types of paint include acrylic resins.

Nylons

The chemical name for this polymer is 'polyamide', a derivative of organic nitrogen-containing acids. There are hence two parts to the monomer—the nitrogen or amino section and the acid section, and nylons are often referred to by the number of carbon atoms in each; for example, nylon 66. Most nylons are chain polymers, hence they are thermoplastic and since there is a degree of polarity in bonding (ionic bonding), there is considerable chain attraction and crystallinity. This leads to a low coefficient of friction and a fairly high melting point (260°C for nylon 66) with a maximum service temperature of 170°C. Nylons are resistant to many organic solvents, alkalis and dilute acids but tend to become brittle by the action of sunlight. Products may be moulded, extruded or drawn. Examples of moulded products are catches; extruded products, microbore central heating tubes; drawn products, nylon ropes. The ease of cutting nylon central heating tubes makes installation very simple, though thermal movement should be allowed for and sharp objects could cause damage in service.

Polycarbonates

These are obtained by reactions of polyhydroxy compounds with carbonic acid derivatives. The polymer has excellent transparency and is tough and rigid up to temperatures of over 100°C. Weathering resistance is good and sheets of the polymer are used as a glazing material of high-impact resistance.

THERMOSETTING PLASTICS

Phenolic resins

Phenol-formaldehyde was one of the earliest synthetic resins to be produced, being given the name Bakelite. The chemical formula of phenol is C_6H_5OH and polymerisation occurs on reaction with formaldehyde (HCHO) to give a condensation product which is extensively cross-linked and therefore hard, brittle and heat resistant.

Being thermosetting, extrusion cannot be carried out. Products are manufactured from low-molecular-weight resins which are normally ground to a powder, mixed with a filler, hardener and other ingredients, compounded by heat or solvent, and moulded. The manufacturing process produces a dark colour—normally brown or black. Widest use of phenolic resins has been electrical goods such as switches and plugs, though use for such components has now decreased and laminates form the largest market for the resin. Such laminates are formed from phenolic resin-impregnated paper and have a sufficient degree of flexibility for use in protective coverings to working surfaces and wall boards, while retaining a hard surface. The laminates themselves are brown and resemble mica but usually have a coloured plastic coating. Phenolic resins are widely used as wood adhesives.

Amino resins

These are resins based on the amino group or amide group. The most important are urea and melamine formaldehydes.

Urea-formaldehyde resins are similar in properties to phenol-formaldehyde resins except that they are lighter in colour (hence a wider range of colours is obtainable). They are also more moisture resistant and have greater impact strength. They are used in electrical fittings, for rigid moulded articles such as toilet seats, and in adhesives. In expanded form, urea-formaldehyde is, on account of its low cost, the chief competitor of polyurethane for *in situ* insulation purposes.

Melamine-formaldehyde resins have extremely good resistance to water, heat and chemicals and can be coloured. They are widely used as surfacing coatings for decorative laminates based on phenolic resins.

Polyester resins

Esters are produced when organic acids are neutralised, in much the same way as salts result when inorganic acids are neutralised. If the acid is unsaturated, then sites for cross-linking are provided and polymerisation will occur, links being made through, for example, styrene molecules. In practice, to reduce brittleness, saturated acids may also be incorporated. Inhibitors are normally mixed with resins which are marketed as viscous liquids in drums. The hardener or catalyst is then added and the resin then hardens at a rate dependent on temperature, giving full strength after about a week. Fully cured resins are hard and tough and are commonly used with glass fibre, which bonds well and gives good impact and strength properties. When used in adhesives, polyester resins have been shown to have greater fire resistance than the other commonly used adhesives—epoxy resins—especially if a limestone filler is used. Polyester resins have also been used in resin cements (see Chapter 6).

Epoxide (epoxy) resins

The chemical components of these resins are complex, involving phenolic and other groups. The epoxide group is, however, the most important; it contains oxygen in the form:

$$R-\overset{\displaystyle O}{\underset{}{CH}}-CH_2$$

which enables cross-linking to take place, usually on addition of a hardener. These resins are characterised by low curing shrinkage, good chemical resistance, particularly to alkalis, and good adhesive properties, though they are more expensive than polyester resins. Resins are prepared in the form of partly polymerised liquids which polymerise more fully on curing. They have been used in flooring compositions, paints, adhesives and for glass-reinforced composites.

Polyurethanes ✓

These are formed as a product of isocyanates and polyesters or polyhydroxy materials. It is not possible to classify polyurethanes as thermoplastic or thermosetting since many different forms exist, some with chain-like molecules and therefore thermoplastic; others heavily cross-linked and therefore thermosetting. Polyurethanes are often used in foamed form; for example, in cavity filling for domestic dwellings and in a more flexible form for spraying on pipes for thermal insulation purposes. In each case, they bond well to the background. Most polyurethane is foamed using carbon dioxide which eventually diffuses outwards from cells, being replaced by air. Polyurethanes may be used up to temperatures of about 120°C depending on grade—an advantage over polystyrene foams; they are also less flammable, though, in common with polystyrenes, more flexible types dissolve in some organic solvents and acids.

Flexible polyester and polyether foams come under the general heading of polyurethanes, being used for upholstery, sponges and cushions. Other polyurethanes are used for resilient gaskets in clay pipes, and in surface coatings.

Rubbers (elastomers)

Rubbers have been described above as a class of material, rather than one having a specific chemical structure. They are obtained when an amorphous thermoplastic is heated above its glass-transition temperature. Thermal energy is then sufficiently great for polymer chains to take up configurations of lowest energy which are often helical (Fig. 5.7(a)). On stretching such a helix, it uncoils so that enormous strains are possible (for example, 1000 per cent) without damage to the polymer. Polyisoprene is a naturally occurring latex rubber and has the formula:

$$-\underset{\underset{\text{H}}{|}}{\overset{\overset{\text{H}}{|}}{\text{C}}}-\underset{\underset{\text{CH}_3}{|}}{\overset{\overset{\text{H}}{|}}{\text{C}}}=\underset{\underset{\text{H}}{|}}{\text{C}}-\underset{\underset{\text{H}}{|}}{\overset{\overset{\text{H}}{|}}{\text{C}}}-$$

Note the double bond, which is an important feature of useful rubbers. A certain number of these may be opened by means of divalent elements such as sulphur, causing increased rigidity (Fig. 5.7(b)). The process is known as vulcanising. Unfortunately, oxygen is also capable of cross-linking the groups in this way so that many rubbers harden naturally on exposure, resulting in eventual brittleness. Whether a rubber is classed as a thermoplastic or thermosetting polymer depends on the extent of cross-linking; a very lightly cross-linked rubber may be thermoplastic while a heavily

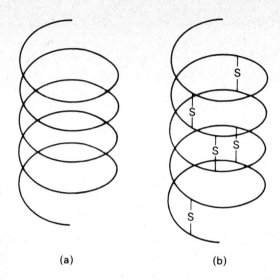

Fig. 5.7 Helical structure of rubbers such as polyisoprene. (a) Unvulcanised; the helix is capable of large extensions. (b) Vulcanised; the sulphur links increase rigidity

cross-linked polymer would be thermosetting. When natural rubber is very heavily cross-linked with sulphur, the rigid and brittle material ebonite is produced. A number of types of synthetic rubbers, notably styrene butadiene (SBR), polysulphide and silicone rubbers, are produced. Rubbers are important in the manufacture of certain fillers and mastics and in special types of paint such as chlorinated rubber paints. They may also be used to modify the mechanical properties of adhesives; for example, to increase the plasticity of phenolic and epoxy resins and even inorganic cements. Rubber 'O' rings are widely used for jointing clay, metal and plastic pipes.

Silicones

These are semi-organic compounds with the following basic structure:

$$\begin{array}{ccc} CH_3 & CH_3 & CH_3 \\ | & | & | \\ -Si-O-Si-O-Si- \\ | & | & | \\ CH_3 & CH_3 & CH_3 \end{array}$$

Note that silicon, like carbon, is tetravalent. According to the degree of polymerisation silicones may exist in liquid, rubbery or solid forms. Fluid forms are stable over a wide range of temperatures and are resistant to dilute acids and alkalis, though their chief importance in building is based on their water-repellent qualities, due to the very low surface tension of silicones. They are used also in protective paper backings for materials with self-adhesive coatings, such as sealing tapes, allowing easy removal of the paper prior to fixing. Resins are used in heat-resistant paints, often with aluminium pigments for painting of boiler flues and in similar high temperature applications.

Silicone rubbers, though inferior mechanically to latex or SBR, have better low- and high-temperature performance, being suitable for gaskets to be used in extreme conditions.

Bitumens

Although these are not plastic in the normal use of the word, they are in many ways similar and may be conveniently described here. The structure of bitumen is extremely complex though it is based on carbon and hydrogen with other elements such as sulphur, oxygen and nitrogen. At room temperature, the material may have consistency varying between that of a hard, brittle solid and a thick, viscous liquid.

Bitumens occur naturally in the form of asphalt, for example, Trinidad Lake asphalt, and in certain rocks and have been used successfully over many centuries in a wide variety of applications. They may alternatively be produced synthetically by distillation of oil—volatile fractions are removed, leaving a residue whose viscosity depends on the heating temperature and period. Bitumens may be of the straight run type, in which the distillation is usually stopped before all the volatile constituents have been removed, or the cut-back variety where distillation is completed, leaving the bitumen as a hard residue. This is then 'cut back' with solvents to restore plasticity.

Bituminous materials have chemical stability characteristic of the paraffin family of materials, being resistant to acids and alkalis. There is, however, some degree of unsaturation in them so that oxygen from the atmosphere tends to cause cross-linking by oxidation and subsequent embrittlement, particularly when exposed to ultraviolet light. Resistance may be increased by using surface coatings of already oxidised bitumen in the case of roofing felts and protecting from the sunlight wherever possible with light-reflecting mineral aggregates such as limestone. Note that many oils, from which bitumens are derived, will seriously soften or erode bituminous asphalts.

Bitumens are examples of *visco-elastic* materials—they are able to flow plastically under gradually applied stresses but may undergo brittle fracture if subjected to sudden stress. Hence, there are two prerequisites for successful use, first, that bituminous materials are not subjected to significant sustained stress which would cause creep; and second, that sudden movements should be avoided. The precise extent of each of these effects depends in practice on the viscosity of the bitumen (measured by penetration values), the temperature and the presence of fibres or stabilising materials such as aggregates.

The following applications are based on the flexibility and water proofing qualities of bitumens:

Roofing felts (BS 747: Part II: 1970). These contain blends of bitumens incorporated in mineral fibres such as asbestos, or glass; or organic fibres such as wood pulp. Felts incorporating organic fibres are suitable for lower layers of built-up roofing or in flat roofs when a bitumen covering is to be applied. Types to which an oxidised bitumen coating has been applied during manufacture are in all cases more satisfactory than unsurfaced saturated grades. A granular mineral surfacing, when applied, increases protection from the sun, allowing use as the external surfacing material on sloping roofs. Reinforced grades are available where felts have to be self-supporting; for example, under tiling.

Other types of felt include sheathing felts containing long fibres which are therefore dimensionally stable, being used under asphalt roofing and flooring; and asbestos and glass fibre felts which are more durable than organic fibre felts. It is important that felt roofs have falls to avoid the possibility of lying water which would eventually cause dampness in the structure.

Asphalts. These consist of bitumens with inert mineral material which increases their rigidity, stability and abrasion resistance. The mineral may already be present in naturally occurring bitumen—for example, lake asphalt—or it may be added, in which case it is usually graded, crushed limestone (BS 988, 1076, 1097, 1451: 1966). Asphalts which are essentially solid and impermeable at room temperature but which soften on heating are known as mastic asphalts. The limestone aggregate is of maximum size, 2·36 mm, graded down to 150 μm. Roofing or tanking grades are normally softer than flooring grades, the former requiring flexibility while the latter require hardness and abrasion resistance. Although bitumens are acid resistant, limestone is susceptible to acids, hence silicaceous fillers and aggregates should be used in such conditions.

Further uses of bituminous materials include damp proof courses, paints, adhesives and thermoplastics flooring tiles. The latter also contain inert fillers, resins and asbestos fibres (BS 2592: 1955).

ADHESIVES AND ADHESION

The advent of synthetic resins has completely revolutionised the field of adhesives and they are quite rapidly finding use in situations where previously there would have been no chance of success. Resins can be used, for example, in load-bearing situations, where moisture, heat or chemical pollution is likely and where there is little in the way of a physical key. It must be emphasised that two surfaces cannot be stuck together without the establishment of bonds between them. In more traditional types of glues and cements, there is little bonding between the adhesive and the surface; the material depends for its action on penetration of the surface so that, on setting such that chemical bonding *within* the adhesive is established, the portions of set material beneath the material surface interlock (rather than bond) with surface layers resulting in tensile strength (Fig. 5.8). Such adhesives are really *cohesive* instead of adhesive.

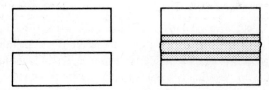

Fig. 5.8 The traditional method of bonding absorbent materials. The 'adhesive' penetrates the surfaces and, on hardening, forms a mechanical key. There is little true adhesion. Examples include inorganic cements and plasters

Hence non-porous surfaces such as glass or metals were very difficult to stick together, and the advent of plastic materials has led to requirements for joining these also. Many resins now produced are however in the true sense of the word, adhesive—they stick *to* the surface by bonding with it, whether or not it is porous. The exact nature of the bond depends on the adhesive and the adherend and though the bonding mechanism in most cases is not fully understood, it is true to say that the existence of primary bonds is not a prerequisite for successful adhesion; van der Waals bonds will result in satisfactory properties provided a sufficient number is established. The bonding properties of materials can be predicted from a knowledge of their surface energies. Surface energy may be defined as the energy required to form unit area of new surface; it is always positive, due to surface tension effects in solids and liquids. It is well known, for example, that two drops of the same liquid on contact will merge to form a larger drop, since, in so doing, the total surface area of liquid will be reduced, resulting in a more stable arrangement (Fig. 5.9). Solid objects behave similarly,

Fig. 5.9 Illustrating surface energy in liquids. On touching, two globules coalesce, forming a single larger globule of surface area less than the original total surface area

though the effect is less obvious. Adhesion between a solid and liquid may be obtained either if the solid is *soluble* in the liquid, in which case the surface solid material migrates into the liquid forming a mixture or alloy (Fig. 5.10); or if one 'wets' the other, in which case adhesion will occur at the interface (Fig. 5.11(a)).

The solubility of one material in another depends on molecular structure of each and in particular the *polarity* of molecular groups; that is, the charge eccentricities of the molecular bonds. A term which summarises polarity is 'solubility factor' which may be used for organic materials and solvents to predict the type of solvent required for, say, solvent welding, or to safeguard against use of plastics in contact with certain organic liquids. To be soluble in a certain solvent, the polymer should have a similar solubility parameter. Table 5.1 shows typical values for some common polymers and

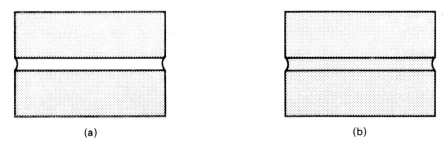

| (a) | (b) |

Fig. 5.10 Joining of surfaces by solvent welding. (a) immediately after application of solvent, (b) some time later; the solid dissolves and diffuses into the solvent until the solvent itself solidifies. The layer of solvent should be thin

Fig. 5.11 Adhesion of a liquid to a solid. (a) If the surface tension of the solid is higher than that of the liquid, the liquid wets the surface. (b) If the surface tension of the solid is lower than that of the liquid, the liquid does not wet the surface. The same effect occurs if there is a thin coating of a low surface tension material on the solid; for example, grease

solvents. Hence, chloroform may be used for solvent welding PVC or polystyrene; phenol will dissolve nylon. (There are exceptions where, for example, due to crystallinity in polymers they are insoluble in solvents of similar solubility parameter. Polyethylene is for this reason insoluble in any organic solvent at room temperature.) This type of solubility should not be confused with, for example, the dissolution of metals in acids; the latter type of reaction is irreversible and due to chemical attack. Unlike the above example, the product is entirely different, having a new molecular

Table 5.1

Solubility parameters of some common polymers and solvents. Polymers usually dissolve in a solvent of approximately equal solubility parameter

Polymer	Approximate solubility parameter
PTFE	6
Polyethylene	8
Polypropylene	8
Polyisoprene	8
Polystryrene	9
Polymethyl methacrylate	9
PVC	9
Amino resins	10
Epoxy resins	10
Phenolic resins	11
Nylon	13
Solvent	
Carbon tetrachloride	8·6
Benzene	9·2
Chloroform	9·3
Acetone	10·0
Phenol	14·5
Water	23·4

structure. Since solution of organic polymers is principally due to separation of molecular chains, heavily cross-linked polymers are much more difficult to dissolve, though swelling may occur if such a material is subjected to potentially active solvents; that is, solvents which would dissolve less heavily cross-linked varieties of the polymer.

Closely related to the solubility parameter of polymers are their surface tension values and this is to be expected, since both derive from molecular properties. Polyethylene, for example, has a much lower surface tension than more polar polymers. The requirement for wetting (and hence adhesion) of a liquid to a solid is that the liquid has a surface tension less than that of the solid, since if it is greater, the liquid would be cohesive, tending to form globules on the solid surface (Fig. 5.11(b)). Surface tensions of solid materials are roughly in the order of solubility parameters with inorganic materials having much higher values. Hence water wets inorganic materials and epoxy resins will adhere to them, as well as to some thermosetting plastics. On the other hand, many of the polymers with low surface tension are water-repellent and cannot be joined by epoxy resins. Surface treatment of polyethylene is required, for example, if epoxy resins are to adhere to it; the surface tension of the material must be increased and this can be achieved by oxidation—by an oxidising acid, for instance. It is important when joining materials with epoxy-type resins that the surfaces be completely clean, since even a very thin coating of grease or similar material may reduce considerably the effective surface tension of the surface, impairing the bond. Appropriate solvents should be used for this purpose. Similar arguments apply to solvent welding.

There are, of course, cases in which water-repellent properties are advantageous. If, for example, the surface tension of stonework could be reduced, it would become water repellent and therefore more resistant to the effect of moisture. This can be easily achieved using silicone resins which have an extremely low surface tension. Release agents for concrete work on a similar principle. If, on the other hand, wetting is required, this can be achieved by *reduction* of the surface tension of the liquid as is obtained by adding surface actants such as soap to water. Some workability aids for concrete work on this principle—the water is able to wet particles more effectively, decreasing interparticle friction.

Types of adhesives

It is not easy to classify adhesives according to use, since many varieties are multipurpose in their application. Hence, they are here divided into natural adhesives (glues) and then thermosetting and thermoplastic synthetic adhesives, though the first five to be described are used mainly for timber products. In this context, durability is of extreme importance and BS 1203 and 1204 give four classifications as to the suitability of timber glues for various situations. They are as follows:

WBP stands for weather- and boil-proof types.
BR indicates boil-resistant types that fail on prolonged exposure to weather.
MR refers to moisture-resistant but not boil-resistant adhesives.
'Int' adhesives are resistant to cold water, but unlike the above, are not required to be
    resistant to micro-organisms.

A further general point which should be considered when selecting an adhesive is the mechanism of curing or hardening. While most of the adhesives described below are truly adhesive (that is, they bond to the adherend), the curing processes of some still require an absorptive surface—to allow removal of water or solvent, for example. Such adhesives would not be effective if used to join *two* non-absorbent surfaces.

Animal glues. These have been used for centuries in carpentry and joinery, being obtained from the skin or bone of cattle and sheep. The major constituents of animal glues are proteins—large molecules occurring in gelatinous form, softening to form a viscous liquid at temperatures above about 40°C and gelling to form a solid at lower temperatures. Animal glues are normally sold in powder form, being melted in warm water to give a solution of suitable viscosity. After application, cooling of the liquid results in rapid gelation, producing some strength, and drying finally produces a tough and rigid product. Note that the removal of water from the glue during curing is essential; wood assists in this process due to absorption. Glued joints in wood should be as strong as the wood, though damp conditions will, of course, reduce strength and animal glues are not suitable for external use unless adequately protected from moisture (BS 1204 'Int' rating). The glue will harden gradually in the pot but can be softened by reheating with water.

Casein glues. Casein glues are of rather similar structure to animal glues, though they are derived as a precipitate from skimmed milk by the action of acids. Glues are obtained in powder form which also contains an alkaline solvent necessary to dissolve the glue on addition of water. Mixing is carried out cold and setting is partly by evaporation or absorption of water and partly by a natural gelation process. The latter reaction results in limited pot life of glues, once mixed—usually about 6 hours. Some degree of water resistance can be obtained by incorporation of formaldehyde, but use is normally confined to dry situations ('Int' rating).

Thermosetting adhesives

Urea-formaldehyde. This is one of the commonest adhesives used in joinery for general purposes. To make the adhesive, formaldehyde and urea in aqueous solution are reacted together to a certain stage and the reaction is then 'stopped' while the resin is still liquid. Hence these resins are generally of two-pack form, since a hardener is required to initiate the final stage of the hardening process. Alternatively, the water may be evaporated, giving a powder which has a longer shelf life than the liquid forms. On addition of water, the original properties are restored and setting commences on adding the hardener. Some varieties contain both the resin and hardener in powdered form, mixed together so that water only need be added. Urea-formaldehyde adhesives have little natural 'tack' so that pressure is essential to hold surfaces together during curing.

One problem which occurs with this and other resins is crazing, which tends to occur with large volumes of adhesive as might be used when gaps of say 1 mm have to be filled. Crazing is caused by shrinkage which occurs during the condensation reaction. It can be reduced by fillers which are used in gap-filling glues. If restricted pot life is a problem, joints can be made by the separate application method in which the resin is applied to one surface and the hardener to the other, so that setting does not commence until the joint is made. In this way, strong bonds can be obtained as quickly as 10 minutes after making the joint, though there is still time to position accurately the components, unlike 'contact' adhesives. Urea-formaldehyde adhesives are used for fabrication of flush doors, laminated timber and decorative laminates. Hardening of 'glue' lines will occur at room temperature but it may be accelerated by hot presses, strip heating or, most recently, radio-frequency heating, which may enable curing times as low as a few seconds to be used. Although urea-formaldehyde has good water resistance at normal temperatures, hot water or prolonged wetting breaks the resin down—it has the MR rating. Hence, laminates, for example, around kitchen sinks, should be bonded by a more resistant adhesive. Further important uses of urea-formaldehyde resins are for particle board and plasterboard partitioning.

Melamine formaldehyde resin adhesives. These are usually in powder form and are mixed with water to give a colourless resin. They set on heating to 100°C and give good weather resistance (BR rating), though they are more expensive than urea formaldehyde adhesives.

Phenol formaldehyde. These are available as liquids which polymerise on heating to temperatures over 100°C, and are used for assembly of plywood sheets. A hardener is added, the sheets formed and compressed and then the laminates subjected to a hot press which causes hardening in a period of about 5 minutes. Film varieties have also been used; these bond the surfaces on warming. Cold-curing phenolic adhesives are also used. These are insoluble in water, and set by addition of strong acids so that the glue is acidic, having pH values as low as 1. They have been used for assembly glueing of wood, though the setting reaction is exothermic and too much hardener tends to reduce pot life on account of the accelerating effect of heat on the curing rate.

Phenolic adhesives are hard but brittle so that fracture in wood joints is possible, especially if thick glue lines exist. Moisture resistance is excellent; they have the WBP rating of BS 1204. Correct mixing, application and curing are important so that they are best suited to factory use.

Resorcinol formaldehydes. These are related to phenol-formaldehyde adhesives but, unlike the latter, will cold cure under neutral conditions by addition of formaldehyde. Adhesives consist of a water-soluble liquid resin obtained by mixing resorcinol with a quantity of formaldehyde which is insufficient to cause cross-linking. The 'hardener' is, or contains, formaldehyde which completes the process. Curing can be carried out cold, or accelerated by moderate heat.

Resorcinol adhesives are important in laminated timber, since they have very good durability in extremes of weather (WBP rating), though, since timber may not stand up to such conditions unprotected, preservatives should be used; most preservatives do not affect the bond obtained. These adhesives are also useful for joining wood products and laminates to brick, concrete and asbestos backgrounds and are tolerant of a certain amount of moisture. Grades containing fillers should be used when bonding to uneven substrates. Like phenoic adhesives, resorcinol types are strong but brittle.

Epoxy resins. These are a most important development, since, with the exception of some thermoplastics, they form a good bond with almost any material, including wood, metal, glass and thermosetting plastics. This is considered to be due, at least in part, to the low shrinkage of these resins on curing, so that surface shear stresses do not arise.

Although most commonly used in two-pack form, lower-molecular-weight epoxy resins can be dissolved by organic solvents so that setting will then occur by solvent evaporation. Hence in this form they need no hardener and can be stored as a liquid for long periods in a well sealed container. They are then used as contact adhesives. Resin is applied to both surfaces and allowed to set for about 20 minutes. On pressing the surfaces together, an immediate bond is obtained; in fact, so rapidly that surfaces must be aligned carefully before pressing together. These adhesives do not have great strength, especially in wet conditions, but are extensively used for bonding laminates. The solvents are highly flammable. Two part resins are universally used in effecting permanent load-bearing joints or repairs in metals and glass.

Polyurethane adhesives. Though not widely used, these have a useful property not possessed by the other adhesives, that they will join unvulcanised rubber to metal. Water-resistant properties are intermediate between those of urea and phenolic adhesives.

Thermoplastic adhesives

The setting action of these may occur as a result of cooling, solvent evaporation or by emulsion coalescence. Hence, the term 'curing', implying chemical changes, is not always appropriate. As is characteristic of thermoplastics themselves, adhesives so based are more flexible but weaker and more prone to creep than thermosetting adhesives so that they are not normally used for 'structural' purposes.

Polyvinyl acetate. This is probably the most important thermoplastic adhesive in building, chief applications being as a wood adhesive and as a bonding agent in concrete. The polymer is obtained from acetylene and acetic acid and is most commonly obtained in emulsion forms. The monomer liquid is emulsified in water, forming very small droplets which are then polymerised by the action of heat and a catalyst. The adhesive sets when the solid particles, on evaporation or absorption of the moisture, cohere to form a tough film which is no longer water soluble. The chief advantage of PVA adhesives is that they are water miscible and do not require the use of a hardener, though one of the materials to be joined must be absorbent. Thin glue lines with absorbent materials set quickly, though gap-filling properties are less satisfactory. Properties of joints are characteristic of thermoplastic adhesives—they have better impact resistance than thermosetting adhesives but prolonged stress will cause creep and ultimate failure.

A further common use of PVA emulsions is as a bonding agent between new and old concrete. The resin may be diluted and applied to the substrate or added to the new mix, in which case it enables thinner sections and screeds to be applied with reduced danger of cracking. Coatings of PVA are often used to seal surfaces such as plaster prior to tiling.

Polystyrene adhesives. These normally operate on the solution principle, possibly containing some dissolved polystyrene also. Polystyrene, PVC and polymethyl methacrylate can be joined in this way, though the solvents are highly flammable.

Bituminous adhesives. These form good bonds with a number of materials, are moisture resistant and flexible. Natural or synthetic rubber and solvents may be included to give the desired combination of elasticity and strength. Adhesives are obtainable in the following forms:

Water-based emulsions. These are used for laying wood block flooring and PVC or thermoplastic tiles.

Solvent types. Used in laying linoleum and for PVC and thermoplastic tiles, though tests should be carried out to ensure that staining does not occur. Both solvent and emulsion types rely on some degree of absorbency in the substrate to allow absorption/evaporation of the water or solvent.

Hot applied varieties. These are used for wood block flooring. Application temperatures are in the region of 150–200°C.

Rubber-based adhesives. Rubbers such as neoprene, dissolved in a solvent, make excellent adhesives for wall panels, tiles and coving, giving good impact properties and resistance to background movement, though adhesives are highly flammable until cured.

Sealing compounds and fillers

There are many situations in building, internally and externally, where gaps are incorporated for any of a variety of purposes or they may occur unavoidably as a result of the construction process; for instance, gaps around window and door frames. Ease of maintenance, weathering or appearance requires that these gaps be filled and sealed. A filler is used to fill the body of larger gaps while the sealant prevents ingress of moisture, draughts or dirt. The sealant must adhere to the sides of the gap and accommodate its likely movement, which may vary from a few microns only (for example, ceramic tiles used internally) to several millimetres (for example, jointing compounds in large glazing units or expansion joints in walls). In some cases, strength may also be required. The requirements of the situation should first be assessed and then selection made of the most suitable filler and sealant. In order of increasing ductility, the following are the main groups:

Brittle materials. Mortars based on cement, gypsum, lime and other materials. These should only be used in situations where movement is minimal or where small cracks are no disadvantage; for example, pointing of brickwork and stonework. Common applications of these materials in situations where they are not likely to give long life are in roofing flaunchings and for fixing w.c. pans to the soil pipe. In each case, cracking of mortar or jointing material is likely due to stresses imposed by relative movement. Ductility of these mortars can be improved by addition of emulsified resins such as polyvinyl acetate.

Preformed fillers. These are usually incorporated at the construction stage of buildings to allow for movement in the finished structure. They must be inert, able to support any stresses imposed during the construction process and yet sufficiently compressible to absorb thermal movement. Expanded polythene is a typical filler, being light and elastic, yet tough and able to support quite large loads. Where more elastic behaviour is required, expanded rubber may be used. Typical applications include joints in floors, walls, infill panels and roads. In all cases, a sealant is required to exclude moisture from the joint. Fibreboard is sometimes used as a filler but its use can only be regarded as a temporary measure, since it is not sufficiently durable to withstand the effect of prolonged dampness.

Mastics and rubber-based sealants. These may be used to seal small gaps or to act as sealants in larger joints in which a separate filler is incorporated. Mastics must exhibit *tack*—a tacky substance will wet the background to which it is applied and immediately bond to it to the extent that it supports its self-weight. The most traditional examples are oil-based and bituminous mastics and putties. These tend to harden with time by oxidation so that in practice a paint coating should be applied some weeks after application, when a surface film will have formed. Even then, brittleness results on prolonged exposure or under rapid loading. A most important innovation are rubber-based mastics. These cure by one of the following processes:

Addition of a hardener. Some varieties containing correct proportions of the sealant and hardener in the same can are available. In this case, mixing only is necessary, though unless the contents of the whole can are used, the method is wasteful.

By the action of moisture in the atmosphere. Some silicone sealants set in this way, though acetic acid fumes may be liberated on curing.

By solvent evaporation. There is a fire hazard from such sealants until cured.

Rubber sealants bond well to metals, brick, glass and many plastics, though two surfaces only should be bonded, since rubbers do not change in volume when stressed;

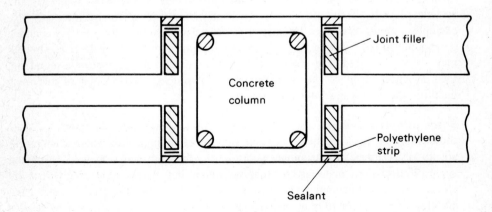

Fig. 5.12 Illustrating the use of joint filler and sealant between concrete column and brickwork panels

tensile stresses must cause waisting and compressive stresses barrelling. Polyethylene film may be used to prevent sealants bonding to the filler if used, and joint depth should not be greater than joint width (Fig. 5.12).

In the case of polysulphide and silicone mastics, a lifetime of 20 years or more may be expected. Caulking compounds based on rubbers have much greater flexibility than the inorganic compounds traditionally used around baths, sinks and similar situations where considerable movement may occur. In some situations, adhesive tapes may be used instead of the above types of sealant.

PAINTS

Paints are surface coatings suitable for site use, marketed in liquid form. They may be used for one or more of the following purposes:

1. To protect the underlying surface by exclusion of the atmosphere, moisture, chemicals, fungi and insects.
2. To provide a decorative, easily maintained surface.
3. To provide light- (or heat-) reflecting properties.
4. To give special effects; for example, inhibitive paints for protection of metals, electrically conductive paints as a source of heat, condensation resistant paints.

Externally, (1) and (2) will be of greatest importance. Internally, (2) and (3) are of greater importance.

Painting forms a small fraction of the initial cost of a building and a much higher proportion of the maintenance cost. It is, on this basis, advisable to pay careful attention to the subject at construction stage. Furthermore, there are a number of situations in which restoration is both difficult and expensive once the original surface coating has failed and weathering has affected the substrate; for example, clear coatings on timber. In these situations, particular care is necessary.

Paints consist essentially of a vehicle and pigment, the former being responsible for setting, gloss and impermeability while the latter is responsible for opacity, colour and, to some extent, strength. Other materials such as driers, solvents and extenders may also be added. Once applied, the coating must harden within a few hours. The hardening process may be due to one of the following:

(a) Polymerisation by chemical reaction with a hardener or by oxygen (or in some cases, moisture) in the air.
(b) Coalescence of an emulsion.
(c) Evaporation of a solvent.

Categories (a) and (b) are referred to as convertible coatings, since, on hardening, chemical bonds are established so that the coating cannot easily be restored to its earlier liquid state. Type (c) is non-convertible, since the liquid state can be restored simply by adding a suitable solvent. The most important paints in the first category are oil-based paints.

Oil-based paints

These were traditionally based on linseed oil (obtained from flax seeds) or tung oil (obtained from soya beans), and although satisfactory properties can be obtained by refining these oils they are now usually modified by alkyd resins. Some understanding of the drying action of oils used in paints can be gained from an examination of the organic acids which form their basis. Vegetable oils such as linseed oil consist of combinations of triglycerides of fatty acids. Glycerol has the formula

$$
\begin{array}{l}
CH_2-OH \\
CH-OH \\
CH_2-OH
\end{array}
$$

while fatty acids have a variety of formulae, each containing the $-COOH$ (acid) radical; for example, stearic acid, $CH_3(CH_2)_{16}COOH$ (no double bonds) and oleic acid, $CH_3(CH_2)_7CH=CH(CH_2)_7COOH$, one double bond. On reaction, these form products of the type:

$$
\begin{array}{l}
CH_2-OOCR_1 \\
CH-OOCR_2 \\
CH_2-OOCR_3
\end{array}
$$

where R_1, R_2 and R_3 are the hydrocarbon sections of the acids. Water is also produced, the OH coming from the glycerol and H atoms from the acid radicals.

Quite large molecules may result from this process and the oil may be made to polymerise if double bonds in the hydrocarbon sections can be opened, causing cross-linking. For example, the chain, $-CH_2-CH=CH-CH_2-$ may combine with a similar chain by means of oxygen to give:

$$
\begin{array}{c}
-CH_2-CH-CH-CH_2- \\
|\quad\ |\ \\
O\ \ \ O \\
|\quad\ | \\
-CH_2-CH-CH-CH_2-
\end{array}
$$

These linkages may occur between any neighbouring hydrocarbon chains, so that oxygen from the atmosphere causes gradual cross-linking of molecules until a solid film is produced. The strength and stiffness of the solid depends on the number of

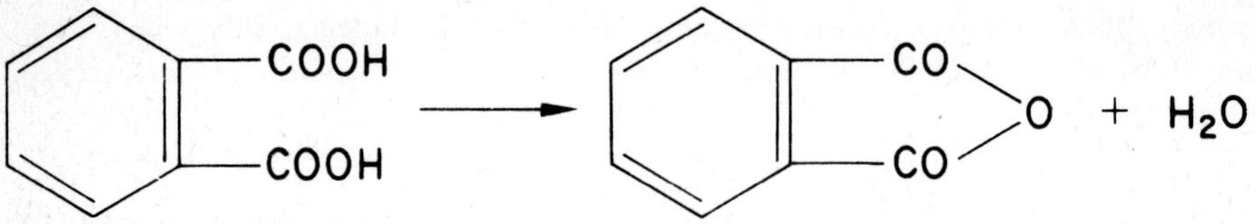

Fig. 5.13 Formation of phthalic anhydride from phthalic acid

unsaturated groups in the original glyceride, and hence on the acid type present. Stearic acid, for example, is saturated, hence it would not form a drying oil; acids containing a small number of unsaturated groups would result in oils which produce soft films, more suitable for mastics, while acids containing a large number of unsaturated groups might produce hard brittle films. Certain metals such as lead, cobalt and manganese can be incorporated in the oils, accelerating curing and being referred to as 'driers'. They are characterised by having more than one valency value, so that they can effectively 'carry' oxygen into the molecular network to assist in polymerisation. Boiled linseed oil, which has superior hardening properties to ordinary linseed oil, contains metal compounds incorporated by heating.

Once hardened, oil-based paints behave as thermosetting plastics, being resistant to solution in the oils from which they are formed. Such paints form films in the can unless a protective coating of, say, white spirit is applied.

Alkyd resins

These play an important part in modern oil paints; they are produced by mixing glycerol with phthalic anhydride (so called because it is derived from phthalic acid by extraction of water molecule (Fig. 5.13)). Reaction of a tri-functional alcohol represented

$$G\begin{matrix} \diagup OH \\ -OH \\ \diagdown OH \end{matrix}$$

with a dibasic acid produces complex molecules (Fig. 5.14). Tetrafunctional alcohols such as pentaerythritol:

$$HOH_2C-\underset{\underset{\displaystyle CH_2OH}{|}}{\overset{\overset{\displaystyle CH_2OH}{|}}{C}}-CH_2OH$$

may also be used. Further cross-linking occurs when two free OH bonds condense (Fig.

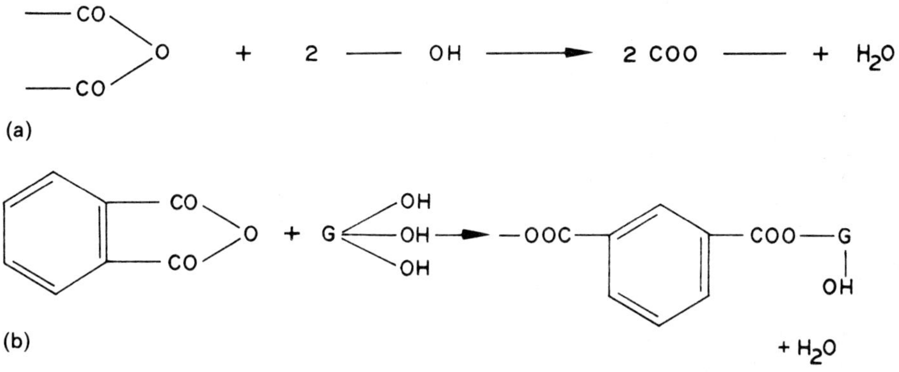

(a)

(b)

$+ H_2O$

Fig. 5.14 (a) The reaction between an anhydride radical and hydroxyl radicals. (b) The same reaction taking place between phthalic anhydride and two of the hydroxyl groups of glycerol

5.15). Unless the reaction is stopped, this process would produce a solid resin by itself without need for oxygen. The incorporation of monobasic acids or monohydric alcohols which effectively terminate chains is therefore common practice. Alkyd resins are, however, white in colour and therefore, in practice, oil-based paints and varnishes

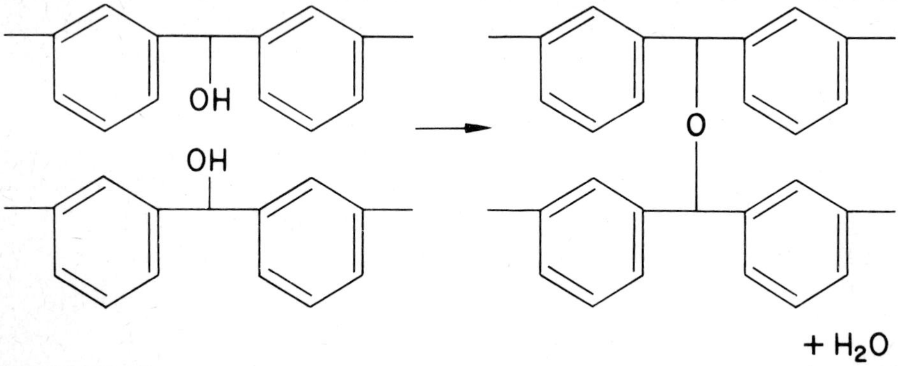

$$+ H_2O$$

Fig. 5.15 Polymerisation of the chains formed from the reaction of Fig. 5.14 by condensation reactions

usually contain combinations of synthetic resins and drying oils. In this form, gloss retention, durability and colour retention properties are much better than those of pure alkyd or pure oil. Vehicles containing a high proportion of oil are known as 'long oil' vehicles and these are tough, flexible and suitable for external use. Medium and short oil types are more suitable for internal use.

Polyurethane paints

These are available in a variety of forms. The hardest films are obtained from two-pack versions of the resin. The resin itself is a polyester, as are the alkyd resins, though produced by a different process involving a dibasic acid

$$R\begin{matrix} \diagup COOH \\ \diagdown COOH \end{matrix}$$

a diol

$$R\begin{matrix} \diagup OH \\ \diagdown OH \end{matrix}$$

and a polyol; for example,

$$R{-}OH\begin{matrix} \diagup OH \\ \diagdown OH \end{matrix}$$

The resulting ester has several OH groups which are reacted with isocyanates (containing NCO groups ($-N{=}C{=}O$)). A typical reaction is

$$HO{-}R_1{-}OH + OCN{-}R_2{-}NCO \longrightarrow HO{-}R_1{-}O{-}\overset{\displaystyle O}{\overset{\|}{C}}{-}\overset{\displaystyle H}{\overset{|}{N}}{-}R_2{-}NCO$$

Further reaction between OH and NCO groups causes cross-linking, and hence film formation. Similar reactions occur when water or acidic groups are present, these giving rise to carbon dioxide gas, used in the formation of expanded polyurethane.

Although two-pack polyurethanes produce extremely good film properties, tolylene diisocyanate vapour can be dangerous if inhaled. Also, temperature tends to affect the curing rate, and two-pack paints which require accurate mixing are themselves a disadvantage for general site use. Various types are available; hardest resins may be used on furniture while more flexible grades are required for external use of flooring. Note that curing of two-pack polyurethanes is not dependent on the atmosphere.

Air-drying polyurethane paints and varnishes

These are commonly used in building for a wide variety of purposes. They are really modified air drying oils. For example, by means of glycerol, hydroxyl groups are introduced into an air-drying oil:

$$
\begin{array}{l}
CH_2-COOR_1 \\
CH-COOR_2 \\
CH_2-COOR_3
\end{array}
\longrightarrow
\begin{array}{l}
CH_2-COOR_1 \\
CH-OH \\
CH-COOR_3
\end{array}
$$

oil $\qquad$ monoglyceride

The glycerol will form a similar product. The addition of a polyisocyanate will cause some polymerisation by action on hydroxyl groups as previously. The polyurethane 'oil' will then dry by oxidation of unsaturated bonds, the film having similar properties to two-pack varieties though not normally as hard or tough. In varnishes in particular, some polyurethane coatings may not withstand the thermal and moisture movements which occur when applied to wood. South-facing aspects exaggerate the problem.

Moist-curing polyurethane varnishes

These are sometimes claimed to react with water in damp timber forming an impervious film. Although the polymerisation process involves moisture, quantities required are only small, approximately 1 per cent by weight of the paint. Hence, they will not 'dry' wet timber. Paints of this variety cannot be produced since pigments normally contain sufficient moisture to cause them to set in the can.

Saponification of oil-based paints and varnishes

It has been explained that oil-based paints are glycerides of organic acids; that is, they are formed from glycerol. If an alkali such as sodium hydroxide contacts such an oil-based film, there is a tendency to revert to glycerol with the production of sodium salts known as soaps.

$$
\begin{array}{l}
CH_2-COOR_1 \\
CH-COOR_2 \\
CH_2-COOR_3
\end{array}
+ 3NaOH
\longrightarrow
\begin{array}{l}
CH_2-OH \\
CH-OH \\
CH_2-OH
\end{array}
+
\begin{array}{l}
NaCOOR_1 \\
NaCOOR_2 \\
NaCOOR_3
\end{array}
$$

glycerol $\qquad$ soaps

This leads to the breakdown of films and formation of a soapy deposit. Hence, oil-containing paints (including polyurethanes) should not be used on alkaline substrates such as Portland cements. Alkali-resistant primers such as PVA emulsion paints should first be applied.

Emulsion paints

These are now very widely used in interior decorating. Examples are polyvinyl acetate (PVA) emulsions which are suitable for application to new cement or plaster. The molecules are very large but are dispersed in water by colloids to give particles of size approximately 1 micron. Hence these paints have the advantage of being water miscible although, on drying out, coalescence of molecules occurs, resulting in a coherent film with moderate resistance to water (Fig. 5.16). The film is, however, not

Fig. 5.16 Coalescence of an emulsion to form a coherent but non-continuous film

continuous so that the substrate can, if necessary, dry out through the film. Acrylic emulsions for painting of timber have now been produced, including a form which results in a gloss finish.

Solvent-based paints

From some points of view, non-convertible coatings are an advantage, since such paints do not form films in the can and subsequent coats bond into one another. On the other hand, the hardened films are much less tolerant of organic solvents than convertible types. Examples of solvent-based paints are cellulose and bituminous paints.

Cellulose paints

The cellulose constituent is the form of nitro-cellulose dissolved in a solvent such as acetone. Plasticisers are added to give elasticity, and synthetic resins to give a gloss, since pure cellulose gives little gloss.

Drying usually occurs rapidly but well ventilated areas are essential and the paint is highly flammable. Cellulose paints are most suited to spray application (though retarded varieties for brushing are available). These properties, together with the fact that paints give off a penetrating odour, tend to restrict the use of cellulose paints to factory application. In these conditions, high-quality finishes can be obtained and the resulting coat has good resistance to fungal attack and to chemicals including alkalis.

Bituminous paints

These are intended primarily for protection of metals used externally and have poor gloss-retention properties. Thick coats give good protection though the solvents used sometimes cause lifting if applied over oil-based paints, or bleeding in subsequently applied oil-based coats. Sunlight softens the paint, though resistance can be improved by use of aluminium in the final coat. Chlorinated rubber paints have similar properties; uses are often based on their resistance to alkalis.

Pigments

The chief object of these is to impart opacity and colour to the paint. In white paints, pigments are used without need for dyes; titanium dioxide being one of the most important. This pigment occurs in two forms, anatase and rutile; the latter having greater resistance to 'chalking'—gradual wearing away of paint due to binder destruction. 'Coloured' pigments are now frequently obtained by use of organic dyes, though these are not as durable as more traditional inorganic pigments. Extenders such as calcium carbonate, known as whiting, are added to cheapen the paint and obtain the desired flow properties.

Painting particular materials

Metals. Steel forms the largest bulk of metals used in building and is one of the most difficult to maintain. Paint systems normally consist of primers, undercoats and finish coats. Primers are intended to grip the substrate, to provide some protection (possibly by inhibition) to the steel and to act as a suitable base for subsequent coats. Inhibitive primers include red lead, zinc rich and zinc chromate primers. Of these, red lead, though toxic, is often still preferred because it is fairly tolerant of poorly prepared surfaces and is amenable to application in thick coats. The type of undercoat/finish coat to be used will depend on the severity of exposure, and decorative requirements, if any. Where a decorative finish is required, an aluminium, stainless steel or alkyd gloss paint may be used. Micaceous iron oxide may be used as an undercoat in such situations or as a finish coat in others. Generally speaking, the wetter the situation and the more aggressive the climate or atmosphere, the more coats should be given. In extreme situations or where extended life without maintenance is required, protection is only likely to be achieved by impregnated wrappings, thick, factory-formed films or prior treatment such as galvanising.

Non-ferrous metals. Zinc and aluminium are the non-ferrous metals most likely to require surface coatings and each provides a poor key to paint unless surface treatment is first carried out. This may take the form of degreasing, using white spirit followed by roughening of unweathered surfaces with emery paper or etching treatment.

Primers containing phosphoric acid are available for this; they often contain an inhibitor as well. For zinc, zinc rich, metallic lead or calcium plumbate (*not* red lead) may be used and for aluminium, zinc chromate is suitable. For sprayed zinc or aluminium surfaces, it is sufficient to clean the surface and apply a zinc chromate primer.

Wood. Preliminary treatment includes stopping holes and treatment of knots with shellac. A primer is essential to penetrate and yet block the pore structure. Undercoats are not normally satisfactory here since they often do not penetrate the wood and may flake off later. Lead-based primers have been replaced by newer types such as aluminium and acrylic emulsion primers, the latter being more tolerant of a rather high moisture content than alkyd types. Undercoats are used to obtain the desired colour, contributing to the film thickness and therefore protection, though the gloss coat provides the bulk of the protection. Alkyds and polyurethanes form the basis of most paints, though newer types such as acrylic emulsions are now available for external use. These may be slightly porous but it may be questioned whether an absolutely vapour-proof surface coating on wood is required externally on account of the tendency for moisture to diffuse *outwards* through the buildings. Modern practice in relation to vapour barriers is to install them as near to the interior side as possible, with *moisture* barriers only externally to allow any vapour in walls to escape. Hence some small degree of porosity in an external paint film might not be a disadvantage.

Plastics. Most plastics in common use do not require painting, and paint coats, once applied, cannot be removed by normal techniques. Paints, on the other hand, will reduce the rate of degradation of plastics such as polyethylene. Adherence is poor unless the surface is first roughened to give a mechanical key.

THE RHEOLOGY OF PAINTS AND RELATED MATERIALS

It is well known that the behaviour of solids under stress is described by the use of stress-strain diagrams and, at least at low stress values, a given stress defines a given strain for a particular material. The relationship is clearly different for liquids since, in the absence of long range order, the application of stress will cause immediate relative motion with the body of liquid; there is no elastic stage. The equivalent of a stress-strain diagram for liquids would therefore be a graph relating shear stress to strain rate and this relationship will depend on the nature of short range bonding, practically observed as the viscosity of the liquid. For many liquids, usually of low molecular weight, a straight line graph would be obtained, at least for low shear stresses (Fig. 5.17). Such liquids are described as Newtonian. A typical consequence of this relationship between shear stress and shear strain is that the velocity of a liquid in a pipe varies parabolically from the maximum value (at the centre) to zero (at the walls) assuming flow is non-turbulent.

As the molecular weight of a liquid is increased, viscosity increases, though interaction between molecular chains alters the relationship between shear stress and shear strain. At small stresses, some such liquids shear at a lower rate than would be expected, while others have the characteristics of a solid, supporting a small shear stress without continuous movement (Figs. 5.18, and 5.19). Such behaviour is non-Newtonian. The form of Fig. 5.18 is obeyed by paints, in which large molecules tend to become tangled together. Small shear stresses are insufficient to cause alignment, while larger stresses achieve this, resulting in decreased viscosity. The viscosity of paints must be carefully controlled by regulation of molecular chain size, since a paint must be sufficiently liquid to brush or spray and yet sufficiently viscous to resist sagging or curtaining on vertical surfaces after application. It is found that these properties are best achieved when there is a grading of molecular weights in a similar way that aggregates for concrete are graded.

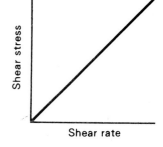

Fig. 5.17 Newtonian liquid. Shear rate proportional to shear stress

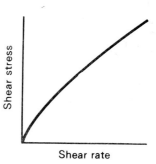

Fig. 5.18 Non-Newtonian, shear rate lower than would be expected at low shear stresses

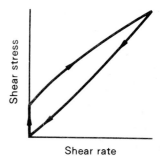

Fig. 5.19 Non-Newtonian, semi-solid properties are displayed at low sheer stresses. Such liquids are thixotropic, the degree of thixotropy being proportional to the area enclosed by the increasing and decreasing sheer stress cycle

Figs. 5.17–5.19 Behaviour under stress of different types of liquid

Some types of paint exhibit colloidal properties and obey the form of Fig. 5.19. This is caused by van der Waals bonds and can be useful, since the gel structure of the paint breaks down under shear stresses due to brushing and reforms afterwards, improving the stability of the fresh film. Such paints, known as *thixotropic* paints, are attractive to the amateur, since they are tolerant of poor application technique, and to the professional, since they allow thicker coats to be applied, if these are required. The area enclosed by the complete stress/strain-rate curve of Fig. 5.19 indicates the degree of thixotropy.

TIMBER

Although one of the earliest materials to be used in building, timber is by no means out-dated and still plays a major part in general building, particularly in domestic dwellings and furniture. Advances in the field of adhesives have increased enormously the potential of the material, and better methods of testing, combined with increased understanding of timber properties, have enabled timber to be used at quite high stress levels. At the same time, the material can be worked with simple hand tools, is resistant to many types of chemical and atmospheric pollution and can be finished to give aesthetically pleasing effects. This section does not attempt to deal exhaustively with all the properties and applications of the wide range of varieties that exists. Instead, the fundamental properties and applications will be described. The reader is referred to specialist works for further information.

The physical and chemical structure of timber

Wood is a naturally occurring fibrous composite, the fibres being of cellulose and occupying about two-thirds of the bulk, and the matrix, lignin, which binds the fibres together. Bonding parallel to the grain is therefore primary in nature and hence very powerful, so that on stressing in this direction failure usually occurs by shear between the cells formed from the cellulose fibres. Bonding across the grain is, on the other hand, of secondary nature so that tensile strengths radically or tangentially are much reduced. From some points of view—for example, working—this is an advantage, but from others it is a disadvantage; for instance, it is responsible for many of the defects arising from moisture-content changes. Cellulose is able to absorb substantial quantities of water—atmospheres of 100 per cent humidity result in a moisture content of about 30 per cent by dry weight and immersion in water may result in 200 per cent absorption. Volume changes result, illustrated for example by the swelling of cellulose wallpaper adhesives on adding water. Drying shrinkage in timber is, however, highly directional, being between 4 and 10 per cent tangentially, about two-thirds of this radially and negligible (about 0·2 per cent longitudinally).

The relative values of these figures are easy to appreciate from the structure of the wood; longitudinally there is great strength due to the cellulose fibres; tangentially timber is relatively free to shrink, while radially the lower movement may be caused by cells in these directions known as rays (Fig. 5.20). Rays grow radially, and as their separation increases new rays form between them, the process repeating indefinitely.

Note also the spring and summer wood layers and the outer 'sapwood' which carries the food.

Timber may be divided into softwoods (obtained from coniferous trees) and hardwoods (obtained from broad-leaved species). The latter are usually, but not always, harder, denser, stronger and more stable, though more difficult to machine than softwoods. They contain a higher proportion of cellulose than the latter.

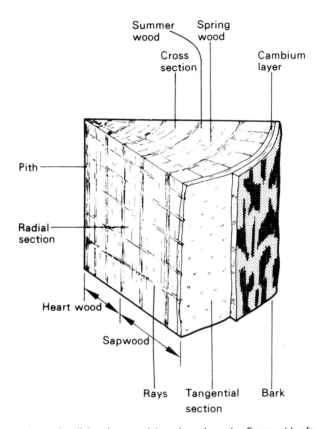

Fig. 5.20 Cross section and radial and tangential sections through a 5-year-old softwood log

Conversion

Conversion is the process by which logs are cut up prior to seasoning. The actual method of cutting individual logs must be a compromise between that which results in most economical use of timber and that which results in the most desirable timber properties. An understanding of the effect of conversion methods on properties requires an examination of the effect of seasoning on the geometry and mechanical performance of timber.

Effects of seasoning and conversion methods on timber.

'Green' timber contains large quantities of moisture, typical figures being 150 per cent (sapwood) and 80 (heartwood), based on dry weight. On conversion, timber begins to dry out, reaching an equilibrium moisture content dependent on the type of timber, the ambient temperature and the humidity, in a time which depends on the above parameters and on the size of timber. Typical average values for the equilibrium moisture content of timber at 20°C are, at 60 per cent relative humidity, 13 per cent; and 90 per cent humidity, 20 per cent. Substantial shrinkage of timber does not begin until moisture content reaches fibre saturation value—about 30 per cent. Below this, shrinkage and moisture content are approximately linearly related. Higher temperatures result in lower moisture contents; for example, at 30°C, the above figures would be reduced by about 10 per cent of their previous value. Timber near to radiators or under floor heating may reach a moisture content as low as 8 per cent. Seasoning may be carried out for the following purposes:

1. To reduce moisture content to a level below that required for fungal attack (about 20 per cent).
2. To obtain with as little distortion as possible the moisture content appropriate to the conditions of use of the timber. Ideally, timber should not be used at a moisture content more than 5 per cent different to that which it will finally assume. Otherwise, further movement is likely with corresponding deformation. Timber for flooring should, for example, be supplied at a lower moisture content than carcasing timber, for which a figure of 20 per cent is acceptable.
3. Some preservatives require fairly low moisture contents prior to application.

It is most important that seasoning be carried out such that the moisture content of timber is reduced progressively. If, for example, drying out is too rapid, surface layers will tend to shrink first, splitting or stretching. Splitting in itself is undesirable and stretching may mean that when the inner sections finally shink, they are restrained by the now deformed outer layers so that inner layers crack. Large timbers are particularly prone to this since internal wood takes some time to dry out. Hence kiln-drying schedules must take account of timber type, size, original moisture content and use. Air seasoning normally avoids these problems but takes some months to complete, so that faster methods such as kilns are more commonly used.

Once timber is seasoned, it is, of course, essential to preserve its low moisture content, otherwise at least part of the benefit will be lost.

The effect of seasoning on various timber sections is shown in Fig. 5.21. Since tangential shrinkage is greater than radial shrinkage and outer layers tend to shrink more than inner layers, growth rings usually straighten on seasoning, producing, for example, cupping in boards. This is often unacceptable, as in flooring, where attempts to straighten the cupped boards would cause splitting. If cupping cannot be prevented, it is often better to relate this to the mode of use of the section; for example, skirting boards are better machined as in Fig. 5.22(b) rather than Fig. 5.22(a), though machining of the latter is more difficult. Wherever possible, timber should be sawn parallel to the longitudinal grain; if growth rings intersect the longitudinal surface, bowing and twisting may occur and strength and wearing properties are adversely

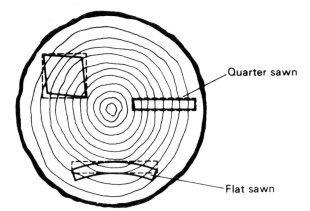

Fig. 5.21 The effect of grain orientation on shrinkage properties of timber. The cheapest way of conversion of timber is to make parallel cuts through the log, known as through-and-through cutting. Most of the resulting timber will then be flat sawn rather than quarter sawn

affected (Fig. 5.23). Quarter sawn boards are preferable generally to flat sawn, though the latter produce a more attractive figure if appearance is important. The ends of timbers also often contain fissures (shakes and checks) due to stresses imposed when end shrinkage is restrained by the body of the timber. Ideally, it might be considered better to season timber before conversion in order to avoid these dimensional changes after machining but this is normally impracticable, since the large bulks of timber would take long periods to season, would be difficult to stack and would give rise to large shrinkage fissures.

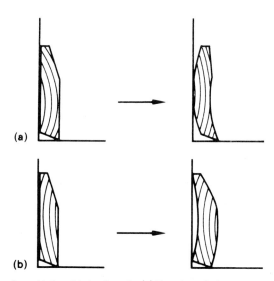

Fig. 5.22 Methods of machining skirting boards. (a) Board on drying cups away from wall at edges. (b) Board on drying cups away from wall at centre. This is preferable

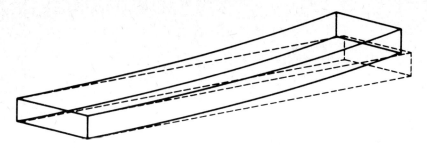

Fig. 5.23 Bowing of timber due to intersection of growth rings with the longitudinal surface. The effect also occurs when seasoned flat sawn timber is machined to size. In this case it is due to shrinkage stresses in the timber

There are, of course, many practical difficulties associated with control of the moisture content of timber in building, but the following general rules should be adhered to as far as possible:

1. Do not store timber on site longer than is absolutely necessary.
2. Specify moisture contents for internal timber, particularly flooring and doors. On specification of certain types of door, additional precautions may be necessary. Panels in panelled doors may split on drying if assembled and glued at high moisture content. Veneered doors should be of the same veneer each side to avoid bowing by differential shrinkage or movement.
3. Store all timber under cover. Units such as doors should be kept in a heated store if possible and not installed until the building is weatherproof, reasonably dry and, if possible, heated in winter.
4. The occupier should not apply severe heating during early stages of occupation.

Preservatives for timber

Although some varieties of timber (for example, oak and cedar) are naturally very durable even when unprotected, most building timbers require protection unless kept dry, and future repair or replacements can be very difficult and expensive if fungal or insect attack gains a positive hold. The National House Builder's Registration Council now requires effective preservative treatment after machining of structural or externally used timber. Timber should be protected in any situation in which the moisture content is likely to exceed about 20 per cent, where inspection or maintenance are not practicable or in areas where specific forms of attack such as insect attack are common. Preservatives should be toxic to fungi and insects, chemically stable, able to penetrate timber and non-aggressive to surrounding materials, particularly metals. There is a very wide range on the market, though basic properties are as follows:

Tar oil preservatives. Creosotes are probably the best-known examples. These are only suitable for external use since they give rise to a noticeable colour and smell and render timber unsuitable for painting. They are, however, cheap and can be applied on timber at a fairly high moisture content. They tend to creep into porous adjacent materials such as cement renderings and plaster.

Water-based preservatives. These consist of salts based on metals such as sodium, magnesium, zinc and copper and also arsenic and boron. Chrome copper arsenate is a common example. They are very tolerant of moisture in the timber, are odourless, non-flammable, non-creeping and do not stain timber, which may be painted on drying out. However, swelling occurs on treatment, which may be a disadvantage in some situations. Drying out may take some time and corrosion of metals in contact with treated timber may occur during this period. Although some types combine chemically to some degree with the wood, these preservatives are not generally suitable for external use since there is a tendency to leach out.

Organic solvent preservatives. Typical are chloronaphthalenes and metallic naphthenates. Penetration is excellent provided timber is fairly dry, hence they are often preferred where only brush or spray application is feasible. They are non-creeping, non-staining and quite suitable for brush application; they do not corrode metal and may be painted over later. Some of the solvents are, however, flammable, so that fire risk is increased until timber has dried out. On account of the organic solvents used in them, they are generally more expensive than the other types.

Application methods

These are described in order of decreasing effectiveness. Pressure methods give greatest penetration. In the 'full cell' method the timber is first evacuated so that preservative is drawn into the cells, being effective but rather wasteful. The empty cell method involves first pressurising the timber then injecting the preservative at greater pressure and finally releasing the pressure, causing cells to eject excess preservative. In the hot and cold tank treatment, the timber is heated to about $85°C$ in the preservative, drawing in more preservative on cooling. The effectiveness depends on the duration of steeping. Dipping usually implies that the timber is submerged for a few minutes only. Brushing and spraying are possible *in situ* but are not as effective as the above methods. Repeated application will to some extent improve protection. A rather different approach—'Timborising'—has been used in which newly felled green timber is dipped into a boron compound, diffusion then taking place over a period of time such that protection to the body of timber is obtained. This type of treatment and the pressure methods are the only ones which give adequate penetration of preservative.

Fungal and insect attack

Fungi grow from spores which are present in the air and which lie dormant in timber until conditions are suitable for growth. All fungi require moisture contents of at least 20 per cent to grow, though once established many fungi can exist and grow at lower values for periods up to about a year. They thrive best at moderate temperatures. There are two chief varieties of fungi: *Coniophora cerebella* (wet rot) and *Merulius lacrymans* (dry rot). The former is not usually important in building since it only occurs in saturated timber. Dry rot is so named because it leaves the wood in a dry, friable condition. It begins as a white fluffy coating, sending out branching strands in search of more water, during the course of which they can penetrate brickwork. The fruit consists of wrinkled, soft, fleshy plates which bear the red spores that propagate the fungus. Timber has little strength once attack has reached this advanced stage. Vulnerable situations include:

1. Roof members, if the roof is not fully waterproof or near eaves.
2. Floor joists bearing on to solid walls.
3. Floor members in contact with concrete or when inadequately ventilated.

Remedial measures involve cutting away and burning all affected timber, replacement with suitably protected new timber, application of preservatives to existing unaffected timber and, most important, eradication of the fault. It is often very difficult to eliminate dry rot which has grown into walls. Speical types of plaster are, however, available to resist growth and further attack. The composition of these is usually complex, including zinc oxide and chlorides, boric acid and ammonium chloride, with whiting (calcium carbonate) and sand as fillers. Problems of this type can in the first place be avoided by careful attention to roofing and flooring details and ventilation. It is in general poor practice to allow timber to contact brick or concrete without some impervious separating membrane, particularly in solid walls or foundation concrete. Careful maintenance of roofing and guttering should avoid problems in roofing timbers. In timber-framed buildings, it is wise to treat all timber with preservative before construction, and the use of an effective vapour barrier near to the internal side of the construction is essential. This prevents diffusion of water vapour from inside the building, where its pressure is often higher, into the structure where, on cooling, it could result in condensation. A *moisture barrier* should be provided externally to prevent rain penetration and yet allow small quantities of moisture in the structure to evaporate. In timber-framed flat roofs, it is unwise to enclose timber between an internal vapour barrier and the impervious bitumen coating unless adequate ventilation is ensured.

Insect attack

There are a number of insects that attack newly felled timber; however, seasoning usually eradicates these so that the chief interest of the builder will be in insect attack in timber in use, and particularly structural timber. Table 5.2 shows some common types of attack. Sapwood is most prone to attack since the cells contain food and are of an open structure, though the latter also results in much better penetration of preservative into sapwood than heartwood. Affected timber is best removed, burned and replaced by adequately protected new timber. Brush treatment of existing unaffected timber may not eradicate the problem. The use of a pressure spray in flight holes will destroy most active beetles or larvae.

Timber and wood products

Recent years have seen an enormous increase in the variety of products, mainly on account of advances in mechanised techniques and the introduction of synthetic resin

Table 5.2
Some types of insect attack on seasoned timber

Beetle	Life cycle	Visual signs	Timber attacked
Common furniture *(Anobium punctatum)*	2 years. Emergence, May–Aug.	Grubs 5 mm long, granular dust, 1 mm diam. flight holes	Sapwood of untreated hardwoods or softwoods
House longhorn *(Hylotupes bajulus)*	3–11 years	A few large holes (4 mm) surface swelling, beetles 10 mm in length	Sapwood of softwoods (Surrey)
Death watch *(Xestobium rufovillosum)*	Several years. Emergence, March–June	Large bun-shaped pellets, ticking during mating period, May–June	Mainly hardwoods, especially if old or decayed

binders. As a result, wastage of timber is minimised and many products are quite cheap. The following are important in building, properties of each being controlled in British Standard specifications:

Fibre boards. These are produced by pulverising of wood down to individual fibres and then compressing them to form large sheets. Small percentages of adhesives—usually phenolic—may be used to act as a binder though fibres have inherent adhesive properties and are to some degree self-binding. Several different types of product are obtained according to the degree of compression of the fibres. Almost all types are, however, very susceptible to moisture content changes and to creep, especially in damp conditions.

The most densely compressed fibre boards are referred to as hardboards. These boards can have quite high bending strengths, for example, 30 N/mm^2, though swelling and strength reductions occur on wetting. They are usually approximately 3 mm in thickness and are used for lining low-cost doors, partitions and in sheeting and cladding in dry situations. Nail and screw retention properties are poor. Oil-tempered grades have greater resistance to dampness and have been used for low-cost external cladding.

A number of medium fibre boards are now available which have moderate bending strength but better thermal insulation properties than hardboards. These are suitable for ceilings and claddings.

The low-density fibre boards (softboards) are used primarily for insulation purposes, having thermal conductivities of approximately 0.05 W/m°C and densities of about 300 kg/m^3. Types suitable for ceilings, sarking and sheathing are obtainable, the latter normally being bitumen impregnated and contributing to the stiffness of timber-framed structures.

All types of board are inherently flammable, though fire retardants can be incorporated.

Particle boards. These consist of small particles or splinters of wood bonded together with synthetic resins. Fibres are usually randomly orientated parallel to the plane of the board so that stability is good and moderate bending strengths can be obtained (for example, 10 N/mm^2). The material is cheap and applications include flooring, roof decking and as a base for veneers. Moisture resistance depends on the type of binder used but normal grades are bonded with an 'Int' grade glue and undergo swelling, strength reduction and softening in damp conditions. Exterior grades have been produced for such uses as shuttering for concrete.

Plywood. Plywood consists of glued wood panels comprising outer and inner sheets, the grains in adjacent sheets being at right angles. An odd number of plies is normally used, since this enables symmetrical distribution of plies about the centre sheet. Hence, if the moisture content changes, equal and opposite bending effects occur due to differential shrinkage of symmetrically opposed sheets. As a result, plywood can be used in situations with variable moisture content with minimum distortion. Sheets behave isotropically in the plane of the sheet, and although flexural strength is not as high as in a solid timber sheet loaded parallel to the grain, it is much greater than a solid timber loaded across the grain. The flexural strength and stability of plywood increases with the number of plies. Also, since the glue lines restrain surface cracking due to the stresses imposed by moisture changes, there is a limit to the thickness of surface plies that can be used. In order to achieve greatest flexural strength, the face grain should be parallel to span.

The working properties of plywood are similar to those of ordinary timber, though it can be nailed or screwed without risk of splitting, since there are no cleavage planes. Impact strengths are much better than those of ordinary timber, for the same reason. Performance standards for plywood tend to be rather complicated since they are often those of the country from which they are imported, but colour codes are now quite commonly used, as they are for other timber products.

When used decoratively, the surface veneers are usually of hardwood. BS 1455 gives three grades—grade 1 indicating knot- and defect-free veneers jointed at the centre, if jointed. Where painting is anticipated, grade 2 veneers are suitable. These, though flat, may be jointed and contain sound knots, fine splits or repairs in the form of smooth inserts. Grade 3 plywoods are used when appearance is unimportant. The above requirements may be applied to either or both faces.

Plywoods are also very widely used for cladding, as formwork for concrete and for structural purposes.

Blockboard. This consists of strips of wood between 7 and 25 mm wide glued together and sandwiched between veneers. The grain of the veneers is at right angles to that of the strips. When long sheets are required, the strips normally run parallel to length, and, in addition to the veneers already described, further veneers are included with outer sheets having grain parallel to the long axis. These boards are generally suitable for internal purposes only. Blockboards are widely used in furniture, for interior doors and shelving.

Laminboard. This is similar to blockboard except that the strips are less than 7 mm in width. As a result, strength and stability are improved. Both laminboard and blockboard are broadly referred to as 'plywoods'.

Finishes used for timber externally

As new advances are made in the fields of protective treatments, timber is being used more widely as a cladding material. In larger structures, this also enables a saving in foundation size compared to brick or concrete. Although the application of preservatives may enable timber to fulfill its protective function in cladding, decorative appearance is usually also important and this requires, at least in the case of softwoods, the exclusion of moisture; if rain reaches surface layers, it tends to dissolve out the water-soluble colouring materials. This process is assisted by sunlight, which increases solubility. The wood therefore changes colour and may also accumulate dirt. Cladding at ground level will be particularly vulnerable to the effects of dirt and moisture.

Moisture-proofing treatments may be divided into those which do or do not form a surface film. The former—paints and varnishes—are described under the heading of paints, though it may be appropriate to point out that varnishes give limited life time, and once peeling and weathering have occurred it is difficult to restore the original appearance. Hence, preventive maintenance must be thorough—coats should be renewed before failure of earlier films. Long oil varnishes give longer, but by no means indefinite, protection. Non-film-forming finishes such as linseed oil are not entirely satisfactory since they take some time to dry and tend to attract dirt. Specially formulated grades containing solvents to increase penetration and a wax or silicone to impart water-repellent properties to the timber surface are available. Maintenance and renewal of such surfaces is necessary, though less difficult than with film-forming types.

Structural uses of timber

The attractive properties of timber for structural purposes are high specific strength, ease of construction and finishing, attractive appearance and durability, especially in aggressive environments. These are offset to some extent by the variability of timber properties which require a statistical approach to obtain the best safe performance. However, stress grading has gone some way towards classifying—and hence using more efficiently—most commonly available timbers. Grading is normally carried out visually, though more recently mechanical methods have been used in which the deflections of pieces of timber on face and on edge are measured under a standard load for that section. Grading may, in this way, be carried out automatically and tends to give more accurate results, especially in relation to the effect of knots.

Visual stress grading (BS 1860; C.P. 112). A grade is ascribed to each piece of timber by measuring the size of knots and fissures, slope of grain and, in the case of softwoods, the spacing of growth rings. BS 1860 describes methods of measurement, grades are then designated by comparison with a perfect or 'basic' timber of the same variety (C.P. 112). The grades 75, 65, 50 and 40 are given accordingly. A composite grade also exists; this contains at least 75 per cent of 50 grade or better, the balance being of 40 grade. Figure 5.24 shows typical requirements of a grade 75, 50 x 150 mm softwood joist. The stress grading requirements for timber to be used in laminated beams are slightly different to those for other forms of structural timbers since some types of defect will have different effects on the overall structure. C.P. 112, for example, does not give growth ring requirements although it is clear that no wane can be permitted for 'architectural' grades. Allowable maximum knot sizes are also rather less. Laminating grades LA, LB and LC are designated. Grading in this way may appear

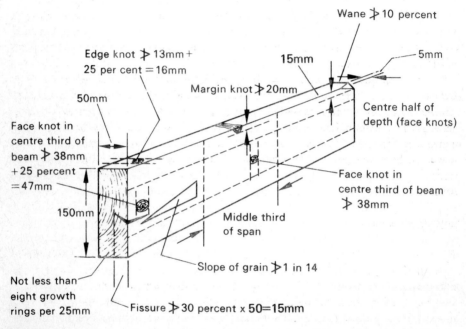

Fig. 5.24 Visual stress grading of a simply supported softwood timber joist using C.P. 112. The requirements given are for Grade 75 timber. Knots of maximum size should be separated by at least 300 mm

to be a time-consuming process, but experienced labour can classify rapidly most timber specimens. Typical (long-term) stress values for a dry basic grade softwood such as pitch pine are approximately 20 N/mm^2 in flexure or tension, 15 N/mm^2 in compression and 1·5 N/mm^2 in shear (parallel to grain). Moduli of elasticity are usually in the range of 5-15 kN/mm^2. As might be expected of a material in which secondary bonds play an important part, long-term strength of timber is considerably below short-term strength. Reductions of 40 per cent or more are necessary on short term test results for components which will be under sustained loads, quite apart from factors of safety introduced to take account of statistical variations and decay hazards. In the 1973 edition of BS 1860, the grades 75, 65, 50 and 40 are replaced by two visual grades—'General structural', GS, and 'Special structural', SS. These are judged to be similar to the 50 and 65 grades respectively, though the method of measurement of knots is rather different, being based on a 'knot area ratio' KAR method. As before, the timber beam sections are divided into centre half and upper and lower quarters but the area of knot in each cross-section is assessed instead of the surface dimensions only. Hence a knot area ratio is established, the permissible value being reduced if the upper and lower quarters have more than a certain proportion of their area occupied by knots.

Jointing methods for timber

Traditionally, nails, wood screws and bolts have been used, the strength of joints so obtained increasing in that order. In the case of wood screws, undersize holes are necessary to minimise danger of splitting, and if joints are subject to bending hardened types will give a stronger joint than mild steel. Bolts (and to some extent, screws) enable transfer of load by friction between wood components, though, on account of the low compressive strength of timber, load-spreading washers are essential. More recently, gusset plates have been introduced, being highly suited to quantity production of roof trusses provided timbers are of consistent thickness at joints. Galvanising is essential for long life. The strongest joints are obtained using timber connectors. These either have teeth to grip both pieces of timber or incorporate rings which fit into pre-cut grooves. Bolting of timbers together then gives great shear strength. Adhesives are of course also important; these are described under that heading.

Laminated timber

This form of construction is by no means new, though it is only recently that its full potential has been realised. The high strength/weight ratio of timber and the ease with which virtually any shape can be produced are the chief reasons behind the success of laminated timber. In fact, the material is highly competitive with steel where larger spans under moderate load are required as in roofing. Spans of over 100 m have been obtained.

Timber may be laminated vertically (that is, in the plane of bending) or horizontally (at right angles to the plane of bending) (Fig. 5.25). The former have been shown to give higher strength, though application is limited to beams of constant section. Horizontal laminations have the advantages that weaker grades of timber can be located at the centre of beams where stresses are likely to be less. The allowable stresses in horizontally laminated timber are in general slightly lower than those in solid, perfect timber so that the chief advantage is gained when the finished laminate is much larger than could be produced from a single piece. Strength increases with the number of laminations for a member of a given section, though costs also increase and wastage of timber in planing is such that there is little point in using a large number of very thin laminates. Thicknesses in the region of 20 mm are usually satisfactory, though smaller values may be necessary when tight bends are required. Joints are normally required to be spaced by at least 24 times the laminate thickness; finger

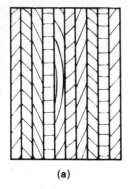 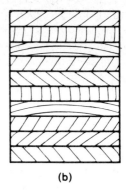

(a)   **(b)**

Fig. 5.25 Sections through a laminated timber beam. (a) vertically laminated. (b) horizontally laminated

joints are now considered to be most satisfactory. If beams or arches taper, best performance is obtained by tapering internal rather than external members. Units are coated with glue and then pressed together such that excess glue is expelled. Radio frequency treatment enables curing to be carried out vary rapidly.

Other forms of timber construction

Developing parallel to space frames in steel construction have been three-dimensional roof structures in timber with essentially similar properties, allowing large spans to be used on account of their low weight and high rigidity. Alternatively, rigidity can be achieved from the shape of the roof itself, as in hyperbolic parabaloid types.

One of the most important timber products in modern building construction is plywood. If laminates are fixed on to a simple timber frame, they impart great rigidity and strength, in fact carrying the bulk of the load. This is known as stressed skin construction and is widely used in the fabrication of beams ('box beams'), in roofing and for the frames of complete structures such as houses and even multi-storey blocks of flats. Although such structures have been extremely successful, it is important to allow for the higher likely movement, especially during and immediately after construction, compared to other materials. If construction is carried out in wet weather, considerable shrinkage will result, and this should be allowed to occur before finishes are applied. Finishes should also be capable of a certain degree of movement if unsightly cracking is to be avoided. Completely 'dry' finishes are in this respect better than more traditional finishes. Sound insulation between timber-framed dwellings and flats might be considered a problem, but by careful design, detailing and construction involving floating floors, structurally independent composite party walls and insulating materials, the grade 1 sound insulation standard can be achieved.

 Thermal properties and fire resistance

The thermal conductivity of timber is low, varying from approximately 0·12 W/m°C for softwood to 0·16 W/m°C for some hardwoods. As a result, heat losses through the material are small (though this has in the past caused pattern staining in otherwise uninsulated roof structures) and timber resists formation of condensation better than metals. The same property is responsible for the relatively good performance of timber in serious fire. 'Burning' of wood occurs due to ignition of flammable gases which are given off when the temperature of the material exceeds about 300°C. On burning, charcoal is produced which though of little strength is valuable in reducing heat flow to underlying wood. Charcoal itself, however, burns at a temperature over 500°C so that, in a severe fire, charring, and hence strength reduction, take place at an approximately linear rate, generally considered to be 0·64 mm/minute for a flat surface. When the fire encroaches from all sides of a member, as for example, in columns, the rate may be slightly higher. The design stresses of C.P. 112 allow a substantial margin—approximately 2·25—between design and failure so that the durability of a beam in fire is often quite large, being the time taken for charring to reach the stage at which, on account of the decreasing cross-sectional area, failure stresses are reached. It is found that laminated beams which are usually bonded with the WBP adhesives phenol or resorcinol formaldehydes have fire resistance similar to that of solid timber of the same dimensions. Metal connectors, on the other hand, greatly accelerate destruction and are a potential hazard in roof structures unless protected. Plywood box beams are also less fire resistant than laminated or solid timber, since the thickness of wood is usually smaller. Although timber floors might also be considered unsatisfactory, the normal first floor construction in houses has usually quite good fire resistance, largely due to its enclosed nature and the underlying plaster ceiling. In this respect, however, plywood is better than tongue and groove boards, which are better than flush boards, since a large number of joints or gaps increases ventilation. In timber-framed buildings, satisfactory fire resistance can be achieved by use of plasterboard on walls and ceilings, though firestops are also necessary in wall structures containing large vertical cavities.

A number of fire-retardant preparations are available. Some types impregnate the timber, increasing the proportion of charcoal and decreasing combustible gases in a fire. This treatment is carried out on seasoned timber cut to its final size. Typical chemicals include aqueous solutions of monammonium phosphate, borax and ammonium chloride and preservatives are often included. Alternatively, intumescent paints, varnishes or pastes may be used. These form protective films under the action of fire, preventing oxygen access. Fire retardants are valuable in reducing surface spread of flame in cladding materials and partitions; Class 1 performance under BS 476, Part 7 can be obtained (Class 3, untreated). Charring rates are, however, not greatly reduced and the best protection against structural failure is the provision of extra (sacrificial) timber to protect underlying material.

Problems

5.1. Compare and explain the reasons for differences/similarities in the properties of polyethylene and polypropylene at various temperatures.

5.2. Classify as thermoplastic/thermosetting and write notes on:
polyvinyl chloride;
phenol formaldehyde polymers;
polyvinyl acetate;
polymethyl methacrylate.

5.3. What are the problems/advantages in the use of plastics for hot water services? Indicate suitable plastics and precautions that would be necessary in design and installation.

5.4. Discuss the likely future of plastics materials in building under the headings:
   (a)   structural,
   (b)   services;
   (c)   finishes.

5.5   Describe the chief mechanisms by which adhesives bond to materials. Indicate the limitations of each and give illustrations.

5.6. Suggest the requirements of adhesives which would be used to join:
   (a)   glass to glass for stained glass windows;
   (b)   phenolic-based laminated to particle board;
   (c)   decorative panelling to brickwork background;
   (d)   new concrete to old concrete;
   (e)   two lengths of PVC.

5.7. By what possible mechanisms can paint harden? Give examples and advantages or disadvantages of each type of paint.

5.8. What considerations dictate the flexibility of sealant required for a given situation? Give illustrations and, in the case of rubber-based sealants, indicate any other requirements necessary for a satisfactory joint.

5.9. Give the chief reasons for seasoning timber and explain why installed timber should be of moisture content approximately equal to its final equilibrium value. In what situations is this particularly important? What steps should be taken to ensure that such timber satisfies this condition?

5.10. Explain why the properties of timber such as moisture movement and strength are directional. How are these properties affected in:
   (a)   fibre board;
   (b)   particle board;
   (c)   chipboard;
   (d)   plywood?

5.11. Compare timber and steel in respect of:
   (a)   strength/weight ratio;
   (b)   durability;
   (c)   fire resistance;
   (d)   aesthetics.
   Hence suggest in what situations they are likely to be used for structural purposes.

5.12. A timber beam 200 m x 300 mm is exposed to fire on its soffit and faces. If charring occurs at a rate of 0·64 mm/minute and the beam was initially under its design load with a factor of safety of 2·25 predict whether or not a fire resistance of 1 hour will be obtained.

References

J. A. Brydson. *Plastics Materials*, Iliffe, 1970.
P. Reboul and R. G. Bruce Mitchell. *Plastics in the Building Industry*, Newnes, 1968.
R. Houwink and G. Salomon, *Adhesion and Adhesives*, Elsevier, 1965.
P. M. Fisk. *Advanced Paint Chemistry*, Leonard Books, 1961.
P. M. Fisk. *The Physical Chemistry of Paints* Leonard Books, 1963.
Introduction to Paint Technology, Oil and Colour Chemist's Association.
H. E. Desch. *Timber, its Structure and Properties*, Macmillan 1968
E. Levin. *Wood in Building*, Architectural Press, 1971.

Relevant British Standards

BS 747: Part II: 1970. *Roofing felts.*
BS 988:1076 1097, 1451: 1966. *Mastic asphalt for building (limestone aggregate).*

BS 1203: 1963 *Synthetic resin adhesives (phenolic and aminoplastic for plywood).*
BS 1204: *Synthetic resin adhesives (phenolic and aminoplastic for wood).*
BS 1444: 1970. *Cold setting casein adhesive powders for wood.*
BS 1455: *Plywood.*
BS 1860: *Structural timber: measurement of characteristics affecting strength.*
BS 2592: 1955. *Thermoplastic flooring tiles.*
C.P. 112: 1967. *The structural use of timber.*

Chapter 6
FIBRE REINFORCED MATERIALS

This chapter is devoted to fibrous composites developed relatively recently and, in addition, a brief description of resin cements is given.

The materials discussed to this point have been divided into three main groups, whose properties may be summarised as follows:

CERAMICS

On a volume basis, these are the cheapest materials. They have high compressive strength and are very rigid. They can be formed, using cements, into large structures of complex shape. They are, however, brittle and exhibit low tensile strength on account of microscopic cracks which are usually present in them. Hence, they cannot be relied upon to withstand, unassisted, large tensile, flexural or impact loads. Chemically, they are relatively stable.

METALS

These have the highest modulus of elasticity and tensile strength of any commonly used building material. Hence, they are, at present, a most important structural material, being the only group which will withstand satisfactorily high tensile stresses. They are also formable, though heavy sections or castings require high temperatures while lighter sections such as sheet or strip can often be worked at ordinary temperatures—these properties result in widespread uses for pressed or craftsman-formed components. Metals are generally the most prone of the three groups to atmospheric attack; they are dense and, on a volume basis, quite costly.

ORGANIC MATERIALS

Plastics, the chief synthetic organic materials, are characterised by low moduli of elasticity, variable ductility and moderate tensile properties. They soften at relatively low temperatures but are resistant to many chemicals and to attack by moisture. They are extremely versatile and, within the general limits given above, can be modified to suit specific requirements. On a cost basis, they are becoming increasingly competitive with other materials

The shortcomings as well as the chief attributes of the three major groups, are evident. Regarding chemical or atmospheric instability, it has been possible by means of a study of the nature of degradation or attack, to select materials according to the situation required or to modify or protect them if the environment is potentially harmful. As regards mechanical properties, there are perhaps two major problems which restrict the use of certain materials:

1. The brittleness/low tensile strength of most ceramics,
2. The low elastic modulus of those plastics which are sufficiently ductile to be viable for structural uses.

Although research is continually taking place into ways of improving metals, it may be said that these two problems have given rise to the most urgent investigations, with the result that a number of new materials have been developed which are certain, in the future, to find increasing application in construction.

It would appear that ceramics and plastics could be regarded as opposites in the sense that one is rigid and brittle while the other is ductile and tough, metals forming an intermediate group. Two chief methods of overcoming the brittleness of ceramics have been undertaken—fibre reinforcement and the incorporation of resinous materials. The former technique is by no means new, lime plasters were traditionally reinforced with horse-hair, while the use of reinforcement in concrete is fundamental to its use in almost all situations. Fibre reinforcement may also be used in certain cases to overcome the second problem the low elastic modulus of plastics. The principles of the use of fibres will be discussed first, followed by types of available fibre and typical applications.

Principles of fibre reinforcement

Fibre reinforcement may be intended to overcome either of the two problems described. In each case, a term 'stiffness' will be required, this may be taken as the ability of the given material to resist deformation due to stress. The stiffness of a composite will be dependent on the volume concentrations and 'E' values of its constituents. For example, a steel wire in concrete at a volume concentration of 5 per cent could hardly be regarded as contributing significantly to stiffness, since, in spite of its relatively high elastic modulus (210 kN/mm^2 compared to approximately 30 kN/mm^2), the cross-sectional area would be insufficient to carry a significant proportion of the load (unless the concrete were cracked).

Fibres in brittle materials

It will be clear that, since the stiffness of brittle materials is usually high, and only small volume fractions, V_f

$$\left(V_f = \frac{\text{volume of fibres}}{\text{total volume of composite}} \right)$$

can normally be incorporated, fibres are not likely to make a major contribution to the stiffness of such materials. Their use is intended to increase tensile and impact strengths, preventing failure by holding crack interfaces together. The action of fibres in such situations may be illustrated by taking a simplified model—for example, a

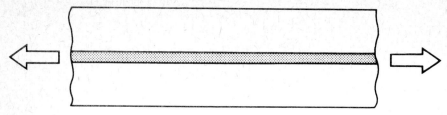

Fig. 6.1 Single continuous fibre in a brittle matrix. Load is applied to the matrix and fibre

single long fibre embedded in a cylinder of brittle material (Fig. 6.1). These, separately, might have stress–strain curves as shown in Figs. 6.2(a) (b), respectively. The gradient of a load-strain diagram will be dependent on the area of cross-section of the specimen. Supposing, for example, matrix and fibre are to be of similar stiffness, the ratio of the gradients in Figs. 6.2(a) (b) would be in the ratio of their cross-sectional areas. The former graph is steeper than the latter since, as already stated, the fibres in brittle materials normally form a small volume fraction and do not usually contribute the major part of stiffness. Figure 6.2(b) indicates much larger strains in the fibre before failure than occur in the matrix. On combining the fibre and the matrix, the load-strain curve would change as follows:

The initial gradient of the curve would be equal to the sum of the individual gradients (Fig. 6.3), since, at a given strain, each part would carry loads as before and the total load would be the sum of these. There will be no shear force on the fibre/matrix interface, since 'E' values are equal. At the same strain as previously, the ceramic will crack. The remainder of the stress–strain curve will depend on the bonding between fibre and matrix.

If there were no bonding, then the matrix would pull off the fibre—hence the fibre would be of no use unless the fibre were itself attached to the testing machine, and this in practice is unlikely.

If the fibre were bonded to the matrix, then when the first crack forms there would be a slight, sudden extension as the fibre at the point of cracking takes all the load.

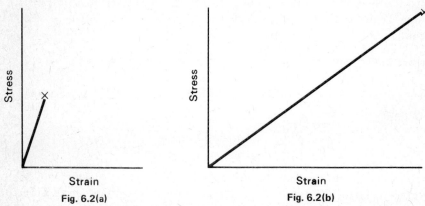

Fig. 6.2(a)   **Fig. 6.2(b)**

Fig. 6.2. (a) Stress–strain relationship for the matrix part of the composite shown in Fig. 6.1. (b) Stress–strain relationship for the fibre part of the composite shown in Fig. 6.1

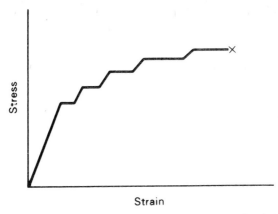

Fig. 6.3 Possible stress–strain relationship for the composite shown in Fig. 6.1. The initial gradient is equal to the sum of the gradients in Fig. 6.2(a) and (b). Failure is supposed to have occurred by pull-out of fibres

The extension would be proportional to the degree of local bond failure in shear around the now heavily stressed fibre-matrix interface at the crack. Figure 6.4 shows the stresses likely to result around the cracked area. The tensile load in the fibre at the crack must be equal to the first crack load on the composite, assuming that the testing machine is able to accommodate the resultant sudden strain increase without load reduction. Shear stress on the fibre will be small (due to friction only) around the central region in which shear failure has occurred; it will then increase rapidly to the

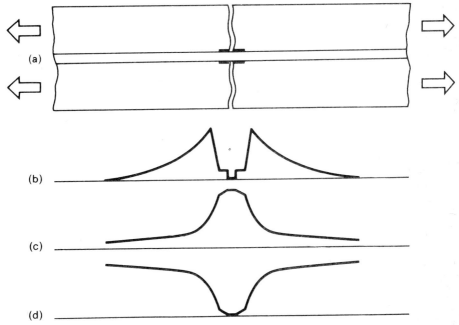

Fig. 6.4 (a) Cracked matrix showing debonded length of fibre. (b) Shear stress on fibre. (c) Tensile stress in fibre. (d) Tensile stress in matrix near to the fibre

maximum stable value and then decrease roughly exponentially towards fibre ends. On continued stress increase, the matrix would continue cracking, weakest areas breaking first, until eventually the fibre would either pull out or break dependent on whether the bonding load or tensile load reaches its ultimate value first. In practice, when large numbers of fibres are used, the step effect of Fig. 6.3 would be less obvious, the above arguments occurring on a smaller scale.

In flexure, the same arguments as above apply though, as the stress is transferred from the matrix to fibre on cracking, the neutral axis would tend to move towards the compression zone in order that, for a given degree of flexure, the total tensile load due to fibres in tension balances the total compressive load of the stiffer matrix. Considerable deflections will therefore occur before failure, which could in some cases be due to crushing of the small, heavily stressed compression area. It might be supposed that this kind of fibre reinforcement would be of little value in increasing *compressive* strengths of brittle materials. However, arguments given in Chapter 3 on the failure of concrete cubes referred to the possibility that compressive stresses may induce tensile strains according to the Poisson ratio of the material, actually resulting in tensile failure. Hence fibres may be of use in such situations and this is borne out by the fact that cube strengths of concrete have been significantly increased even by the use of relatively soft fibres such as polypropylene. The degree of improvement in performance in compression will, of course, depend in practice on the exact nature of the loading system and the geometry of the structure.

A further use of fibre reinforcement emerges from the fact that the area under the load–strain curve of Fig. 6.3 is higher than the combined areas under Figs. 6.2(a) and (b). This represents the energy absorbed during the test and gives an indication of impact properties. Hence, impact strength of fibre-reinforced materials is often much greater than that of the pure matrix.

Each of the above modes of behaviour will be influenced by the fibre length and diameter since, for a given bond strength per unit area of fibre/matrix interface, a shorter, thicker fibre will have less resistance to pull out, which will then occur well before its ultimate tensile strength is reached. This represents inefficient use of the fibre, though there are practical difficulties associated with the use of long fibres. The bond strength of a fibre should therefore be such that, if possible, it is almost sufficient to cause failure of the fibre itself at the maximum length which can be used. This requires a certain minimum value of the length/diameter ratio, known as the 'aspect ratio'. If, for example, a model similar to that of Fig. 6.1 were made in steel and concrete, the fibre would certainly pull out well before failure on account of the low bond strength of steel to concrete (the order of 5 N/mm^2) compared to the yield stress of a drawn steel fibre (perhaps 1000 N/mm^2). Much higher aspect ratios are required, and hence in fibrous materials the fibres are usually quite fine. If very high aspect ratios are used, the gradient of Fig. 6.3 may, in the latter stages of the test, increase to a value corresponding to the stiffness of the fibres themselves. Final fracture would then occur at the normal fracture stress of the fibres.

Fibres in flexible materials

In these cases, the main object of fibres is to increase the *stiffness* of the matrix. This poses several requirements—that the fibre itself be as stiff as possible, that it be capable of being used in a sufficient volume concentration to achieve the desired effect and that it bond well to the matrix. The approximate 'E' value of the composite during its elastic stage can be shown by energy considerations to be theoretically equal to the sum of the 'E' values of its components, weighted according to their respective volume fractions. For example, suppose parallel fibres of 'E' value 50 kN/mm² are incorporated at volume fraction 0·3 into a matrix of 'E' value 5 kN/mm². The resultant 'E' value in the direction of the fibres would be

$$0·3 \times 50 + 0·7 \times 5 = 15 + 3·5 = 18·5 \text{ kN/mm}^2$$

The first term here, which represents the fibre contribution, must be modified by an *efficiency factor* if the fibres are not all parallel to the stress direction (see below). On loading such a composite containing discontinuous fibres in tension, the matrix will tend to strain more than the fibre, so that shear forces between them will arise. These will fall off roughly exponentially towards the centre of the fibre as the load carried by the fibre increases and that carried by the matrix decreases, until, if the fibre is long enough, the strain in each is the same and the load carried by each would be in the ratio of their stiffness (15 : 3·5, fibre : matrix, in the example above).

When the heavily stressed matrix material at fibre ends reaches its yield stress, it usually gives rise to a certain maximum shear force on fibres at fibre ends. Any subsequent increase of load is transferred to fibres, and the region of yielded matrix material will extend along each fibre. The associated shear stress will increase proportionately the load on fibres until finally the shear force operates across each complete half length of fibre (Fig. 6.5). The tensile load in the fibre will then be (shear area × shear stress) = $\pi d \frac{l}{2} f_s$. The fibre is best utilised if, as in Fig. 6.5, its length is such that its tensile strength f_c is exceeded at about the same load as that corresponding to shear along its entire length; That is

$$\frac{\pi d^2 f_t}{4} = \pi d \tfrac{l}{2} f_s$$

or

$$l = \frac{d f_t}{2 f_s}$$

or

$$\frac{l}{d} = \frac{f_t}{2 f_s}$$

(For a given fibre diameter this corresponds to a *critical fibre length* l_c required for efficient use of the fibres.) Minimum aspect ratios, determined in practice by inspection of fractured specimens, tend to be higher than those suggested by the latter equation possibly because:

1. if fibres are kinked, their benefit is partly lost,
2. flaws in fibres often result in premature fracture, decreasing effective aspect ratios.

The above arguments also presuppose that the volume fraction and disposition of fibres, if non-continuous, is such that shear planes in the matrix are interrupted by fibres and are therefore too small to allow shear failure (Fig. 6.6). Continuous fibres

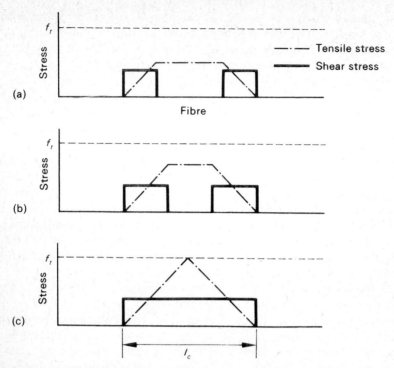

Fig. 6.5 Shear and tensile stresses due to friction in a fibre of length l_c in a yielding matrix. (a) low stress. (b) Intermediate stress. (c) Stress sufficient to cause fibre failure at the centre

will result in higher stiffness as well as higher strengths, since discontinuous fibres cannot support loads at their ends. This argument is, of course, an extrapolation of that given above regarding fibre length. Assuming fibres to be parallel to tensile stress and ignoring matrix contribution, the maximum theoretical tensile strength of these composites is $V_f f_t$ (V_f = volume fraction of fibre), though this may be accompanied by high strains, up to 5 per cent, so that the most important reason for incorporating fibres in a ductile matrix is normally to increase stiffness rather than ultimate tensile strength. These arguments apply in principle to fibre-reinforced metals and polymers, though the latter are of chief importance in building.

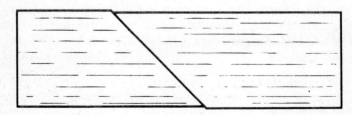

Fig. 6.6 Shear, a possible cause of failure in tension or compression when discontinuous fibres are used

Effects of randomness of fibre orientation on benefit obtained—efficiency factors

In order to contribute to stiffness, the most advantageous fibre orientation would be parallel to the direction of the stress. Hence, for example, in a beam subject to bending the fibres would best be aligned with the beam axis. In a slab subject to flexural stresses, they should be evenly distributed in the plane of the slab, if flexure in different vertical planes is likely. In this case, to obtain a given improvement in performance, more fibres would be required than if they were all arranged parallel to a single plane of flexure. Hence, if the same number of fibres were used, randomly orientated in the plane of the slab, less benefit would be obtained—experiments show that the proportion of the load carried by the fibres in an uncracked fibre-reinforced material, when randomly arranged in a plane, is approximately one-third of that carried by the fibres when fully aligned in the loading plane. Nevertheless, except where specific stress systems are experienced, this is the safest way of incorporating fibres—in the form of matting or sprayed on to the matrix. Where fibres are arranged in three dimensions, the load carried is reduced to approximately one-sixth of that carried by fully aligned fibres, though in some materials this is the only way fibres can be incorporated; for example, concrete, where semi-fluid properties of the material are essential for placing. (Subsequent treatment such as vibration may reorientate fibres, but this may not always be in the desired direction.)

In relation to control of cracking, the arguments are more complex, though it seems likely that the above effects of fibre orientation will apply at least qualitatively, most benefit being obtained when the fibre is parallel to the tensile stress—at right angles to the direction of cracking.

TYPES AND PROPERTIES OF FIBRES

The three basic groups of materials each make contributions to the range of fibres which exists for reinforcement of materials. In the 'ceramic' group there are glass and asbestos fibres; in the 'metallic' group steel fibres and in the 'organic' group carbon and polypropylene fibres. Properties are summarised in Table 6.1.

Ceramic fibres

The low tensile stress of ceramics has been explained by reference to the existence of microscopic flaws in the material which result in very high localised stresses when an external tensile stress is applied. Griffith showed that the stress f_R at the tip (root) of a crack is given by

$$f_R = 2f_A \sqrt{\frac{L}{R}}$$

where L = crack length, R = radius of root of crack, f_A = applied stress. (See Fig. 6.7.) In metals or ductile plastics, where plastic flow is possible, the crack becomes blunted by plastic flow, relieving stress, but in ceramics the absence of any plastic flow mechanism results in very high stresses at the crack tip due to the very small root radius of the flaw. If the propagation of a crack requires more energy to produce new

Table 6.1

Typical properties of some common fibres in order of decreasing elastic modulus

Fibre type	Specific gravity	Modulus of elasticity (kN/mm²)	Ultimate tensile strength (N/mm²)	Specific modulus of elasticity (kN/mm²)	Specific tensile strength (N/mm²)	Strain at failure (per cent)
Carbon high modulus	2·0	420	2100	210	1050	0·5
Carbon low modulus	1·7	240	2400	140	1410	1
Steel	7·8	210	1300	27	167	Necks
Asbestos (crocodilite)	2·5	160	3000	64	1200	2
'E' glass	2·5	70	1200	28	480	2–3
Polypropylene	0·91	8	550	8·8	605	7

surfaces than is released as elastic energy by the advancing crack, then the crack is stable. Note, however, that this depends on the crack geometry, and that since the crack's lengths themselves obey statistical laws, tensile strengths are likely to fluctuate considerably. This is well known from experimental results on ceramics. The size of flaws, which are due to the imperfections occurring in molecular packing and/or

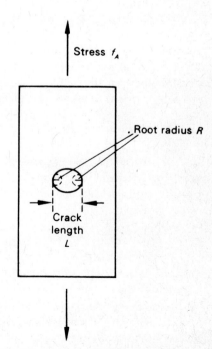

Fig. 6.7 Griffith's model for estimation of stress concentration due to a small crack in a brittle material

surface structure, can be reduced enormously by production of fine filaments. Such filaments will also have much greater flexibility than a larger component, since, for a given radius of curvature, the extreme 'fibre' stress is proportional to the distance of that 'fibre' from the neutral axis. In thin fibres, all parts of the material are near to the neutral axis, hence much tighter bends can be formed without fracture and ceramic fibres are apparently quite ductile. A typical minimum bending radius for a 10 μm diameter glass fibre is, for example, only 100 μm.

Glass fibres

These are, of course, non-crystalline, though the above arguments apply on account of surface defects. Glass fibres are manufactured by drawing filaments from the base of platinum crucibles (bushings) containing molten glass. Each bushing contains several hundred holes and the filaments so formed are collected to form strands and then wound onto a drum. Individual filament diameters depend on glass properties, hole size and drawing speed, though they are usually about 10 μm. A 'size' such as polyvinyl acetate is used to bind filaments together and protect them from damage during fabrication at a later stage (these fibres should not be confused with glass fibres for thermal insulation purposes, which are much coarser and produced by a different process). The strand may be formed into continuous lengths called roving, woven into cloth or chopped to form matting. Cloth consists of continuous fibres and therefore gives greater strength than chopped strand matting (fibre length approximately 40 mm). The 'E' value for the glass fibres in tension is approximately 70 kN/mm^2, tensile strength is 1200 N/mm^2 and strains at failure are 2–3 per cent, though strength figures are variable, as explained above. It is unfortunate that ordinary ('E') glass is slightly attacked by Portland cements on account of their alkalinity. The very small diameter of the filaments in glass fibre may result in complete dissolution of fibres in a short space of time. Alkali-resistant varieties are, however, available.

Asbestos fibres (see also asbestos, Chapter 2)

Since they occur naturally, their use is perhaps more traditional than that of other fibre types. They have an elastic modulus of approximately 160 kN/mm^2, 40-mm length fibres having tensile strengths between 1000 N/mm^2 (amosite) and 3000 N/mm^2 (crocidolite). Shorter fibres may give slightly higher strengths. The superior heat and chemical resistance of these fibres over glass gives them advantages in relevant situations.

Metal fibres

The most common metallic fibres used are steel. They are usually relatively coarse—for example, 300 μm in diameter—and since it is unusual for failure of steel fibre-reinforced materials to be caused by failure of the fibres themselves (failure is usually by pull-out of fibres), there is little point in aiming for higher tensile strength than is possessed by drawing ordinary low carbon steel. Tensile strengths are approximately 1300 N/mm^2, though metals are different to ceramic fibres in that failure involves necking and consequently larger strains. The 'E' value of steel fibres is similar to that of larger steel components—about 210 kN/mm^2. Fibres may be plated to increase corrosion resistance.

Organic fibres

Polypropylene. This material has great flexibility and toughness combined with light weight and imparts great improvements to impact strength in materials it reinforces. It is normally marketed as a film, fibrilated by drawing to orientate molecular chains. The 'E' value is the lowest of any common fibre, approximately 8 kN/mm^2, so that it would be of no use in stiffening materials. Tensile strengths are approximately 550 N/mm^2.

Carbon fibres. These are new and highly promising materials based on the strength of the carbon–carbon bond in graphite and the lightness of the carbon atom. Carbon fibres are produced by heat treatment of plastic fibres such as acrylic fibres so that the carbon atoms link together to form small graphitic crystallites. The fibres are about 10 μm in diameter but consist of tiny 'fibrils' stranded together in quantities of up to 100,000. There are two chief varieties: high *strength* fibres with ultimate tensile strength of approximately 2400 N/mm^2 and 'E' value of 240 kN/mm^2 and high *modulus* fibres with ultimate tensile strength of 2100 N/mm^2 and 'E' value of 420 kN/mm^2. With strengths of this order, it is clearly important that high bond strengths with the matrix are essential if the fibres are to be used for reinforcement. Unfortunately, the more perfect the graphitic structure, the less likely the fibre is to bond to other materials, so that treatment is required to obtain maximum benefit from this material. The above figures will give, however, an indication of the importance of the fibres once technological advances result in price reduction, though at present fibres are very expensive—the order of £100 per kg!

Fibre-reinforced cement products

Materials based on Portland cements form a natural choice for application of fibrous materials, since they are usually cheap but leave much to be desired in respect of ductility, impact resistance and tensile strength, the latter being 3–5 N/mm^2. All the above-named fibres have been used in attempts to improve these properties, though the elastic modulus of the composite is in each case similar to that of the unreinforced material, since the fibres form small volume fractions of the total. Table 6.2 summarises properties of typical composites based on Portland cement and, for comparison, glass-reinforced gypsum.

Glass-reinforced cements (g.r.c.)

Glass fibres have been included in certain types of cement product, notably precast units, with a view to increasing flexural strength and impact resistance. Manufacture is on the lines of asbestos cement goods—by spraying chopped glass fibres 10–50 mm in length on to a perforated base and, at the same time, spraying on a cement slurry.

Table 6.2

Properties of typical fibre-reinforced cements compared to glass-reinforced gypsum and semi-compressed asbestos cement sheet

Material	Modulus of rupture (N/mm^2)	Tensile strength (N/mm^2)	Strain at failure (Tension) (per cent)	Impact strength
Glass-reinforced cement (5 per cent by volume of alkali-resistant sprayed 40-mm fibres)	35	15	1	High
Steel fibre-reinforced concrete (2 per cent by volume of 40-mm fibres)	7	5	High	High
Polypropylene fibres in concrete (0·2 per cent by volume of 40-mm fibres)	5	4	High	High
Glass-reinforced gypsum (Class B) (4 per cent by volume sprayed 40-mm fibres)	30	15	0·7	Very High
Semi-compressed asbestos cement sheet (15 per cent by weight of fibres)	20	14	0·2	Medium

When a sufficient thickness is built up, excess water is vacuumed off and the flexible composite sheet can be shaped and then cured. Fibres may, alternatively, be introduced by mixing a small percentage of the shorter fibres directly with cement slurry before moulding, but since the resultant orientation is completely random, the tensile strength would only be about half that of products containing fibres orientated in a plane. The resulting material has very much better impact strength than either unreinforced cement or asbestos cement, 5 per cent by weight of glass fibre, giving an impact strength about five times that of the latter. Resistance to fire is also much better than the unreinforced material, particularly if a proportion of p.f.a. is included. Thermal shocks are also absorbed more satisfactorily.

The main problem with g.r.c. is that ordinary ('E' glass) glass fibres are attacked by the hydrating cement. Figure 6.8 shows that after a short time in air storage, flexural strength decreases steadily until a very low value, about half its previous maximum, is reached. Impact strength is similarly affected. A newer type of glass which includes zirconium oxide, ZrO_2, has been produced; this is alkali resistant and therefore not as severely affected as 'E' glass. A typical curve is also shown in Fig. 6.8.

Tensile strength is in the region of 15 N/mm^2 for 5 per cent by volume of alkali-resistant glass and the strain at failure in tension is the order of 10,000

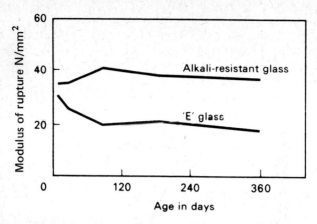

Fig. 6.8 The effect of age on the modulus of rupture of alkali resistant and 'E' glass fibres in cement. Composite contains 4 per cent by volume of 34-mm length fibres and is stored in air. (Courtesy of the Building Research Establishment)

micro-strain—indicative of good bonding between fibre and matrix. Possible applications of g.r.c. are as follows:

1. In precast units allowing thinner, lighter units to be produced for given strength/ impact resistance properties. Aggregate finishes can be applied where appearance is important.
2. In reinforced concrete units. G.r.c. is very dense, so that the surface layers carbonate only at a slow rate, allowing more economic positioning of reinforcement nearer the concrete surface.
3. In cladding panels for protection of structural members from damage by fire.
4. Very rapid wall construction has been achieved by assembly of dry concrete blocks and then spraying the surfaces with a fibre–mortar mixture. A strong, waterproof structure is formed.

Steel fibre-reinforced concrete

Steel is preferable to other metals for fibre reinforcement of concrete on account of its high elastic modulus and reasonable cost.

It would, at first sight, seem reasonable to assume that a good bond would be obtained between steel and concrete in much the same way as in conventional reinforced concrete. However, the bond in the latter is known to be at least partly due to surface irregularities produced by hot rolling and the presence of thin, adherent rust films. Surface irregularities are virtually absent in steel fibres, which are less than 1 mm in diameter and produced by cold drawing. This, together with the fact that it is not possible to reproduce the corrosion effect in a fine fibre, results in a relatively poor bond between fibre and matrix in steel fibre-reinforced concrete. As a result, long fibres would theoretically be required in order to produce sufficient anchorage to utilise fully the strength of the steel. There are practical problems here since long fibres tend to 'ball up', resulting in increased porosity and reduced strength in the resultant composite. There are, in fact, advantages in having a composite system in which failure occurs by pull-out of fibres, since there is often more warning of failure than when failure takes place by fracture of fibres (as, for example, in asbestos cement), although it clearly represents inefficient use of a composite if fibres pull out when well below their yield stress. To this end, many fibres used to reinforce concrete are deformed (crimped) to increase resistance to pull-out. Alternatively, surface oxidation by heating or controlled acid attack may be used to increase the bond.

Mixing of fibre-reinforced concrete requires careful attention. 'Balling up' of fibres is likely to occur if more than 2 per cent by volume of fibres is used or if fibres are not added gradually to the mix (best carried out through a coarse mesh sieve). Long, thin fibres (for example, 50 mm in length and 150 μm in diameter) aggravate the situation. The fibres themselves make the concrete unpleasant to handle due to their stiff, prickly nature.

Compaction is best achieved by vibration, though with higher fibre concentrations pokers are not suitable since, on withdrawal, it is difficult to fill the cavity that remains. Vibration tends to orientate the fibres parallel to the plane of the slab, which is not always advantageous, though the precise effect—especially on more complex shapes—has not been fully investigated.

Properties of the hardened composite

Impact and flexural strengths of concretes are increased considerably by incorporation of steel fibres. Figure 6.9 shows, for example, the approximate relationship between flexural strength and per cent by volume of fibres and indicates that, assuming full compaction can be achieved, flexural strengths will be doubled by incorporation of 2 per cent by volume of fibres. An important advantage is that failure is much more gradual than in unreinforced concrete, with ample visual warning. Increasing fibre length increases flexural strength but decreases the percentage of fibre content at

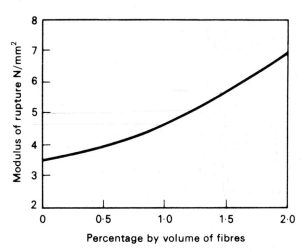

Fig. 6.9 Relationship between modulus of rupture and volume concentration of fibres in steel fibre-reinforced concrete. Fibre length 40 mm; diameter 300 μm

which balling up in the mixer occurs, so that in practice fibre lengths greater than about 50 mm are not normally used.

It is important to appreciate that the action of steel fibres in increasing flexural strength of concrete is different to that by which conventional reinforcement works. The latter is not designed primarily to prevent cracking; it carries the tensile load when cracking has occurred. Fibres, on the other hand, do not carry all the tensile load in concrete—they tend to bridge the microcracks which under tension grow to form observable cracks. However, as in the case of conventional reinforced concrete, they do carry some of the load after cracking has taken place, so that a cracked fibre-reinforced concrete may be stressed further before failure occurs.

Though quantitative results are not available, impact properties are considerably improved, particularly in thin slabs, probably by the same microcrack control that results in flexural strength improvements. Significant improvements in fatigue resistance are also obtained.

When used in exposed situations, the steel fibres which are adjacent to the surface inevitably corrode, owing to exposure or carbonation of the concrete surface. Such exposure does not affect the mechanical properties of the composite though it results in rust staining which might be unacceptable if appearance is important. This could be avoided by use of stainless steel or coated fibres—brass may be used for the latter.

In order to utilise more efficiently the fibres to improve flexural strength, experiments have been carried out in which fibres have been concentrated at positions of highest tensile stress. This could be by placing of fibres separately during pouring of concrete or by post treatment as in guniting (a cement mortar sprayed on to a solid background). The latter could be very effective, provided safety precautions are taken against injury by the steel fibres.

Uses

Most applications are based on situations which require a greater degree of impact and flexural strength than can be provded by ordinary concrete. Examples are in factory floor slabs, aircraft aprons or runways, and surface screeds. The durability of the concrete and particularly resistance to cracking are considerably improved. Further possible applications include precast units such as pipes or panels, for general reinforcement of structural concrete or to reduce cracking caused by drying shrinkage.

The high cost of steel has been a drawback in the use of steel fibres in concrete—a concrete containing, for example, 2 per cent by volume of fibres is likely to cost up to six times as much as an ordinary mix. Such a figure could on the other hand, be misleading since the material cost is usually a fairly small fraction of the cost of the structure, which might be only slightly increased. Also, the enhanced properties of the concrete may a'low the use of thinner sections for a given specification, enabling some saving to be made on the quantity of concrete.

Polypropylene fibres in concrete

It might seem surprising that polypropylene be used in concrete at all, since its modulus of elasticity is only about 8 kN/mm^2 compared to at least double this figure for most concretes, so that flexural properties are unlikely to be improved. These fibres are, however, cheap and have marked effects on two other properties of concrete which are of importance in certain situations.

1. *Plastic properties.* A system has been devised commercially to improve the properties of concrete in the plastic stage. The addition of about 0·1 per cent by volume of short fibres (less than 20 mm in length) leads to a heavily air-entrained mix containing up to 45 per cent air. This gives the fresh concrete thixotropic properties having, perhaps, zero slump and yet flowing and compacting readily under vibration. At the same time, it is resistant to bleeding and segregation which would normally occur in concrete mixes with such high quantities of air. The mix appears 'fatty' so that finishing is easily carried out and textured finishes with fine detail can be achieved, one method being to use patterned rollers. Mixes of varying strengths and densities using dense or lightweight aggregates can be produced. The hardened material is said to have improved frost resistance (due to the entrained air), lower permeability to water and increased resistance to surface crazing and impact compared to normal concretes. This type of concrete is likely to have particular application in precast products such as cladding panels, though wider use in pre-finishing flooring and walling units, or structural concrete may arise.

2. *Impact strength.* Impact strengths similar to or slightly greater than conventional steel reinforcing techniques can be obtained by incorporation of approximately 0·2 per cent by volume of fibrillated film fibres about 400 mm in length. The cement mortar penetrates the filaments so that a key is obtained, though it is found that pure polypropylene rather than processed varieties gives greatest improvement in impact properties. Small cracks which occur in the concrete terminate at fibres and hence allow absorption of energy on impact. Eventually, failure occurs by multiplication and joining of cracks until larger visible cracks form. Such concrete has been used in situations where replaceable components subject to severe impact are required, for example, a patented system for 50 mm thick circular concrete pile shells, polypropylene in this case being more economical to use than steel and of slightly better performance.

Glass-reinforced gypsum (g.r.g.)

A brief description of gypsum will first be given.

Gypsum is the common name for calcium sulphate, $CaSO_4$, which is the material normally used for plastering. In the natural state, it exists as the dihydrate $CaSO_4.2H_2O$, but in the manufacture of plasters, some or all of the water is removed by heating. If three-quarters of the water is removed, the hemihydrate, $CaSO_4 \cdot \frac{1}{2}H_2O$ (more strictly, $2CaSO_4 \cdot H_2O$) is formed, being commonly known as plaster of Paris. On mixing with water, this powder sets quickly by crystallisation to form the dihydrate again. It is known as Class A Plaster. On addition of a retarder such as keratin, a slower setting plaster (Class B) is obtained, being used widely for undercoat and lightweight plasters. If all the original water is removed, anhydrite—Classes C and

D—are obtained, the former being used for finish coat plaster and the latter, which is harder burnt, for projections such as arrises where a harder surface is essential.

The most suitable plaster for reinforcement is Class B—retarded hemihydrate. This material may have a high compressive strength; up to 50 N/mm^2 or more at low water contents with an elastic modulus of about 20 kN/mm^2 though tensile strength is low, approximately 6 N/mm^2. Fibres can therefore be profitably used; they will not contribute significantly to stiffness but will improve considerably tensile, flexural, impact and fire-resistant properties. Mixing methods are as for g.r.c., maximum flexural strength occurring with about 7 per cent by volume for sprayed fibres. Impact strength is improved remarkably—by over twenty times—while flexural strengths increase to approximately 30 N/mm^2 for 4 per cent by volume of fibres, though the flexural stress at the elastic limit occurs at only 10 N/mm^2 approximately. Compressive strength reduces as fibre content increases probably because fibre interference causes reductions in density. The bond strength between fibre and matrix in g.r.g. is known to be lower than that in g.r.c., and this is the likely reason for the improved impact strength of the former, especially at high fibre contents. Impacts are absorbed by causing partial bond failure between fibre and matrix. Higher bond strengths produced by better compaction are known to result in lower impact strengths (cf. the effect of lowering the temperature of steel on (a) its yield strength and (b) its impact strength).

One most important property of gypsum is its high water of crystallisation content. As a result, it has a high specific heat and very good fire resistance in the form of g.r.g.

The material has almost no shrinkage, though gypsum is slightly soluble in water, so that g.r.g. could not be used externally unless adequately protected.

Possible applications include:

For fire-resistant partitions; a 10-mm thickness has a fire resistance of approximately 1 hour. Ceiling tiles of Class O (Building Regulations) have been produced.

In precast flooring units; strength and fire resistance are both satisfactory.

For precast components such as ducts; g.r.g. could be used in similar situations to asbestos cement (internally only) but without the health hazard associated with the latter on drilling or cutting.

In sandwich construction; for example, timber doors to improve fire resistance, or with foamed plastics to give fire-resistant partitions with good heat insulation properties.

Glass fibre-reinforced polyester resin (g.r.p.)

Great advances have been made in recent years in reinforcement of plastics, and at present g.r.p. forms the largest bulk of these materials. The mechanical properties of polyester resins are dependent on the polymerisation process, on the presence of plasticisers, fillers and the temperature. However, the tensile strength of polyester resins lies in the range 40–100 N/mm^2 and the tensile modules of elasticity varies between 1 and 4 kN/mm^2, the latter being too low for efficient structural use. The 'E' value of glass fibre is about 70 kN/mm^2 in tension, so that considerable improvements in stiffness can be obtained by incorporation of glass fibres, this being the chief reason for their use. A property of glass which is most important in the context of reinforcing resins is its high affinity for water. Water is adsorbed in a thickness of twenty or more molecules to the surface of glass on account of its polar bonding; indeed, experiments have shown that water is partly responsible for their low tensile strengths. Hence, if a tensile stress is applied to glass, fracture will occur over a period of time unless the glass is completely dry, presumably by the action of stress corrosion due to water in flaws. The exact nature of the glass/resin bond is not fully understood though water appears to affect the bond even when keying agents are used, since these rarely cover the whole surface and must, in any case, penetrate adsorbed water layers. Fibres are covered with a protective size after manufacture which is generally removed before keying agents are applied. An exception is P.V.A. size, into which keying agents can be incorporated.

It is found that relatively high aspect ratios, for example 2000, are required to utilise most efficiently the tensile properties of glass fibres. For example, a 10-μm diameter fibre should be at least 20 mm in length to obtain sufficient stress transfer.

Manufacture of g.r.p.

Hand lay-up. The laminate is produced by building up layers of resin and fibre in an open mould, often itself made of g.r.p. A 'gel' coat may then be added and will improve appearance and weathering performance. This method only produces one smooth face. It may be used for small numbers of mouldings or for very large products.

Pressure moulding. The composite is built up on one-half of the mould and then a second matching mould is applied which presses the composite into shape. A higher proportion of fibre can be used, giving greater strength than in lay-up processes. Two smooth surfaces are obtained.

Continuous processes. These can be used for such products as corrugated sheeting.

Properties of g.r.p.

By the techniques described above, large volume fractions of fibres can be incorporated in the polyester resin, 50 per cent being a typical figure. The resulting modulus of elasticity is about 6 kN/mm^2 with tensile strengths of over 100 N/mm^2. On stressing in tension a randomly reinforced resin, an initial high value of 'E' is obtained appropriate to relative elastic moduli and volume fractions, modified by orientation and fibre length factors. G.r.p. containing discontinuous fibres strains plastically at quite small loads due to adhesion failure at the ends of the fibre. Further stressing results in a reduction in elasticity due to crazing of the resin component so that its contribution to stiffness gradually reduces. Figure 6.10 shows a typical stress–strain curve which is representative of curves for reinforced ductile materials. On loading in flexure, the neutral axis moves towards the compression zone, giving apparently higher flexural strengths than are obtained in direct tension. Continuous fibres—that is, fibres in the form of roving or cloth—result in the highest strengths. It

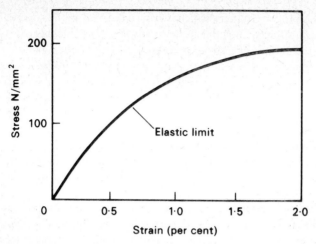

Fig. 6.10 Typical stress–strain curve for glass reinforced polyester composite loaded in tension. The exact relationship depends on the rate of loading

might be expected that since the stiffness of a resin is increased significantly by fibre reinforcement, the impact strength would be reduced. In fact, impact strength is increased and this is due to the increase in tensile strength that can be obtained even after crazing in the resin matrix has commenced. Although creep properties of resins are improved by fibre reinforcement, creep is still a significant phenomenon and 'E' values taken over long periods of time are inevitably less than those obtained by short term measurements.

A most important property of g.r.p. is its low density compared to other similar materials (approximately 1600 kg/m^3). Light transmission of the composite is about 85 per cent when new, slightly lower than that of glass, but g.r.p. is stronger and tougher than the latter.

Weathering resistance depends on the type of resin used, the proportion of resin and the nearness of fibres to the surface. Resins shrink on curing (this is, in fact, thought to be at least partly responsible for the glass/resin bond), tending to leave fibres standing on the surface so that water may penetrate by capillarity, destroying the resin/fibre bond. Some resins themselves are able to absorb water, resulting in the same effect. Alternatively, weather may erode the surface of the resin, exposing the fibres. The ingress of moisture may be prevented by use of gel coats on the surface of laminates though these should be lightly reinforced with glass monofilaments to prevent cracking. Acrylic resins are often used as gel coatings. If, after a time, fibres become exposed, it is best to rub the surface down and apply a sealer resin. The procedure should then be repeated periodically. Lives of 30 years or more may be obtained in this way.

Applications

G.r.p. is the most important plastic composite in the field of structures. Although the stiffness of the material is not high, the production of the complex shapes which are therefore essential for rigidity is easily and cheaply carried out. A multitude of three-dimensional shapes has been produced, some of which have considerable architectural merit. Small, lightweight buildings such as filling station canopies, shelters and even domestic dwellings, have been constructed from g.r.p. mouldings and on account of the low density of the material allow substantial savings in foundation costs. The use of sandwich constructions containing cellular plastics increases stiffness where necessary. The design of all structures requires careful attention to stress transfer at fixings to avoid local failure of g.r.p.

Roofing. The translucency of g.r.p. makes it an attractive material for roofing for buildings which have a daylight requirement. The simplest form is corrugated sheeting, which can be used in place of single sheets in an ordinary corrugated roof. Specially designed dome lights are now often used and, by fabrication of sections, large spans such as over swimming pools, warehouses and arcades can be obtained without need for a supporting frame. Light-transmission qualities are impaired over a number of years.

Concrete moulds. Concrete is being used increasingly as a facing material for structures, and the high quality of patterned finishes that can be obtained with g.r.p. moulds can be a major contribution. For small numbers of units, moulds may be hand made while for a larger number of slabs or columns it may be worthwile to use presses. Moulds may be used many times over though choice of release agent is important and moulds may require stiffeners, especially if large components are involved. A further possibility is the use of g.r.p.-moulded units as permanent shuttering for concrete; units containing locating ducts for reinforcement are assembled and concrete is then poured in and compacted. This provides perfect curing conditions and eliminates formwork removal. This method is most likely to be used for large numbers of *in situ* units; for example, columns where the mould would also make some contribution to strength.

Other applications. G.r.p. is used in a large number of products in building. Plumbing applications include tanks and cisterns and even hot water cylinders. In all cases, stresses due to inadequate supports or poorly aligned pipework should be avoided. Other uses include window frames, cladding panels, garage doors, and ventilators.

Fire resistance of g.r.p.

In some of the above applications, fire resistance may be important. All grades of g.r.p. will be destroyed by severe fire though chlorinated polyester resin composites having the BS 476: Part III Ext AA rating are available. These, however, have been shown to have somewhat inferior weathering resistance. Where fire resistance for elements of building construction is required (BS 476: Part VIII) g.r.p. could be used as a sandwich material with asbestos or concrete.

Uses of glass fibre in other forms of plastics

Epoxy resins have also been used in reinforced form; they adhere well to glass fibres and produce a composite of superior strength and chemical resistance to g.r.p. They also shrink less on curing so that initial stresses in composites are reduced. They are, however, more expensive than polyester resins. Typical applications include moulds for concrete products such as posts, when the moulds, on account of their toughness and strength, can be used time after time.

Resin concretes

These have been introduced in an attempt to improve the tensile properties of concrete and have also enabled the use of very thin sections of concrete, well bonded to their background.

Polyester, and particularly epoxy, resins bond well with most aggregates either by adhesion or by penetration in the case of porous aggregates, and this is probably the mechanism by which tensile properties are improved—the weakness of ordinary concrete in this respect is due chiefly to failure of the aggregate/cement interface. On account of the lower stiffness of resins compared to concretes (approximately 3 kN/mm^2 compared to 20 kN/mm^2 in tension), the stiffness of the composite is likely to be, if anything, less than that of ordinary concretes. Flexural strengths have, however, been increased by up to four times though deflections at failure will clearly be relatively larger and failures are usually sudden.

Experiments have been carried out on beams using ordinary concrete for compression zones, bonded to resin concrete in tensile zones and improved performance is obtained. Disadvantages of resin concretes in structural situations are their susceptibility to fire and their high thermal movement.

Perhaps the most important uses of resin cements are in surfacing and repair work. Epoxy resin-based floors have long been used in situations where impact and abrasion resistance combined with chemical durability are required. Epoxy resins are also used for repair work to existing concrete structures damaged by weathering or fire. Extremely good bonds to concrete and steel are obtained even when wet and when small thicknesses are used. Resins are available in water-dispersable forms that can be mixed in with water in a normal concrete mixer. Resulting properties are intermediate between ordinary concrete and those containing 100% resin binder. Such mixes may be used in thicker sections; for example, granolithic toppings, improving wearing qualities and crack resistance. Resins containing Portland cement have been produced; these contain a dispersed catalyst which, like the cement, is activated by water so that the whole sets. Curing times are much reduced, tensile strengths are much better than ordinary concretes while compressive strengths are better than those of either Portland cement concretes or neat resin. These types of cement are also likely to be useful for repair work or other situations where good bond to substrate is essential. More general use of resin cements is at present unlikely, since they are at least one order of magnitude more costly than ordinary cements.

Theoretical strengths

In compression there is theoretically no limit to stresses which could be imposed, although in practice compressive stresses give rise to tensile or shear stresses which may in some cases lead to their destruction. Even in such cases, very high strengths could be obtained if a triaxial compression system could be devised (Fig. 6.11). For example, concrete has been made to withstand compressive stresses of over 200 N/mm^2 by enclosing in a steel cylinder which provides the necessary lateral restraint. Such a system could conceivably be used in concrete columns, though lateral stability would of course still have to be satisfactory.

In tension, the theoretical strength must be related to the stress at which crystal slip or bond failure occurs. Theoretical calculations show that in ceramic-type materials fracture due to bond failure of materials should not occur until quite large strains corresponding to the maximum value of the bonding force of Fig. 4.8(b)—the order of 20 per cent—are encountered. Hence, the theoretical strengths should be in the region

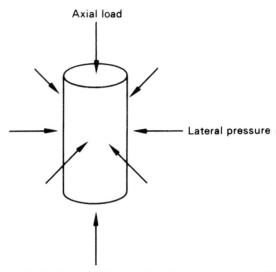

Axial load

Lateral pressure

Fig. 6.11 Increase of axial load when a simultaneous lateral pressure is applied. The increase is equal to three times the lateral pressure. For example, concrete of axial strength 50 N/mm^2 and subject to a lateral pressure of 50 N/mm^2 would fail at a stress of about 200 N/mm^2

of 20 per cent of their 'E' value. Such strengths require flawless crystals and these can be produced, though they are normally in the form of very thin single crystal fibres or 'whiskers'. Aluminium oxide whiskers have been produced having, for example, tensile strengths of over 20 kN/mm^2. Iron whiskers may give strengths of 10 kN/mm^2 (cf. tensile strengths of pre-stressing wires: Table 4.10), though their elastic modulus is unchanged from that of pure iron.

The above will give some indication of ceiling strengths of materials, but although in the future such materials may find application for specialised purposes, they are unlikely, on account of cost, to be used in constructional engineering or building, where structural problems are usually on a relatively large scale.

Problems

6.1. Explain the purpose of incorporating fibres in (a) brittle materials and (b) ductile materials. Give, in each case, requirements of fibres and the volume fractions necessary to achieve the desired effects. Illustrate by reference to actual composites.

6.2. Explain Griffith's theory of strength of brittle solids. A ceramic material has a theoretical tensile strength of 20 kN/mm^2 and is known to contain flaws of root radii 10^{-9}m. Calculate from Griffith's theory the crack length which would be necessary to result in an actual tensile strength of 1000 N/mm^2. What limits the application of these arguments to ductile solids?

6.3. A thin strip of resin having a Young's modulus 2 kN/mm^2, loaded uniformly, undergoes a deflection of 10 mm when a certain load is applied. What deflection would be obtained if 30 per cent by volume of glass fibres having an 'E' value of 70 kN/mm^2 were incorporated randomly in the plane of the strip? (Efficiency factor $\frac{1}{3}$).

6.4. A certain fibre of diameter of 10 μm has an ultimate tensile strength of 1200 N/mm^2 and a bond strength with the matrix of 10 N/mm^2. What minimum aspect ratio would theoretically be required to prevent pull-out of the fibre? Give reasons why, in practice, higher values might be required.

6.5. Compare the properties of glass-reinforced gypsum and glass-reinforced cement, in situations where: impact strength, fire resistance, long-term strength, weather resistance, are required. Suggest applications of each in general building purposes.

6.6. Discuss the following in relation to fibre reinforced concretes:
  (a) Aspect ratio,
  (b) Fibre orientation,
  (c) Volume fraction.
  Show how these affect or are affected by formation technique (that is, conventional mixing and lay- or spray-up methods).

6.7. Give reasons why glass should be the fibre type normally incorporated with polyester resins. Describe the properties of g.r.p., comparing with those of competitive materials.

6.8. Discuss the properties and applications of cements reinforced with:
  (a) glass.
  (b) steel,
  (c) polypropylene.

References

'Prospects for Fibre Reinforced Construction Materials'. *Proceedings of the International Building Exhibition Conference,* 1971. Building Research Establishment.

G. S. Hollister and C. Thomas, *Fibre Reinforced Materials,* Elsevier, 1966.

A. Kelly. *Strong Solids,* Oxford, 1966.

L. Holliday, Ed. *Composite Materials,* Elsevier, 1966.

A. J. Majumdar. 'Glass Fibre Reinforced Cement and Gypsum Products', *B.R.S. Current Paper* 12/71.

✓Fibre Reinforced Concrete'. *Concrete Building and Concrete Products,* Vol. XLIV, No. 10, 1969. Cement & Concrete Association.

M. Ali and F. J. Grimer. 'Mechanical Properties of Glass Fibre Reinforced Gypsum', *B.R.S. Current Paper* 13/69.

B. Parkyn. *Glass Reinforced Plastics,* Iliffe.

R. J. Towler and R. I. T. Williams. 'Resin Concrete', Vol. I. No. 4, *Construction Research and Development Journal.*

Polypropylene Fibres in Concrete. Patent: Shell International Chemical Company.

Use of Polypropylene in Pile Shells. West's Piling and Construction Company Ltd.

Polypropylene Fibres in Concrete: Faircrete. John Laing Research and Development Ltd.

References—General

L. Holliday, Ed. *Composite Materials,* Elsevier, 1966.

J. B. Moss. *Engineering Materials,* Butterworth, 1971.

L. Addleson. *Materials for Building,* Iliffe, 1972.

R. M. E. Diamant. *Chemistry of Building Materials,* Business Books, 1970.

J. C. Anderson and K. D. Leaver. *Materials Science,* Nelson, 1969.

T. J. Lewis and P. E. Secker. *Science of Materials,* Harrap, 1965.

B. R. E. Digests, published by H.M.S.O.

R. A. Burgess, P. J. Horrobin, Norman McKee and J. W. Simpson. Eds. *The Construction Industry Handbook,* Medical and Technical Publishing Co. Ltd.

J. W. Simpson and P. J. Horrobin. *Weathering and Performance of Building Materials,* Medical and Technical Publishing Co. Ltd, 1970.

R. A. Burgess, P. J. Horrobin and J. W. Simpson, Eds. *Progress in Construction Science and Technology,* Medical and Technical Publishing Co. Ltd., 1971.

Index